Drugs and Cosmetics Act, 1940 and Rules, 1945

Second Edition

Drugs and Cosmetics Act, 1940 and Rules, 1945

Second Edition

Ranjan Magazine

Plant Head—Manufacturing and Marketing
Sunny Allied Industries
Jammu, J&K

CBSPD

CBS Publishers & Distributors Pvt Ltd

New Delhi • Bengaluru • Chennai • Kochi • Kolkata • Lucknow • Mumbai
Gujarat • Hyderabad • Jharkhand • Nagpur • Patna • Pune • Uttarakhand

Disclaimer
Science and technology are constantly changing fields. New research and experience broaden the scope of information and knowledge. The author has tried his best in giving information available to him while preparing the material for this book. Although, all efforts have been made to ensure optimum accuracy of the material, yet it is quite possible some errors might have been left uncorrected. The publisher, printer and author will not be held responsible for any inadvertent errors or inaccuracies.

Drugs and Cosmetics Act, 1940 and Rules, 1945
Second Edition

ISBN: 978-93-88527-76-7

Second Edition: 2019
Reprint: 2025
First Edition: 2014
Reprint: 2018

Published by **Satish Kumar Jain** and produced by **Varun Jain** for

CBS Publishers & Distributors Pvt Ltd

4819/XI Prahlad Street, 24 Ansari Road, Daryaganj, New Delhi 110 002, India
Ph: 011-23289259, 23266838   Website: www.cbspd.com
                                                          e-mail: delhi@cbspd.com
Corporate Office: 204 FIE, Industrial Area, Patparganj, Delhi 110 092
Ph: 011-4934 4934   Fax: 011-4934 4935   e-mail: publishing@cbspd.com; publicity@cbspd.com

Branches

- **Bengaluru:** Seema House 2975, 17th Cross, K.R. Road, Banasankari 2nd Stage, Bengaluru 560 070 Karnataka, India
  Ph: +91-80-26771678/79   Fax: +91-80-26771680   e-mail: bangalore@cbspd.com
- **Chennai:** 18/8B, Subbarayan Street, Shenoy Nagar, Chennai 600 030, Tamil Nadu, India
  Ph: +91-44-42032115, 26681266   e-mail: chennai@cbspd.com
- **Kochi:** 42/1325, 1326, Power House Road, Opp KSEB, Power House, Ernakulam 682 018, Kerala, India
  Ph: +91-484-4059061-65   Fax: +91-484-4059065   e-mail: kochi@cbspd.com
- **Kolkata:** 147, Hind Ceramics Compound, 1st Floor, Nilgunj Road, Belghoria, Kolkata-700056 West Bengal, India
  Ph: 033-25633055, 033-25633056   e-mail: kolkata@cbspd.com
- **Lucknow:** Basement, Khushnuma Complex, 7-Meerabai Marg (Behind Jawahar Bhawan) Lucknow 226001, India
  Ph: 0522-4000032   e-mail: tiwari.lucknow@cbspd.com
- **Mumbai:** PWD Shed. Gala no. 25/26, Ramchandra Bhatt Marg, Next to JJ Hospital Gate no. 2 Opp. Union Bank of India Noorbaug, Mumbai-400009, Maharashtra, India
  Ph: 022-66661880/89   e-mail: mumbai@cbspd.com

Representatives

- **Gujarat** 0-9879558667   • **Hyderabad** 0-9885175004   • **Jharkhand** 0-9811541605   • **Nagpur** 0-8692091830
- **Patna** 0-9334159340   • **Pune** 0-9664372571   • **Uttarakhand** 0-9716462459

Printed at: Chaman Interprises, Daryaganj, Delhi, India

Preface to the Second Edition

This is an important book on *Drugs and Cosmetics Act, 1940 and Rules, 1945* for the use of students, laboratory practice, pharmacists, formulators, marketers and person in manufacturing and marketing. Book is updated, authentic and easy to study. The Chapters cover all aspects of Act and Rules, for example AYUSH, ayurvedic, siddha, homeopathy, cosmetics, drugs, veterinary, Unani, laboratory, clinical trials, sehedule A to Y, banned drugs, price control, project report, flowcharts and decision taken by high courts which is most useful in daily needs in order to avoid criminal activities. In order to remain away from crime, everyone must know Drugs and Cosmetics Act and Rules for his or her better life and prosperity of nation.

Two chapters are added in this edition. Medical Devices Rules are meant for various organs like teeth, heart, bone and joint which are explained. The drugs and magic remedies are objectionable advertisement which means drugs must have right product information, and wrong product information shall be banned which is explained.

Ranjan Magazine
ranjan.magazine@gmail.com

Preface to the First Edition

This is an important book on *Drugs and Cosmetics Act, 1940 and Rules, 1945* for the use of students, laboratory practice, pharmacists, formulators, marketers and personnel in manufacturing and marketing. Book is updated, authentic and easy to study. The chapters cover all aspects of the Act and Rules, for example AYUSH, ayurvedic, siddha, homeopathy, cosmetics, drugs, veterinary, Unani, laboratory, clinical trials, Schedule A to Y, banned drugs, price control and decision taken by Supreme Court of India and High Court which is most useful in daily needs in order to avoid criminal activities.

Everyday we see several persons trapped in criminal activities due to the fact that they are not aware about Act and Rules. Such persons spoil their lives by undergoing imprisonment and fine because these people have adulterated, misbranded and spurious work. Criminal activities are always a loss to person and nation because they spoil the image of both person and nation. In order to remain away from crime, everyone must know Drugs and Cosmetics Act and Rules for his or her better life and prosperity of nation.

Ranjan Magazine
ranjan.magazine@gmail.com

Contents

1

AYUSH
Government of India

Department of Indian Systems of Medicine and Homoeopathy (ISM&H) was created in March, 1995 and re-named as Department of Ayurveda, Yoga and Naturopathy, Unani, Siddha and Homoeopathy (AYUSH) in November, 2003 with a view to providing focused attention to development of Education and Research in Ayurveda, Yoga and Naturopathy, Unani, Siddha and Homoeopathy systems. The department continued to lay emphasis on up gradation of AYUSH educational standards, quality control and standardization of drugs, improving the availability of medicinal plant material, research and development and awareness generation about the efficacy of the systems domestically and internationally.

2

Ayurvedic Formulation

Ayurvedic drugs are developed from Ancient Ayurvedic System of medicine prevalent in India since the Vedic period. The word Ayurveda is made up of two components. 'Ayush' meaning Life and 'Veda' meaning Science, hence Ayurveda is the 'Science of Life'. The origin of this ancient science dates back to Vedic period, about 5000 years ago, Brahma, the creator was the originator of this system who  passed if on to the Ashwini Kumars (Physicians of God) who in turn imparted it to the Rishis, from where it was promoted among the people through generations.

OBJECTIVE OF AYURVEDA

The main objective of Ayurveda is maintenance and promotion of positive health and cure of diseases, through medicine, dietary restrictions and regulated life style.

BASIC PRINCIPLES OF AYURVEDA

The basic principles of Ayurveda involve two theories, one is the Panchamahabhuta theory and the other is the Tridosha theory. According to Ayurvedic philosophy all the living and non-living matters are made up of five basic elements in various proportions, they are Prithvi (earth), Jala (water), Teja (fire), Vayu (air) and Aakash (ether). Even the human body is made up of these elements known collectively as the Panchamaha-bhutas. According to Ayurveda again, all the physiological functions of the body are governed by three biological units namely Vata, Pitta and Kafa each of which in turn is made up of the Mahabhutas, physiologically these three doshas are responsible for various specific functions. Vata is responsible for all voluntary and involuntary movements in the human body. Pitta is responsible for all digestive and metabolic activities. Kafa provides the static energy (strength) for holding body tissues together. It also provides lubricants at the various points of friction. When these doshas are in the normal state of functioning, it is health and when they lose their equilibrium and get vitiated by various internal and external factors they produce varied diseases in the human body. Hence, Ayurvedic treatment of any disease is aimed at restoring the equilibrium of the doshas.

BRANCHES OF AYURVEDA

Ayurveda is mainly classified into eight branches which specialize in different fields of medicine.

DISEASE PROCESS

Ayurveda has very distinctly dealt with the disease process which has six stages. These stages have been referred to as the Sat Kriya Kalas (Time for treatment) and includes:

1. Sanchaya (stage of accumulation)
2. Prakopa (state of provocation)
3. Prasara (stage of spreading)
4. Sthana Sanshrey (stage of localization)
5. Vyakti (stage disease manifestation)
6. Bheda (stage of complications or chronic). It has been emphasized in Ayurveda to diagnose and treat a disease in its early stages so that its complications can be prevented and at times the manifestation of a disease too can be averted.

DEFINITION OF HEALTH

Health is a state of physical, mental and social well-being and not merely a state free from disease. Considering the objective and the above therapeutic principles of Ayurveda, it provides the best alternative in promoting health of an individual and curing the diseases of the afflicted. Ayurveda has also defined health as equilibrium of the three biological units (Doshas) and body tissues (Dhatus) and a state of pleasure or happiness of the soul, senses in the mind. These states will certainly lead to the social and spiritual well-being of an individual. This is very much in conformity with the above definition of health as stated by WHO. Hence, Ule importance of Ayurvedic treatment is relevant in modern time as well. In today's fast life and competitive world there has been a revolution in our eating habits and life style. We are exposed more to various types of stress and strain which affects upon our health. Even our diet has become more synthetic; than the natural one which exposes us to the toxins, resulting in various disorders. Even the modern curative agent are synthetic, therefore, in addition to having specific therapeutic action they also create the adverse reactions in the human body, while curing one disease they might be the cause for another disease. With the growing awareness of the dangers and limitations of the allopathic system of treatment the answer now is Ayurveda.

TREATMENT PROCEDURES

Ayurveda lays great emphasis on the preventive and dietary methods during times of good health and illness. Charaka classifies medicines into two kinds:

1. Promotion of vigour in the healthy and
2. Cure of disease in the afflicted.

Ayurvedic medicines besides the herbal and mineral drugs offers a variety of comprehensive treatment procedures structured to the needs of a patient. These include such procedures as oil massage, fermentation, application of medicated pasts, etc. Considerable success has been recorded in the healing of chronic illnesses through Ayurveda in diseases like metabolic and systemic disorders, skin and allergic disorders and psychological disorders which are generally not amenable to other forms of treatment. Ayurvedic medicines are accepted by the human organism in much the same way as it accepts the nourishment from food. "Ayurvedic drug" includes all medicines intended for internal or external use for or in the diagnosis, treatment, mitigation or prevention of [disease or disorder in human beings or animals, and manufactured] exclusively in accordance with the formulae described in, the authoritative books of (Ayurvedic, specified in the First Schedule;) of the Drugs and Cosmetics Act, 1940.

CATEGORIES OF AYURVEDIC MEDICINES

Avaleha and Pak

Avaleha or leha is prepared by repeatedly boiling the decoction and extract of a and condensing it with sugar, etc. This preparation which can be taken by licking is called Avaleha.

Bati

Those drugs, which have been evolved from plants are pulverized initially and added to honey or any other liquid substances to make up pills and tablets. After mixing, these preparations are eithenlried directly under the sun or by indirect heat while keeping them in open air if in shade to retain the efficacy of these drugs.

Bhasma

Powder of a substance obtained by calcinatioll is called Bhasma. The process of oxidation of the raw material by heat is regulated scientifically. The raw materials for manufacturing Bhasmas are subjected to test and analysis before processing. The 18 processes in Indian Chemistry namely shodhan, Maran, Jaran, Tiryakptan, Urdhwapatan, Adhahpaljn, Niyaman, Bodhan, etc. are strictly followed while manufacturing different preparations under modern conditions.

Churna

Churna is a coarse powder made by certain drugs or combination of drugs. Ayurvedic medicines derived from plants, are prepared either inform of powders or decoctions. Before these plants are subjected to processing they are thoroughly examined by specialists and proper identification is made. Each of the ingredients is pulverized separately as tlie different ingredients when pulverized, together do not pass through the sieve equally which affects the composition.

MEDICATED GHRITA

These are the preparations in which ghee is boiled with prescribed drugs according to the formula. The medicated Ghritas are more effective than ordinary Ghritas. In order to prepare Ghrita in accordance with Ayurvedic system, Ghrita of a particular animal is subjected to several processings. After which Kwath, milk, etc. are added with proper proportion and slowly heated with controlled temperature. The medicated Ghrita from Dabur is manufactured strictly according to the Ayruvedic principles smaller doses. In processing the tablets with finer forms, the ingredients attain special effectiveness in the treatment of diseases.

MEDICATED OIL

The oils are boiled along with the certain drugs as prescribed in the formula. These oils have the property and efficacy almost in the same manner as of the medicines. It is used generally for inunctions and massage. The process of preparing medicated oils includes addition of Kwath, Swaras and Kalka subjecting the mixture in a regulated temperature.

PRAVAW KWATH

Certain drugs or combination of drugs are made into coarse powder (JA VKUn and kept for preparation of Kasaya. Such powders are called Kwath. Drugs are cleaned and dried and coarsely powdered. Weighed as per formula and mixed well before packing.

Ark

Ark is a liquid preparation obtained by distillation of certain liquids or drugs soaked in water using the Arkayantra or any convenient modern distillation apparatus.

SHODHIT DRAVYA AND SATVA

Satva is water extractable solid substance collected from a drug. The drug is cut into small pieces, macerated in water and kept overnight then it is strained through cloth and solid matter is allowed to settle. The supernatant liquid is decanted and Satva washed by repeating the process adding water and decanting. The Satva so sedimented is dried and powdered.

PARPATI

It is prepared by mixing of purified mercury with sulphur, i.e. Kajjali or with other drugs mentioned in formula and subjecting them to heat according to the Ayurvedic principles. During processing the whole mass takes the shape of a cocktail which is indicative of perfection. Due to the presence of mercury and sulphur in combination, the drug has the efficacy to kill bacteria.

PISHTI

The ingredients prescribed in the texts are grinded into fine particles in a pestle and mortar made of Mug un I stone and tritura Hng it with rose water for 8, 14 or 21 days, drying them at night under the moon orin the day time under the sun. It is therefore, either called 'Chandraputit' or 'Suryaputit' accordingly. The adjuncts are used exactly the same way as those of Bhasma.

RAS-RASAYAN

Preparation containing mineral drugs as main ingredients are called Ras Yogas, Mercury, Sulphur, Yatsanabha, Hingu-Tankan, Alum, Kuchila, Opium, Dhatura, Siddhi and laypal are fully tested and purified and a method of manufacture of complete Ras (Tablets) is established to give more effect in...

ASAVA AND ARISHT

A Either decoction or water extract is made from the crude drug to which molasses, honey, sugar and certain astringents – such as Dhatakipushp, Babbul, etc. are mixed for a certain period. In this condition fermentation takes place and these original drugs undergo chemical changes and develop into one drug—such a preparation is called Arishta. Asava–Arishta of higher potency is clear liquids with pleasant odour. It is said that the more these Asava-Arishtas become old the more effective they are in their action.

Prior to 1964, definition of 'drug' under Section 3(b) of the Act had the excluding clause "other than medicines and substances exclusively used and prepared for use in accordance with the Ayurvedic or Unani system of medicines. Therefore, the Ayurvedic drugs were not covered by the Act. The Ayurvedic and Unani drugs have been brought within the scope of the Act. The Ayurvedic and Unani drugs were brought within the scope of the Act because of the following reasons:

- The commercialization of Ayurvedic and Unani drugs by the firms.
- Difficulty in exercising control over Ayurvedic drugs under the Drugs and Cosmetics Act, 1940 because of growing tendency on the part of certain manufacturers to market preparations containing partly modern drugs and partly Ayurvedic drugs.
- Costly raw materials such as gold, musk, pearl, saffron, etc. which are ingredients in the various preparations were either not used or substituted by imitation products.
- The raw materials used in the preparation of drugs should be genuinely and properly identified.
- The formula or the true list of all the ingredients contained in the drugs should be properly displayed on the label of every container.
- The manufacture should be carried under prescribed hygienic conditions, under supervision of a person having prescribed qualification.

By amending the Act 13 of 1964, the excluding clause in the definition of drug under Section 3(b) of the act has been deleted and definition of Ayurvedic drug has been incorporated under Section 3(a) of the act. Definition of Ayurvedic, Siddha or Unani drug as per Section 3(a) of the Drugs and Cosmetics Act, 1940. "Ayurvedic, Siddha or Unani drug" includes all medicines intended for internal or external use for or in the diagnosis, treatment, mitigation or prevention of [disease or disorder in human beings or animals, and manufactured] exclusively in accordance with the formulae described in, the authoritative books of Ayurvedic, Siddha and Unani Tibb systems of medicine [specified in the First Schedule]

THE FIRST SCHEDULE AYURVEDIC SYSTEMS

Sr. No	Name of book
1.	Arogya Kalpadruma
2.	Arka Prakasha
3.	Arya Bhishak
4.	Ashtanga Hridaya
5.	Ashtanga Samgraha
6.	Ayurveda Kalpadruma
7.	Ayurveda Prakasha
8.	Ayurveda Samgraha
9.	Bhaishajya Ratnvali
10.	Bharat Bhaishajya Ratnakara
11.	Bhava Prakasha
12.	Brihat Nighantu Ratnakara
13.	Charaka Samhita
14.	Chakra Datta
15.	Gada Nigraha
16.	Kupi Pakva Rasayana
17.	Nighantu Ratnakara
18.	Rasa Chandanshu
19.	Rasa Raja Sundara
20.	Rasaratna Samuchaya
21.	63[Rasatantra Sara Va Siddha Prayoga Sangraha –Part I]
22.	Rasa Tarangini
23.	Rasa Yoga Sagara
24.	Rasa Yoga Ratnakara
25.	Rasa Yoga Samgraha
26.	Rasendra Sara Samgraha
27.	Rasa Pradipika
28.	Sahasrayoga
29.	Sarvaroga Chikitsa Ratnam
30.	Sarvayoga Chikitsa Ratnam

31.	Sharangadhara Samhita
32.	Siddha Bhaishajya Manimala
33.	Siddha Yoga Samgraha
34.	Sushruta Samhita
35.	Vaidya Chintamani
36.	Vaidyaka Shabda Sindu
37.	Vaidyaka Chikitsa Sara
38.	Vaidya Jiwan
39.	Basava Rajeeyam
40.	Yoga Ratnakara
41.	Yoga Tarangini
42.	Yoga Chintamani
43.	Kashyapasamhita
44.	Bhelasamhita
45.	Vishwanathachikitsa
46.	Vrindachikitsa
47.	Ayurvedachintamani
48.	Abhinavachintamani
49.	Ayurveda-ratnakar
50.	Yogaratnasangraha
51.	Rasamrita
52.	Dravyagunanighantu
53.	Rasamanjari
54.	Bangasena
54-A	Ayurvedic Formulary of India (Part I)
54-B	Ayurveda Sara Samgraha
55.	Siddha Vaidya Thirattu
56.	Therayar Maha Karisal
57.	Brahma Muni Karukkadai (300)
58.	Bhogar (700)
59.	Pulppani (500)
60.	Agasthiyar Paripuranam (400)
61.	Therayar Yamagam
62.	Agasthiyar Chenduram(300)
63.	Agasthiyar (500)
64.	Athmarakshmrutham
65.	Agasthiyar Pin (80)
66.	Agasthiyar Rathna Churukkam
67.	Therayar Karisal (300)

68.	Veeramamuni Nasa Kandam
69.	Agasthiyar (600)
70.	Agasthiyar Kanma Soothiram
71.	18 Siddhar's Chillari Kovai
72.	Yogi Vatha Kaviyam
73.	Therayar Tharu
74.	Agasthiyar Vaidya Kaviyam (1500)
75.	Bala Vagadam
76.	Chimittu Rathna (Rathna) Churukkam
77.	Nagamuni (200)
78.	Agasthiyar Chillari Kovai
79.	Chikicha Rathna Deepam
80.	Agasthiyaar Nayana Vidhi
81.	Yugi Karisal (151)
82.	Agasthiyar Vallathi (600)
83.	Therayar Thaila Varkam
84.	Siddha Formulary of India (Part I)

Customized formulations are for various disorders. These formulations are made from a mixture of pure natural herbs processed under the most hygienic conditions. The customized formulations are available in special packages in different quantities as per the requirement of the clients. Various actual examples are mentioned below.

Contents for HIV/Aids Treatment

Each capsule contains	Wt/unit
Cressa cretica	20 mg
Leptadenia reticulate	20 mg
Tinospora cordifolia	20 mg
Picrorhiza kurroa	20 mg
Asparagus adscendens	20 mg
Zingiber officinale	20 mg
Tribulus terrestris	20 mg
Caesalpinia crista	20 mg
Asparagus racemosus	20 mg
Piper longum	20 mg
Swertia chirata	20 mg
Phaseolus radiatus	20 mg
Piper nigrum	20 mg

Withania somnifera	20 mg
Ocimum sanctum	20 mg
Mineral pitch	20 mg
Mucuna prurita	20 mg
Commifera mukul	20 mg
Glycyrrhiza glabra	20 mg
Holarrhena antidysenterica	20 mg
Feroso revie oxide	20 mg
Pueraria tubeursa	20 mg
Curcuma longa	20 mg
Azadirachta indica	20 mg
Terminalia chebula	20 mg

Contents for the Treatment of Black Spots or Pigmentation

Composition	Wt (%)
Pterocarpus santalinus	10%
Symplucos recemosa	10%
Santalum album	10%
Inula racemosa	10%
Nelumbo nucifera	10%
Berberis Aristata	10%
Myristica fragrans	10%
Termanalia arjuna	10%
Multani	10%
Khapariya	10%

Contents for the Treatment of Sperm Production

Each capsule contains	Wt/unit
Cressa cretica	200 mg
Mineral pitch	200 mg
Mucuna prurita	200 mg
Withania somnifera	100 mg
Asparagus racemonus	100 mg
Zinc	100 mg
Boitite	50 mg
Iron	50 mg

Contents for the Treatment of Hypertension

Each capsule contains	Wt/unit
Rauwolfia serpentina	150 mg
Convolvulus pluricaulis	100 mg
Santalum album	50 mg
Symplocos racemosus	50 mg
Tinospora cordifolia	50 mg
Terminalia chembulla	25 mg
Piper longum	100 mg
Termanalia arjuna	25 mg
Hyoscymus niger	25 mg

Contents for the Treatment of Type 2 Diabetes

Composition	Wt (%)
Cressa cretica	10%
Vitex negundo	10%
Terminatia chebula	10%
Elugenia jamboloma	10%
Picrorhiza kurroa	20%
Enicostama littorale	20%
Azadirachta indicas	20%

Contents for Increasing Strength

Each capsule contains	Wt/unit
Mineral pitch	50 mg
Feroso revie oxide	50 mg
Piper longum	50 mg
Pueraria tubeursa	50 mg
Swertia chirata	50 mg
Asparagus adscendens	100 mg
Cressa cretica	150 mg

Contents for the Treatment of Allergy

Each capsule contains	Wt/unit
Solanum indicum	150 mg
Cressa cretica	150 mg
Ocimum sanctum	100 mg
Piper longum	100 mg

Contents for the Treatment of Strong Hair

Composition	V/V (%)
Cressa cretica	5 %
Berberis aristata	5 %
Eclipta alba	5 %
Vitex negundo	5 %
Bacopa monniera	5 %
Azadirachta indica	Q.S.

Contents for the Treatment to Reduce Cholesterol (LDL)

Each capsule contains	Wt/unit
Termanalia arjuna	300 mg
Annona cherimolia	150 mg
Piper longum	50 mg

Contents for the Treatment of Baldness

Composition	V/V (%)
Cressa cretica	10%
Berberis aristata	10%
Eclipta alba	5%
Vitex negundo	5%
Bacopa monniera	5%
Azadirachta indica	Q.S.

3

Yoga

Yoga is a physical, mental, and spiritual discipline, originating in ancient India. The goal of yoga, or of the person practicing yoga, is the attainment of a state of perfect spiritual insight and tranquility while meditating on the Hindu concept of divinity or Brahman. The word is associated with meditative practices in Hinduism, Jainism, and Buddhism.

1. *Yama (The five "abstentions"):* Ahimsa (non-violence), Satya (truth, non-lying), Asteya (non-covetousness), Brahmacharya (non-sensuality, celibacy), and Aparigraha (non-possessiveness).
2. *Niyama (The five "observances"):* Shaucha (purity), Santosha (contentment), Tapas (austerity), Svadhyaya (study of the Vedic scriptures to know about God and the soul), and Ishvara-Pranidhana (surrender to God).
3. *Asana:* Literally means "seat", and in Patanjali's Sutras refers to the seated position used for meditation.
4. *Pranayama ("suspending breath"):* Prâna, breath, "âyâma", to restrain or stop. Also interpreted as control of the life force.
5. *Pratyahara ("abstraction"):* Withdrawal of the sense organs from external objects.
6. *Dharana ("concentration"):* Fixing the attention on a single object.
7. *Dhyana ("meditation"):* Intense contemplation of the nature of the object of meditation.
8. *Samâdhi ("liberation"):* Merging consciousness with the object of meditation.

The three main focuses of modern yoga (exercise, breathing, and meditation) make it beneficial to those suffering from diseases. Overall, studies of the effects of yoga on diseases suggest that yoga may reduce high blood pressure, arthritis, mental sickness, pain, and stomach and kidney pain. Yoga is best exercise which works on whole body and mind.

4

Siddha Formulation

The drugs used by the Siddhars could be classified into three groups: *thavara* (herbal product), *dhathu* (inorganic substances) and *jangamam* (animal products). The dhathu drugs are further classified as: *uppu* (water-soluble inorganic substances or drugs that give out vapour when put into fire), *pashanam* (drugs not dissolved in water but emit vapour when fired), *uparasam* (similar to *pashanam* but differ in action), *loham* (not dissolved in water but melt when fired), *rasam* (drugs which are soft), and *ghandhagam* (drugs which are insoluble in water, like sulphur).

The drugs used in siddha medicine were classified on the basis of five properties: *suvai* (taste), *guna* (character), *veerya* (potency), *pirivu* (class) and *mahimai* (action).

According to their mode of application, the siddha medicines could be categorized into two classes:

- *Internal medicine* was used through the oral route and further classified into 32 categories based on their form, methods of preparation, shelf-life, etc.
- *External medicine* includes certain forms of drugs and also certain applications (such as nasal, eye and ear drops), and also certain procedures (such as leech application). It also classified into 32 categories.

Siddha Medicine List

Thailam

1. Aswagandha Balalakshadhi Thailam
2. Neeli Bhrungadhi Thailam

Ghirutham/NEI

- Serankottai Nei

Legiyam

1. Aswaganthi Legiyam
2. Dhathukalpa Legiyam
3. Narasimha Legiyam
4. Nellikkai Legiyam
5. Thoothuvalai Legiyam
6. Vallarai Legiyam
7. Venpoosani Legiyam

Rasayanam

1. Thippili Rasayanam
2. Thiraathchai Rasayanam

Tablet

1. Amukkara Choorana Mathirai
2. Karisalai Karpam tablet
3. Kasthoori Mathirai
4. Ponnavarai Choorana tablet
5. Seerana Sanjeevi Choorana tablet
6. Thaleesathi Vadagam tablet
7. Thiripala Karpam tablet
8. Vilvam tablet

Capsule

1. Gnanavalli (Vallarai) capsule
2. Marudham capsule
3. Nandhi Mezhugu capsule
4. Rasagandhi Mezhugu capsule
5. Rathinapurush capsule

Honey

- Honey

Ointment

- Seemai Agathi paste

List of New Siddha Medicines

Chooranam

- SKM Orocare

Thailam

1. Kaya Thirumeni Thailam
2. Vasavu Eannai
3. Vathakodari Thailam

Legiyam

- Prasava Nadakaya Legiyam

Tablet

1. Adhimadhuram tablet
2. Irumal Sanjeevi tablet
3. Skin Sanjeevi tablet
4. Thiripala Choorana tablet
5. Urai tablet
6. Vallarai tablet

Manappagu

- Adathodai Manappagu

Capsules

1. Neeradimuthu Vallathy capsule
2. Sivanvembu Kuzhi Thaila capsule

5

Homeopathy Formulation

Homeopathy has its foundations in all natural and organic ways of life. The system for centuries, offers the greatest benefits through safe mechanism of action.

Our Mission

To become a global source for catering the growing demands for natural alternatives by offering homeopathic and organic formulations produced using organically grown herbs in bulk as well as customer specified packings

Product-contain	Spacking	Indication
Pills Chamomilla 200 C Kreosotum 30 C Cal.phos. 200 C Calc flour 30 C Merc. sol. 30 C	20 gm	For smooth dentition, stone and caly eaters
Pills/Tablets Rhus tox 200 C Bryonia 200 C Colchicum 200 C Causticum 200 C Arnica 200 C Calc. flour 200 C	20 gm/ 60 tab.	Joint pain, backache, etc
Pills/Tablets Borax 200 C Sepia 30 C Kreosotum 200 C Acid nit 200 C Thuja 200 C Hydrastis 200 C	20 gm/ 60 tab.	Uterine disorders, excessive white discharge from female genitals

Pills/Tablets Kale brom 200 C Berb aq. 200 C Hep. sul.200 C Nat. mur 200 C Sulphur 30 C Calc. phos 30 C	20 gm/ 60 tab.	Pimples acne and complexion
Pills/Tablets Nux vomica 200 C Acid nit 200 C Iris ver. 200 C Pulsatilla 200 C Arg. nit. 200 C Carb. veg. 200 C Nat. phos. 200 C Lycopodium 200 C Cinchona 200 C	20 gm/ 60 tab.	Gastric disorders, hyper- acidity, gas trouble, constipa- tion, etc.
Pills/Tablets Flouric acidum 30C Acid phs 30C Natrum mur. 30C Wiesbaden 200C Badiaga 30C	20 gm/ 60 tab.	Falling of hair, premature greying and to increase the growth of hair
Tonic Alfalfa Q 1 Ml Avena sativa Q 5 Ml Hydrasstis Q .05 Ml Nux vomica 2x-0.25 China off. Q 0.25 Ml Cinnamon Q 0.50 Ml Acid phos 2s-5.00 Ml Succharin alb. 25 Gm Aqua dist to make 100 Ml	110 Ml 450 M.	General tonic
Syrup Aconite-q Justicea Ad-3 Drosera-3, Ipecae-3 Ocimum sant-3	110 Ml 450 Ml	Cough syrup of various etiology

Gelsemiou-3
Allium cepa-3
Euhrasia-3
Kali sulph-6x
Kali phos-3x
Mag phos-6x

Tonic	110 Ml	Heametinic
Ashwagandha Q	450 Ml	
Alfalfa Q, China Q		
Hydrastis Q, acid formic 6		
Ferrum met 6		
Five phos 3x		
In syrup base Qs		
Liver tonic	110 Ml	Liver tonic. For curative and preventive of all liver disorders
Chelidonium Mq	450 Ml	
Ceonanthus Aq		
Cardus. mq Dolichos Q, Kalmegh Q		
Syrup	100 Ml	Infestations
Chenopodiun Q		
Cina Q, santonine 3x		
Stanum met 3x		
Nat.phos-2x-worm		
Syrup	110 Ml	Gastric problems, gas trouble, acidity, constipation, etc.
Nux Vomica 200 chpi	450 Ml	
Acid Sul 200 chpi		
Iris Ver 200 chpi		
Pulsatilla 200 chpi		
Carb. veg 200		
Chpi, Nat.phos 200 chpi		
Lycopodium 200 chpi		
Cinchona Off 200		
Syrup	110 Ml	Joint pain, backache, stiffness F Joints
Arnica Montana 200 chpi		
Calc Flour 200 chpi		
Bryonia Alba 200 chpi		
Rhus Tox 200 chpi		

Causticum 200 chpi Colchicum 200 chpi		
Baby tonic Chamomilla 200 chpi Kreosote 200 chpi Calc Phos 200 chpi Calc Flour 30 chpi Merc Sol 30 chpi	110 Ml	Baby tonic
Syrup Gelsemium –200 chpi Eupt.per 200 Baptisia 200 chpi Ars.alb –30 chpi	110 Ml	Running nose, sneezing, etc.
Syrup Lycopodium 200 chpi Selen 200 chpi Phosphorus 30 chpi Damiana 200 chpi Agn.cac 200 chpi	110 Ml	Sex tonic for men
Drops Mag.phos 200 chpi Colocynth 200 chpi Dios Vul 200 chpi	60 Ml	Antispasmodic syrup for infants, children and adults.
Syrup Avena Sative 6 chpi Kali Phos 6 chpi Anacar. or. 6 chpi Lyco 6 chpi	110 Ml	To improve memory power, anxiety, tension, for bed wetting babies.
Syrup Nux Vomica 200 chpi Tabacum 200 chpi Calc Sul 200 chpi Avena Sative 200 chpi	110 Ml	For deaddiction
Syrup Calc Carb-d3 Thuja Oc.-d6 Kali Mur-d3	110 Ml	For lowering cholesterol

Syrup Aesc.hip. 200 chpi Nux Vomica 200 chpi Acid Nit 200 chpi Collin 200 chpi	110 Ml	For bleeding or nonbleeding piles
Syrups Baryta Carb 200 chpi Phytolacca 200 chpi Belladona 200 chpi He.sul. 200 chpi Kali Mur 200 chpi Ferr.phos. 200 chpi	110 Ml	Recurrent tonsillitis
Syrup Calc.carb 30 chpi Agnus.cact. 30 chpi	110 Ml	To increase feeding mother's milk
Syrup Ars.alb. 30 chpi Rhus Tox 30 chpi Sulphur 30 chpi Thuja 30 chpi Apis Mel 30.	110 Ml	For skin diseases
Syrup Thuja oc 200 chpi Causticum 200 chpi Acid Nit. 200 Anti.crud 200 chpi	110 Ml	For warts and corns
Heart tonic Crat.ox. 6c, Cact.gr.6c Stro.his 30c Conv.maj. 6c	110 Ml	Heart tonic
Syrup Fucus.vis. 200 chpi Thyroidin 6 chpi Calc.carb 200 chpi Amm.mur 200 chpi Ant.crud. 200 chpi	110 Ml	For reducing extra fat from body

Syrup Chin.sul 200 chpi Nat.mur. 200 chpi Eup.per. 200 chpi Gelsemium 200 chpi Ipecae 200 chpi Baptisea 200 chpi	110 Ml	For treatment of fever
Syrup	110 Ml	For renal calculi
Syrup Coff.cruda 200 chpi Passiflora 200 chpi Scutell 200 chpi Kali Phos 200 chpi Arnica.mont 200 chpi	110 Ml	For sound sleep
Cream	30 gm	Hypericum Q 10 Ml. cream base
Hair queen-kit (Hair oil, shampoo, tablet vitalizer)		For long and silky hair
Powder	200 gm	Energetic milk powder
Ointment	25 gm	Immediate cooling and rapid healing in burns
Drops	30 Ml	For treatmentof diabetes
Lotion Plantago Q Kreosote Q Calendula Q Borex 6x Glycerine base	10 Ml	Apthous, stomatitis, gingivitis, ect.
Syrup	110/450 Ml	Gastric irritation
Syrup	110 Ml	Help in high BP
Syrup	110 Ml	Migraine
Ointment	30 gm	White spots

6

Drug Formulation

LIST OF ALL FORMULATIONS ARRANGED ALPHABETICALLY

A

Azithromycin suspension (500 mg/10 ml)

Azulene solution (1%)

B

Barium sulfate oral suspension (23%)

Basic cream for different active. *Ingredients:* Benzhexol tablets (5 mg)

Benzoyl peroxide + alpha-bisabolol gel (5.0% + 0.2%)

Benzyl benzoate solution (10%)

Benzylpenicillin + dihydrostreptomycin injectable suspension (200,000 units + 200 mg/ml)

Berberine tablets (5 mg)

Beta carotene + vitamin C + vitamin E chewable rablets (10 mg + 500 mg + 250 mg)

Beta carotene + vitamin C + vitamin E tablets (6 mg + 100 mg + 30 mg)

Beta carotene + vitamin C + vitamin E tablets (7 mg + 60 mg + 15 mg)

Beta carotene + vitamin C + vitamin E tablets (12 mg + 250 mg + 125 mg)

Beta carotene effervescent tablets (7 mg)

Beta carotene tablets (15 mg)

Beta carotene tablets (20 mg)

Betamethasone + neomycin gel-cream (0.1% + 0.6%)

Betamethasone cream (0.1%)

Betamethasone gel (0.1%)

Bifonazole cream (1%)
Bran tablets (250 mg), DC
Bran tablets (250 mg), WG
Bromhexine tablets (8 mg)
Bromocriptine tablet cores (6 mg)

C

Calcium carbonate tablets (500 mg)
Calcium effervescent tablets (250 mg)
Calcium gluconate tablets (350 mg)
Calcium glycerophosphate tablets (200 mg)
Calcium glycerophosphate tablets (500 mg)
Calcium pantothenate see vitamin B_5
Calcium phosphate tablets for cats and dogs (400 mg)
Captopril tablets (25 mg)
Carbamazepine tablets (200 mg)
Carbonyl iron + manganese sulfate + copper sulfate tablets
(24 mg + 3.5 mg + 0.16 mg)
Carnitine + coenzym Q solution (4.0% + 0.1%)
Caroate dispersible cleaning tablets (880 mg)
Caroate effervescent cleaning tablets (650 mg)
Charcoal tablets (250 mg)
Chloramphenicol ophthalmic solution (3%)
Chloramphenicol palmitate oral or topical emulsion (2.5% =
250 mg/10 ml)
Chloramphenicol palmitate oral or topical emulsion (5.0% =
500 mg/10 ml)
Chlorhexidine gel (2%)
Chlorhexidine lozenges (5 mg)
Chloroquine tablets (250 mg)
Choline theophyllinate tablets (100 mg)
Chymotrypsine tablets (27 mg)
Cimetidine tablets (200 mg)
Cimetidine tablets (280 mg)
Cimetidine tablets (400 mg)
Clenbuterol tablets (20 µg)

Clobazam tablets (10 mg)
Clomifen tablets (50 mg)
Closantel veterinary injectable solution (12–20 g/100 ml)
Clotrimazol topical solution (3%)
Clotrimazole cream (1%)
Crospovidone effervescent tablets (1000 mg)
Crospovidone water dispersible tablets (1000 mg)
Cyanocobalamin *see* vitamin B$_{12}$
Cyproheptadine tablet (4 mg)

D

Dexpanthenol gel-cream (5%)
Diazepam injectable solution (2.5 mg/ml)
Diazepam tablet (10 mg)
Diclofenac gel (1%)
Diclofenac gel-cream (1%)
Diclofenac injectable solution (75 mg/3 ml)
Diclofenac oral solution (1.5%)
Diclofenac tablet cores (50 mg)
Diclofenac tablets (50 mg)
Diltiazem tablets (50 mg)
Dimenhydrinate tablet cores (100 mg)
Dimenhydrinate tablets (50 mg)

E

Enteric film coating
Ephedrine tablets (100 mg)
Erythromycin gel (1%)
Ethambutol tablets (400 mg), DC
Ethambutol tablets (400 mg), WG
Ethambutol tablets (800 mg)
Etophylline + theophylline tablets (100 mg + 22 mg), DC
Etophylline + theophylline tablets (100 mg + 22 mg), WG
Eucalyptol solution (8%)

F

Famotidine tablets (40 mg)
Ferrous fumarate tablets (200 mg)
Ferrous sulfate + manganese sulfate + copper sulfate tablets
(65 mg + 3.5 mg + 0.16 mg)
Ferrous sulfate tablets (200 mg)
Fir needle oil solution (3%)
Folic acid tablets (5 mg)
Fucidine tablet cores (125 mg)
Furaltadone injectable solution (50 mg/ml)
Furosemide tablets (40 mg)
Furosemide tablets (200 mg)

G

Garlic tablets cores (100 mg)
Glibenclamide tablets (5 mg)
Glutaminic acid tablets (550 mg)
Gramicidin ophthalmic solution (1.3 mg/10 ml)
Griseofulvin tablets (125 mg)
Griseofulvin tablets (500 mg)

H

Heparin gel (30,000 iu/100 g)
Horsetail extract tablets (450 mg)
Hydrochlorothiazide + potassium
Chloride tablet cores (50 mg + 300 mg)
Hydrochlorothiazide tablets (50 mg), DC
Hydrochlorothiazide tablets (50 mg), WG
Hydrocortisone aqueous gels (1%)
Hydrocortisone cream (1%)
Hydrocortisone ethanolic gel (0.5%)

I

Ibuprofen gel-cream (5%)
Ibuprofen gels (5%)

Ibuprofen solution (2%)
Ibuprofen suspension (4% = 400 mg/10 ml), I
Ibuprofen suspension (4% = 400 mg/10 ml), II
Ibuprofen tablets (400 mg), DC
Ibuprofen tablets (400 mg), WG
Ibuprofen tablets for children (150 mg)
Indomethacin gel (1%), I
Indomethacin gel (1%), II
Indomethacin powder for hard gelatin capsules (160 mg)
Indomethacin suppositories (50 mg)
Indomethacin tablets (50 mg), DC
Indomethacin tablets (50 mg), WG
Indomethacin tablets (100 mg)
Inosin tablet cores (200 mg)
Isosorbide dinitrate tablets (5 mg)

K

Khellin tablets (25 mg)

L

Levamisole tablets (150 mg)
Levothyroxine tablets (0.05 g)
Lidocain gel (2%)
Lidocain gel-cream (5%)
Lisinopril tablets (10 mg)

M

Magaldrate chewable tablets (500 mg)
Magaldrate dispersible tablets (700 mg)
Magaldrate instant powder or dry syrup
Magaldrate suspension (10%)
Magnesium carbonate tablets (260 mg)
Mebendazol tablets (100 mg)
Mebendazole suspension (2% = 200 mg/10 ml)
Mefenamic acid tablets (250 mg)

Meprobamate + phenobarbital tablets (400 mg + 30 mg), DC
Meprobamate + phenobarbital tablets (400 mg + 30 mg), WG
Meprobamate tablets (400 mg), DC
Meprobamate tablets (400 mg), WG
Metamizol tablets (500 mg)
Metformin tablets (500 mg)
Methyl cysteine tablets (100 mg)
Methyl salicylate + menthol gel (11% + 5%)
Metoclopramide tablets (10 mg)
Metronidazole effervescent vaginal tablets (500 mg)
Metronidazole injectable solution (500 mg/10 ml)
Metronidazole tablet cores (400 mg)
Metronidazole tablets (200 mg)
Metronidazole tablets (500 mg)
Metronidazole vaginal Gel (1.2%)
Miconazole cream (2%)
Miconazole injectable solution (1%)
Miconazole mouth gel (2%)
Mint mouth wash solutions
Mint oil solution (3.5%)
Multivitamin + calcium + iron + tablets
Multivitamin + calcium syrup
Multivitamin + carbonyl iron tablets
Multivitamin + minerals tablets with beta carotene
Multivitamin chewable tablets for children
Multivitamin drops
Multivitamin effervescent granules
Multivitamin effervescent tablets with beta carotene (food)
Multivitamin effervescent tablets (I)
Multivitamin effervescent tablets (II)
Multivitamin injectable for veterinary application
Multivitamin instant granules
Multivitamin oral gel (vet.)
Multivitamin oral gel with linoleic acid and linolenic acid
Multivitamin syrup I
Multivitamin syrup II

Multivitamin tablets (I)
Multivitamin tablets (II)
Multivitamin tablet cores with beta-carotene
Multivitamin tablets for dogs
Multivitamin tablets with beta carotene
Multivitamin two chamber ampules

N

Nalidixic acid tablets (500 mg)
Naproxen tablets (250 mg)
Naproxen tablets (450 mg)
Neomycin gel (0.05%)
Neomycin tablets (250 mg)
Nicotinic acid tablets (200 mg)
Nicotinamide *see* vitamin B_3
Nifedipine tablet cores (10 mg)
Nitrendipine tablets (25 mg)
Nitrofurantoin tablet cores (100 mg)
Nitrofurantoin tablets (100 mg)
Norephedrine syrup (40 mg/10 g)
Nystatin suspension (100,000 iu/ml)
Nystatin tabet cores (200 mg)
Nystatin tablets (50 mg and 100 mg)

O

Omega fatty acids tablet cores (10 mg EPA + DNA)
Oxytetracycline injectable solution for veterinary application
(500 mg/10 ml)
Oxytetracycline sustained release injectable for veterinary
application (2.2 g/10 ml)
Oxytetracycline tablets (250 mg)

P

Pancreatin tablet cores (30 mg)
Pancreatin tablet cores (130 mg)

Pancreatin tablet cores (300 mg)

Paracetamol (= acetaminophen) + caffeine tablets (500 mg + 50 mg) paracetamol (= acetaminophen) + doxylamine + caffeine effervescent granules (500 mg + 5 mg + 33 mg/2.1 g)

Paracetamol (= acetaminophen) instant granules (250 mg or 500 mg)

Paracetamol (= acetaminophen) + ibuprofen + orphenadin tablets (250 mg + 200 mg + 100 mg)

Paracetamol (= acetaminophen) + norephedrine + phenyl-toloxamine tablets (300 mg + 25 mg + 22 mg)

Paracetamol (= acetaminophen) + phenprobamat tablets (200 mg + 200 mg)

Paracetamol (= acetaminophen) chewable tablets (300 mg)

Paracetamol (= acetaminophen) effervescent tablets (500 mg)

Paracetamol (= acetaminophen) instant granules (500 mg)

Paracetamol (= acetaminophen) suppositories (150 mg and 500 mg)

Paracetamol (= acetaminophen) suspension (5% = 500 mg/10 ml)

Paracetamol (= acetaminophen) syrup (5% = 500 mg/10 g)

Paracetamol (= acetaminophen) syrup for children (2.5% = 250 mg/10 ml)

Paracetamol (= acetaminophen) tablet cores (500 mg)

Paracetamol (= acetaminophen) tablets (500 mg)

Paracetamol (= acetaminophen) tablets for children (200 mg)

Phendimetrazin tablets (35 mg)

Phenindion tablets (50 mg)

Phenolphthalein tablet cores (200 mg)

Phenytoin oral suspension (5%)

Phenytoin sodium tablets (100 mg), DC

Phenytoin sodium tablets (100 mg), WG

Phenytoin tablets (100 mg)

Piroxicam + dexpanthenol gel (0.5% + 5.0%)

Piroxicam water dispersible tablets (20 mg) placebo tablets

Polidocanol wound spray

Povidone-iodine + lidocain gel (10%)

Povidone-iodine bar soap (5%)
Povidone-iodine bar soap (5%)
Povidone-iodine concentrates for Broilers and cattles (20%)
Povidone-iodine cream (10%)
Povidone-iodine effervescent vaginal tablets (350 mg)
Povidone-iodine foam spray (10%)
Povidone-iodine gargle solution concentrate (10%)
Povidone-iodine gel-cream (10%)
Povidone-iodine gels (10%)
Povidone-iodine glucose ointment (2.5%)
Povidone-iodine lipstick or after shave stick (10%)
Povidone-iodine liquid spray (10%)
Povidone-iodine lozenges (5 mg)
Povidone-iodine mastitis cream (10%)
Povidone-iodine mouth wash and
   Gargle solution concentrate (7.5%)
Povidone-iodine ophthalmic solutions (0.4%)
Povidone-iodine ophthalmic solutions (1.0%)
Povidone-iodine powder spray
Povidone-iodine pump spray (1%)
Povidone-iodine seamless solutions (10%)
Povidone-iodine shampoo (7.5%)
Povidone-iodine soft gel (1%)
Povidone-iodine solution (10%), I
Povidone-iodine solution (10%), II
Povidone-iodine surgical scrubs (7.5%), I
Povidone-iodine surgical scrubs (7.5%), II
Povidone-iodine teat-dip solution (3%)
Povidone-iodine transparent ointment (10%)
Povidone-iodine vaginal douche concentrate (10%)
Povidone-iodine vaginal ovula (5%)
Povidone-iodine vaginal ovula (10%)
Povidone-iodine viscous solution (1%)
Prazosin tablets (5 mg)
Prednisolone tablets (20 mg)

Prednisone tablets (10 mg)
Probenecid tablets (500 mg)
Procain penicillin injectable suspension (300 mg/ml)
Propanidide injectable solution (50 mg/ml)
Propranolol hydrochloride tablets (10 mg, 50 mg and 100 mg)
Propranolol tablets cores (40 mg)
Protective film coating with ethylcellulose + kollidon VA 64
Protective film coating with HPC + kollidon VA 64
Protective film coating with HPMC + kollidon VA 64
Protective film coating with kollidon VA 64
Protecitive filmcoating with polyvinyl alcohol + kollidon VA 64
Protective film coating with shellac + kollidon 30
Pseudoephedrine tablets (60 mg)
Pyrazinamide tablets (500 mg), DC
Pyrazinamide tablets (500 mg), WG
Pyridoxine *see* vitamin B_6

R

Ranitidine tablet cores (150 mg)
Ranitidine tablet cores (300 mg)
Riboflavin *see* vitamin B_2
Rifampicin tablets (450 mg)

S

Saccharin effervescent tablets (15 mg)
Saccharin tablets (15 mg)
Selegiline tablets (5 mg)
Serratio peptidase tablets (10 mg)
Silimarin tablets (35 mg)
Simethicone chewable tablets (70 mg)
Simethicone chewable tablets (80 mg)
Simethicone instant granules (6%)
Sobrerol injectable solution (75 mg/5 ml)
Sodium fluoride tablets (0.5 mg)

Sodium fluoride tablets (1.3 mg)
Spironolactone tablets (25 mg)
Spirulina extract chewable tablets (250 mg)
Subcoating of tablets cores sucralfate tablets (500 mg)
Sugar coating, automatic
Sugar coating, manual
Sugar film coating
Sulfadiazine + trimethoprim veterinary oral suspension (40% + 8%)
Sulfadiazine tablets (450 mg)
Sulfadimethoxine veterinary injectable solution (250 mg/10 ml)
Sulfadimidine tablets (500 mg)
Sulfadoxine + trimethoprim veterinary injectable solution (1000 mg + 200 mg/10 ml)
Sulfadoxine solution (2% = 20 mg/ml)
Sulfamethoxazole + trimethoprim tablets (400 mg + 80 mg)
Sulfamethoxazole + trimethoprim dry syrup (400 mg + 80 g/10 ml)
Sulfamethoxazole + trimethoprim oral suspension (400 mg + 80 mg/5 ml)
Sulfamoxole + trimethoprim veterinary injectable solution (400 mg + 80 mg/10 ml)
Sulfathiazole tablets (250 mg)
Sulfathiazole veterinary injectable solution (8 mg/ml)
Sulfathiazole veterinary oral solution (8 mg/ml)

T

Tannin-crospovidone complex tablets (55 mg + 230 mg)
Terazosin tablets (1 mg and 5 mg)
Terfenadine suspension (60 mg/5 ml = 1.2%)
Terfenadine tablets (60 mg)
Tetracycline tablets (125 mg)
Tetracycline tablets (250 mg)
Tetrazepam tablets (50 mg)
Theophylline + ephedrine tablets (130 mg + 15 mg)
Theophylline tablets (100 mg)

Theophylline injectable solution (200 mg/5 ml)
Thiamine *see* vitamin B_1
Tretinoin + alpha bisabolol gel (50 mg + 100 mg/100 g)
Tretinoin + dexpanthenol gel (50 mg + 2.5 g/100 g)
Tretinoin cream (50 mg/100 g)
Tretinoin gel (50 mg/100 g)
Tretinoin solution (50 mg/100 g)
Triamcinolone tablets (4 mg)
Trifluoperazine tablets (5 mg)
Trihexylphenidyl *see* benzhexol

U

Ultrasonic adhesive gel

V

Valeriana extract + passiflora extract tablet cores (44 mg + 30 mg)

Valproate sodium tablets (500 mg)

Verapamil tablets (120 mg)

Vitamin A + vitamin B_6 + vitamin E tablets (40,000 iu + 40 mg + 35 mg)

Vitamin A + vitamin C + vitamin D_3 chewable tablets for children (2,000 iu + 30 mg + 200 iu)

Vitamin A + vitamin C + vitamin E tablets (1200 iu + 60 mg + 30 mg)

Vitamin A + vitamin D_3 + calcium + magnesium injectable solution (33,000 iu + 6,000 iu + 100 mg + 200 mg/g)

Vitamin A + vitamin D_3 + vitamin E + beta carotene veterinary injectable solution (100,000 iu + 20,000 iu + 10 mg + 8 mg/g)

Vitamin A + vitamin D_3 + vitamin E aqueous injectable emulsion for cattles (500,000 iu + 75,000 iu + 50 mg/ml with solutol HS 15)

Vitamin A + vitamin D_3 + vitamin E aqueous injectable emulsion for cattles (500,000 iu + 75,000 iu + 50 mg/ml with cremophor EL)

Vitamin A + vitamin D_3 + vitamin E concentrates, water-miscible (120,000 iu + 60,000 iu + 40 mg/ml)

Vitamin A + vitamin D_3 + vitamin E injectable solution in organic solvents for cattles (500,000 iu + 75,000 iu + 50 mg/ml)

Vitamin A + vitamin D_3 + vitamin E

Veterinary injectable solution (100,000 iu + 20,000 iu + 10 mg/g)

Vitamin A + vitamin D_3 concentrate, water-miscible (100,000 iu + 20,000 iu/ml)

Vitamin A + vitamin D_3 concentrate, water-miscible (120,000 iu + 12,000 iu/g)

Vitamin A + vitamin D_3 drops (30,000 iu + 3,000 iu/g)

Vitamin A + vitamin D_3 injectable solutions (30,000 iu + 5,000 or 10,000 iu/ml)

Vitamin A + vitamin D_3 oral solution for children (1,000 iu + 100 iu/ml)

Vitamin A + vitamin D_3 syrup (30,000 iu + 10,000 iu/ml)

Vitamin A + vitamin E chewable tablets (30,000 iu + 35 mg)

Vitamin A + vitamin E drops (25,000 iu + 50 mg/ml)

Vitamin A + vitamin E drops (5,000 iu + 50 mg/ml)

Vitamin A + vitamin E injectable solution for sheeps (250,000 iu + 25 mg/ml)

Vitamin A + vitamin E tablets (33,000 iu + 70 mg)

Vitamin A chewable tablets (100,000 iu)

Vitamin A concentrate, water-miscible (100,000 iu/ml)

Vitamin A drops (50,000 iu/ml)

Vitamin A ethanolic veterinary injectable solution (500,000 iu/ml)

Vitamin A suppositories (150,000 iu)

Vitamin A tablet cores (50,000 iu)

Vitamin A tablets (25,000 iu)

Vitamin A tablets (50,000 iu)

Vitamin B complex + amino acid + magnesium effervescent granules

Vitamin B complex + carnitine tablet cores

Vitamin B complex + minerals + linoleic/linolenic acid syrup

Vitamin B complex + vitamin C + calcium effervescent tablets

Vitamin B complex + vitamin C + ferrous sulfate tablets

Vitamin B complex + vitamin C effervescent tablets

Vitamin B complex + vitamin C instant granules

Vitamin B complex + vitamin C syrup, I
Vitamin B complex + vitamin C syrup, II
Vitamin B complex + vitamin C tablets
Vitamin B complex injectable solution
Vitamin B complex syrup
Vitamin B complex tablets I
Vitamin B complex tablets II
Vitamin B_1 + caffeine tablets (500 mg + 100 mg)
Vitamin B_1 + vitamin B_2 + vitamin B_3 + vitamin B_6 injectable solution (100 mg + 6 mg + 40 mg + 4 mg/2 ml)
Vitamin B_1 + vitamin B_6 + vitamin B_{12} tablets (100 mg + 10 mg + 100 µg)
Vitamin B_1 + vitamin B_6 + vitamin B_{12} tablets (100 mg + 200 mg + 100 µg)
Vitamin B_1 + vitamin B_6 + vitamin B_{12} tablets (250 mg + 250 mg + 1 mg)
Vitamin B_1 tablets (50 mg), I
Vitamin B_1 tablets (50 mg), II
Vitamin B_1 tablets (100 mg), DC
Vitamin B_1 tablets (100 mg), WG
Vitamin B_1 tablets (300 mg)
Vitamin B_{12} tablets, coloured (50 ìg)
Vitamin B_2 tablets (3 mg)
Vitamin B_2 tablets (10 mg)
Vitamin B_2 tablets (75 mg)
Vitamin B_2 tablets (100 mg)
Vitamin B_2 tablets (150 mg)
Vitamin B_3 (Nicotinamide) tablets (300 mg)
Vitamin B_5 (calcium D-pantothenate) chewable tablets (600 mg)
Vitamin B_5 (calcium D-pantothenate) tablets (100 mg)
Vitamin B_5 (calcium D-pantothenate) tablets (280 mg)
Vitamin B_5 (calcium D-pantothenate) tablets (300 mg)
Vitamin B_6 tablets (40 mg), DC
Vitamin B_6 tablets (40 mg), WG
Vitamin B_6 tablets (100 mg)
Vitamin B_6 tablets (250mg)
Vitamin B_6 tablets (300 mg)

Vitamin C + calcium carbonate effervescent tablets (500 mg + 300 mg)

Vitamin C + vitamin E lozenges (100 mg + 50 mg)

Vitamin C chewable tablets (100 mg, 500 mg, 1,000 mg)

Vitamin C chewable tablets (500 mg)

Vitamin C chewable tablets with dextrose (100 mg)

Vitamin C chewable tablets with fructose (120 mg)

Vitamin C chewable tablets with sucrose (500 mg)

Vitamin C effervescent tablets (100 mg and 1000 mg)

Vitamin C effervescent tablets (500 mg)

Vitamin C tablets (100 mg)

Vitamin C tablets (200 mg)

Vitamin C tablets (250 mg)

Vitamin C tablets (400 mg)

Vitamin E + benzocaine solution (5% + 2%)

Vitamin E + selenium veterinary injectable solution (60 mg E + 3 mg Se/ml)

Vitamin E chewable tablets (100 mg)

Vitamin E chewable tablets (150 mg)

Vitamin E chewable tablets (200 mg)

Vitamin E chewable tablets (400 mg)

Vitamin E concentrate, water-miscible (10% = 100 mg/ml)

Vitamin E drops (50 mg/ml)

Vitamin E gel-cream (10%)

Vitamin E solution with ethanol (0.01% = 1 mg/10 ml)

Vitamin E tablets (50 mg)

Vitamin K1 phytomenadion) injectable solution (10 mg and 20 mg/ml)

Size and Optimization of the Formulations

All the formulations were developed exclusively on a laboratory scale of the order of 1 kg maximum. For this reason, scale-up for production must therefore be checked and revised, as necessary.

It is only in very exceptional cases that the formulations have been optimized by a systematic study involving a comparison between different excipients or by varying the amounts of excipients. Thus, the formulations are merely suggestions that require further optimization.

Active Substances

The active substances are almost exclusively generic. They were mostly supplied free of charge as samples by pharmaceutical companies. Since the manufacturer's name was mostly not mentioned, it unfortunately cannot be listed here.

Significant differences in the properties of the preparations may occur if the same active substance is used, but has a different grain size or originates from another manufacturer. The reason for this is that the difference in physical properties may exert a strong effect particularly on solid drugs.

Stability Data

It is only in exceptional cases or when certain groups of active substances are present that data are given on the chemical and/or the physical stability of the formulations. The reasons are as follows:

a. The formulations are practically always modified by the customer when they are scaled up to meet the demands of industry.

b. Aromas or colorants are added to the formulations in amounts depending on the particular taste of the target group.

c. In view of the very number of formulations presented here and for capacity reasons, the long-term stability of all of them cannot be checked. The stability of the preparation may change as a result of items a. and b. Thus the final formulation must be checked in any event. Data on the chemical stability are often available for sensitive materials, e.g. PVP-iodine or vitamins. They mostly concern either storage at room temperature (20–25°C) over a period of one year or a stress test that lasts at least just as long. In a number of formulations, data are also listed on the physical stability.

7

Cosmetics Formulation

COSMETICS

Cosmetic means any article intended to be rubbed, poured, sprinkled or sprayed on, or introduced into, or otherwise applied to, the human body or any part thereof for cleansing, beautifying, promoting attractiveness or altering the appearance, and includes any article intended for use as a component of cosmetic.

Object

- To ensure safety of components used in cosmetics.
- To study different cosmetics products for their adverse and toxic effects on body.
- To protect the consumer from misleading and exaggerated advertisements.
- To interact and exchange ideas, notes experiences with experts in different fields and conduct joint studies.
- To study the suggestions made and problems faced by the stake holders.
- To educate consumers for safe use of cosmetics acts implemented.

Acts Implemented

The Drugs and Cosmetics Act, 1940 and Rules, 1945.

Regulate

1. To grant and renew licenses for the cosmetics manufacturing units.

2. To approve plan of manufacturing premises for cosmetics.
3. To issue various certificates for tenders, *Exports:* No conviction certificate, performance certificate, free sale certificate, certificate of compliance of schedule M-II.
4. To investigate complaints received regarding cosmetics.
5. To carry out inspections of manufacturing units.
6. To draw samples of cosmetics.
7. To conduct raids for those manufacturing spurious/substandard cosmetics.
8. To take legal action against the offenders and prosecute.
9. To give approval to personnel as competent technical person for manufacturing and testing.
10. To educate the consumers for the safe use of cosmetics.
11. To take cognizance of news items appearing in newspapers, magazines, etc. and take necessary steps/actions.

ACTIONS
Substandard Cosmetics

On samples which are reported to be of substandard quality, depending upon the findings of government analyst the action of suspension, cancellation of licenses, prosecution is taken.

Noncompliance of Conditions of Licenses

FDA calls for explanation/issues show cause notice for the suspension or cancellation of licenses and wherever necessary files prosecutions.

Dos and Don'ts for Cosmetic

What precautions should you take during purchasing cosmetics?

Consumer should purchase the cosmetic under cash memo/bill. The consumer should verify the details of following particulars on label.

A Cosmetic shall Carry

1. *On both the inner and other labels*

a. The name of the cosmetics

b. The name of the manufacturer and complete address of the premises of the manufacturer where the cosmetic has been manufactured. Provided that if the cosmetic is contained in a very small size container where the address of the manufacturer cannot be given, the name of the manufacturer and his principal place of manufacture shall be along with pin code.

2. *On the outer label:* A declaration of the net contents expressed in terms of weight for solids, fluid measure for liquids, weight for semi-solids, combined with numerical count if the content is sub-divided: Provided that this statement need not appear in case of a package of perfume, toilet water or the like, the net content of which does not exceed 60 ml or any package of solid or semi-solid cosmetic the net content of which does not exceed 30 grams.

3. On the inner label; where a hazard exists:

a. Adequate direction for safe use

b. Any warning, caution or special direction required to be observed by the consumer

c. A statement of the names and quantities of the ingredients that are hazardous or poisonous.

4. A distinctive batch number, that is to say, the number by reference to which details of manufacture of the particular batch from which the substance in the container is taken are recorded and are available for inspection, the figures representing the batch number being preceded by the letter "B" : Provided that this clause shall not apply to any cosmetic containing 10 grams or less if the cosmetic is in solid or semi-solid state, and 25 milliliters or less if the cosmetic is in a liquid state. (Provided further that in the case of soaps, instead of the batch number, the month and year of manufacture of soap shall be given on the label.)

5. Manufacturing license number, the number being preceded by the letter 'M'

6. Where a package of a cosmetic has only one label such label shall contain all the information required to be shown on both the inner and the outer labels, under these rules.

7. Toothpaste containing fluoride:
   a. Date of expiry should be mentioned on tube and carton
   b. Fluoride content in term of ppm should be mentioned on tube and carton and shall not be more than 1000 ppm.

What precautions should you take when using any cosmetics?
If you use cosmetics, FDA urges you to follow these safety tips:

- If any eye cosmetic causes irritation, stop using it immediately. If irritation persists, see a doctor.
- Avoid using eye cosmetics if you have an eye infection or the skin around the eye is inflamed. Wait until the area is healed. Discard any eye cosmetics you were using when you got the infection.
- Be aware that there are bacteria on your hands that, if placed in the eye, could cause infections. Wash your hands before applying eye cosmetics.
- Make sure that any instrument you place in the eye area is clean.
- Do not share your cosmetics. It may be hazardous to you.
- Do not allow cosmetics to become covered with dust or contaminated with dirt or soil. Keep cosmetics containers clean and closed.
- Do not use old containers of eye cosmetics. Manufacturers usually recommend discarding mascara two to four months after purchase.
- Discard dried-up mascara. Do not add saliva or water to moisten it. The bacteria from your mouth may grow in the mascara and cause infection. Adding water may introduce bacteria and will dilute the preservative that is intended to protect against microbial growth.
- Do not store cosmetics at temperatures above 85 degrees F. Cosmetics held for long periods in hot cars, for example, are more susceptible to deterioration of the preservative. · When applying or removing eye cosmetics, be careful not to scratch the eyeball or other sensitive area. Never apply or remove eye cosmetics in a moving vehicle.
- Do not use any cosmetics near your eyes unless they are intended specifically for that use. For instance, do not use a

lip liner as an eye liner. You may be exposing your eyes to contamination from your mouth, or to color additives that are not approved for use in the area of the eye. It may cause hazard.

What precautions should be taken if you dye your hair?
Purchase the product labeled with the prescribed caution statement indicating that the product may cause irritation in certain individuals, that a patch test for skin sensitivity should be done, and that the product must not be used for dyeing the eyelashes or eyebrows. The patch test involves putting a dab of hair dye behind the ear or inside the elbow, leaving it there for two days, and looking for itching, burning, redness, or other reactions. Whether applying hair chemicals at home or in a hair salon, consumers and beauticians should be careful to keep them away from the eyes. FDA has received reports of injuries from hair relaxers and hair dye accidentally getting into eyes. When using all hair chemicals, it is critical to keep them away from children to prevent ingestion and other accidents, and to follow product directions carefully. Consumers should be aware that applying more than one type of chemical treatment, such as coloring hair one week and then relaxing it the next, can increase the risk of hair damage.

8

Naturopathy Medicine

Naturopathy, or Naturopathic Medicine, is a form of alternative medicine based on a belief in vitalism, which posits that a special energy called vital energy or vital force guides bodily processes such as metabolism, reproduction, growth, and adaptation. Naturopathic philosophy favors a holistic approach, and like conventional medicine seeks to find the least invasive measures necessary for symptom improvement or resolution, thus encouraging minimal use of surgery and unnecessary drugs.

The particular modality used by an individual naturopath varies with training and scope of practice. The demonstrated efficacy and scientific rationale also varies. These include: acupuncture, applied kinesiology, botanical medicine, brainwave entrainment, chelation therapy for atherosclerosis, colonic enemas, color therapy, cranial osteopathy, hair analysis, homeopathy, iridology, live blood analysis, nature cure — a range of therapies based upon exposure to natural elements such as sunshine, fresh air, heat, or cold, nutrition (examples include vegetarian and wholefood diet, fasting, and abstention from alcohol and sugar), ozone therapy, physical medicine (includes naturopathic, osseous, and soft tissue manipulative therapy, sports medicine, exercise and hydrotherapy), psychological counseling [examples include meditation, relaxation, and other methods of stress management], public health measures and hygiene, reflexology, rolfing and traditional Chinese medicine.

A 2004 survey determined the most commonly prescribed naturopathic therapeutics in Washington State and Connecticut were botanical medicines, vitamins, minerals, homeopathy, and allergy treatments.

9

Veterinary Formulation

Veterinary medicine is the branch of *science* that deals with the prevention, diagnosis and treatment of disease, disorder and injury in *non-human animals*. The scope of veterinary medicine is wide, covering all animal species, both *domesticated* and *wild*, with a wide range of conditions which can affect different species.

A

- *Acepromazine:* Neuroleptic drug related to chlorpromazine used as a sedative and antiemetic.
- *Amantadine:* As an analgesic for chronic pain.
- *Amitraz:* Antiparasitic used to control ticks, mites, lice and other animal pests. Cannot be used on horses.
- *Amitryptyline:* Tricyclic antidepressant used to treat separation anxiety, excessive grooming and spraying in dogs and cats.
- *Amlodipine:* Calcium channel blocker used to decrease blood pressure.
- *Amoxicillin:* Antibiotic indicated for susceptible gram-positive and gram-negative infections. Ineffective against species that produce beta-lactamase.
- *Artificial tears:* Lubricant eye drops used to treat keratoconjunctivitis sicca.
- *Atenolol:* To treat arrhythmias, hypertension, and other cardiovascular disorders.
- *Atipamezole:* Alpha 2-adrenergic antagonist used to reverse the sedative and analgesic effects of dexmedetomidine and medetomidine in dogs.

B

- *Benazepril:* ACE-inhibitor used in heart failure, hypertension, chronic renal failure and protein-losing nephropathy.
- *Boldenone:* Anabolic steroid for treatment of horses.
- *Buprenorphine:* Narcotic for pain relief in cats after surgery.
- *Butorphanol:* Used for a muscle relaxation effect in horses.

C

- *Carprofen:* COX-2 selective NSAID used to relieve pain and inflammation in dogs. Annedotal reports of severe GI effects in cats.
- *Cefovecin:* Cephalosporin-class antibiotic used to treat skin infections in dogs and cats.
- *Cephalexin:* Antibiotic, particularly useful for susceptible *Staphylococcus* infections.
- *Chloramphenicol:* Particularly useful for anaerobic bacterial infections, both gram (+) and (–). Crosses blood–brain barrier, useful in treatment of meningitis.
- *Cimetidine:* H_2 antagonist used to reduce GI acid production aids in the treatment of gastric and duodenal ulcers as well as esophageal reflux. Newer agents may be more appropriate as they have a longer duration of action and fewer drug interactions (i.e. ranididine, famotidine, omeprazole). It is starting to be recommended for treatment of Melanoma in horses.
- *Clamoxyquine:* Antiparasitic to treat salmonids for infection with the myxozoan parasite, myxobolus cerebralis.
- *Clavulanic acid:* Adjunct to penicillin-derived antibiotics used to overcome resistance in bacteria that secrete beta-lactamase.
- *Clenbuterol:* A decongestant and bronchodilator used for the treatment of recurrent airway obstruction in horses.
- *Clindamycin hydrochloride:* Antibiotic with particular use in dental infections. Effective against most aerobic gram positive cocci (not *Strep-faecalis*), *Corynebacterium diptheriae, Nocardia asteroides, Erysepelothrix, Toxoplasma,* and *Mycoplama.* Anaerobic bacteria susceptible: *Clostridium perfringins, C. tetani, Bacteroides, Fusobacterium, Actinomyces.*

- *Clomipramine hydrochloride:* Primarily in dogs: Obsessive-compulsive disorders, dominance aggression and anxiety, may be useful in spraying cats.

D

- *Deracoxib:* Postoperative pain management and osteoarthritis. Interest in use as adjunctive treatment to transitional cell carcinoma.
- *Dexamethasone:* Antiinflammatory, diagnostic tool for Cushings (low and high dose dexamethasone suppression test).
- *Diazepam:* Benzodiazepine used to treat status epilepticus, also used as a preanesthetic and a sedative.
- *Dichlorophene:* Fungicide, germicide, and antimicrobial agent used for the removal of parasites such as ascarids, hookworms, and tapeworms from cats and dogs.

E

- *Enalapril:* ACE-inhibitor used to treat high blood pressure and heart failure.
- *Enrofloxacin:* Broad-spectrum antibiotic (gram-positive and gram-negatives) not recommended for streptococci, or anaerobic bacteria.
- Equine chorionic gonadotropin–gonadotropic hormone used to induce ovulation in livestock prior to artificial insemination.

F

- *Flunixin:* NSAID used as an analgesic and antipyretic in horses.
- *Furosemide:* Diuretic used to prevent exercise induced pulmonary hemorrhage in horses.

H

Hydromorphone: Analgesia, premed.

I

- *Isoxsuprine:* Vasodilator used for laminitis and navicular disease in horses.
- *Ivermectin:* A broad-spectrum antiparasitic used in horses and dogs.

K

- *Ketamine:* Anesthetic and tranquilizer in cats, dogs, horses, and other animals.
- *Ketoprofen:* Non-steroidal anti-inflammatory drug (NSAID).

L

Lufenuron: Insecticide used for flea control.

M

- *Marbofloxacin:* Antibiotic.
- *Maropitant:* Antiemetic.
- *Medetomidine:* Surgical anesthetic and analgesic.
- *Meloxicam:* Non-steroidal anti-inflammatory drug (NSAID).
- *Metoclopramide hydrochloride:* Potent antiemetic, secondarily as a prokinetic.
- *Metronidazole:* Highly effective against anaerobic bacteria. Has good activity against protozoa, but fenbendazole may be a better choice (more effective, less side effects).
- *Milbemycin oxime:* A broad-spectrum antiparasitic used as an anthelmintic, insecticide and miticide.
- *Mirtazapine:* Antiemetic and appetite stimulant in cats and dogs.

N

- *Neomycin.*
- *Nitenpyram:* Insecticide.
- *Nitroscanate:* Anthelmintic used to treat *Toxocara canis, Toxascaris leonina, Ancylostoma caninum, Uncinaria stenocephalia, Taenia,* and *Dipylidium caninum* (roundworms, hookworms and tapeworms).
- *Nystatin.*

O

- *Ofloxacin.*
- *Omeprazole:* For the treatment and prevention of gastric ulcers in horses.
- *Oxibendazole:* Anthelmintic.

P

- *Panacur:* Dewormer.
- *Pentobarbital:* Humane euthanasia of animals not to be used for food.
- *Phenobarbital:* Antiseizure medication.
- *Phenylbutazone:* Non-steroidal anti-inflammatory drug (NSAID).
- *Pimobendan:* Used to manage heart failure in dogs.
- *Pirlimycin:* Antimicrobial.
- *Ponazuril:* Anticoccidial.
- *Praziquantel:* Treatment of *Dipylidium caninum, Taenia pisiformis, Echinococcus granulosis.*
- *Prednisone.*
- *Propofol:* Short acting anesthetic drug.
- *Pyrantel pamoate:* Effective against ascarids, hookworms and stomach worms.

S

- *Selamectin.*
- *Sentinel flavor tabs:* Antiparasitic.
- *Sucralfate:* NSAID associated ulcers — coats existing ulcers, but probably not useful in prevention.
- *Synulox:* Antibiotic.

T

- *Theophylline:* Brochospasm and cardiogenic edema.
- *Thiostrepton.*
- *Thiabendazole.*
- *Triamcinolone acetonide.*

- *Trimethoprim:* Used widely for bacterial infections, is in the family of sulfa drugs.
- *Trilostane:* Canine Cushing's.
- *Tylosin:* Antibiotic.

Drugs of Animal Origin

FIXED OILS

Cod-liver Oil (Oleum Morrhuae)

Sources is a **fixed oil** extracted from the **fresh liver of the cod**, **Gadus morrhua**, family: Gadidae.

Geographical

Sources: The oil is produced in Iceland, Britain, Norway, Germany and Denmark.

Beeswax (Yellow and White Beeswax)

Sources is obtained by melting and purifying the honeycomb of the live bee, **Apis mellifica** and other species of **Apis**, family: Apidae.

Spermaceti

Sources is a solid wax obtained from the fixed oils derived from the head of the sperm whale, Physeter **macrocephalus**, Fam: Physteridae and the bottle-nosed whale, hyperoodon rostratus

Wool Fat (Anhydrous lanolin)

Sources is a waxy substance prepared from the wool of the sheep, **Ovis aries**, Fam: Bovidae.

Description is a pale yellow, tenacious substance with a faint but characteristic odour.

Unani Formulation

These drugs may be any substance or product including herbs, minerals, etc. for animals and human beings and can even be that prescribed by practitioners of **Unani** system of medicine. In recent days, awareness has been created related to safety and adverse drug reaction monitoring of Unani drugs.

Formulation Composition
Majoon-e-Sandal by Liquid Extract Method

Unani Name Botanical/English Name/Part used Quantity

1. Sandal Safaid/*Santalum album* Linn./Heart wood 110 g
2. Aab-e-Zulal Tamar. *Hindi*—Tamarindus indica. Linn./Fruit pulp 250 ml
3. Aab-e-Anar/Trush *Punica granatum* Linn./Seed extract 350 g
4. Tabasheer Safaid/*Bambusa bambos.* Druce./Bamboo manna 15 g
5. Ood Kham/*Styrax benzoin* Benz./Resin 15 g
6. Zafran/*Crocus sativus* Linn./Dried stigmas and top of styles 5 g
7. Qand Safaid/Sugar—750 g

List of Unani Medicine

Name of medicine desies packing size.

1. Dia-eaz	Diabetes	50 tab
2. Khamira Khas Jawahar Wala	brain tonic	60 and 125 gm
3. Baqai Cough Cour	Cough, cold	100 and 200 ml
4. Baqai Haelthtone	Health tonic	200 and 500 ml
5. Sharbat-E-Nauijad	Natural refresher	700 ml

6. Liveen	Liver problem	200 and 500 ml
7. Indige-Cure	Indigestion syrup	200 and 500 ml
8. Akseer-E-Hazim	Indigestion powder	50 gm
9. Baqai ARQ-E-Musaffi Azam (ARQ)	Blood purifier	500 ml
10. Musaffi Azam (syrup)	Blood purifier	200 and 500 ml
11. Baqai Ghutti	Baby tonic	50 ml
12. Baqai Artho-cure	Arthritis	50 tab
13. Rehuma act oil	Joint pain	50 and 100 ml
14. Lady act syrup	Gyne problems	200 and 500 ml
15. Lady act tablet	Gyne problems	50 tab
16. Muqavvi Azam	Sexual disorder for male	60 and 125 gm
17. Redium Pills	Vigour and vitality	50 pills
18. Habb-E-Nemat	Premature ejaculation	50 pills
19. Baqai Consti Cour	Constipation tablets	50 tab
20. Daf-E-Qabz	Constipation powder	50 gm
21. Baqai beuty care	Face pack, dark circles, pimples	50 and 200 gm
22. Baqai healthy hair	Hair oil, hair falling, etc.	100 and 200 ml
23. Baqai herbal tooth powder	Tooth powder	50 gm
24. Sunoon-E-Pyorrhea	Tooth powder for gums	50 gm

List of Baqai's Classical Unani Medicine

Araqiyat

1. Araq-E-Ajwayin
2. Araq-E-Ambar
3. Araq-E-Afsanteen
4. Araq-E-Badiyan
5. Araq-E-Bed Mushk
6. Araq-E-Baranjasif

7. Araq-E-Chiraita
8. Araq-E-Chobchini
9. Araq-E-Dasmool
10. Araq-E-Gaozaban
11. Araq-E-Gulab
12. Araq-E-Gazar Sada
13. Araq-E-Heel Khurd
14. Araq-E-Kasni
15. Araq-E-Mako
16. Araq-E-Ma-Ul-Laham Khas
17. Araq-E-Ma-Ul-laham Mako Kasni Wala
18. Araq-E-Musaffi Khoon Qawi
19. Araq-E-Mundi
20. Araq-E-Nana
21. Araq-E-Nilofar
22. Araq-E-Pudina
23. Araq-E-Shahtra
24. Araq-E-Sheer-E-Murakkab
25. Araq-E-Ushba

Dawa

26. Dawa-Ul-Misk Motadil Sada
27. Dawa-Ul-Misk Motadil Jawahar Wali

Haboob

28. Habbe-E-Ahmar
29. Habbe-E-Ambar Momyaee
30. Habb-E-Asgand
31. Habb-E-Ayarij
32. Habb-E-Azaraqi
33. Habb-E-Bawaseer Badi
34. Habb-E-Bawaseer Khooni
35. Habb-E-Hilteet
36. Habb-E-Jalinoos
37. Habb-E-Jawahir

38. Habb-E-Kabid Naushadri
39. Habb-E-Khas
40. Habb-E-Leemu
41. Habb-E-Marwareed
42. Habb-E-Muqil
43. Habb-E-Musaffi Khoon
44. Habb-E-Nishat
45. Habb-E-Papita
46. Habb-E-Pechish
47. Habb-E-Raal
48. Habb-E-Rasaut
49. Habb-E-Seen
50. Habb-E-Shifa
51. Habb-E-Suranjan
52. Habb-E-Surfa
53. Habb-E-Sumaq
54. Habb-E-Tankar
55. Habb-E-Tursh Mushtahi
56. Habb-E-Zeequn Nafas

Halwa

57. Halwa-E-Baiza-E-Murgh
58. Halwa-E-Gazar
59. Halwa-E-Gheekwar
60. Halwa Salab
61. Halwa Supari Pak

Itrifalat

62. Itrifal Deedan
63. Itrifal Kishneezi
64. Itrifal Mulaiyyin
65. Itrifal Muqil
66. Itrifal Muqawwi Dimagh
67. Itrifal Shahtra

68. Itrifal Ustukhuddus
69. Itrifal Zamani

Jawarishat

70. Jawarish-E-Aamla Sada
71. Jawarish-E-Anarain
72. Jawarish-E-Bisbasa
73. Jawarish-E-Jalinoos
74. Jawarish-E-Kamooni
75. Jawarish-E-Kamooni Kabir
76. Jawarish-E-Mastagi
77. Jawarish-E-Pudina
78. Jawarish-E-Shahi
79. Jawarish-E-Tabasheer
80. Jawarish-E-Tamar Hindi
81. Jawarish-E-Ood Shireen
82. Jawarish-E-Ood-tursh
83. Jawarish-E-Zanjabeel
84. Jawarish-E-Zarooni Sada
85. Jawarish-E-Zarooni Ambari Ba Nuskha Kalan

Khamira

86. Khamira-E-Abresham Hak. Arshad Wala
87. Khamira-E-Abresham Sada
88. Khamira Abresham Sheera Unnab Wala
89. Khamira-E-Banafsha
90. Khamira-E-Gaozaban Ambrijadwar Ud-E-Saleeb Wala
91. Khamira-E-Gaozaban Ambri Jawahar Wala
92. Khamira-E-Gaozaban Sada
93. Khamira-E-Khashkhash
94. Khamira-E-Marwareed
95. Khamira Marwareed Khas
96. Khamira-E-Sandal Sada

Luboob

97. Luboob-E-Barid
98. Luboob-E-Kabir
99. Luboob-E-Sagheer

Laooq

100. Laooq Aab Tarbuzwala
101. Laooq-E-Badam
102. Laooq-E-Katan
103. Laooq-E-Motadil
104. Laooq-E-Nazli
105. Laooq-E-Sapistan Khiyarshambri
106. Laooq-E-Zeeq-Un-Nafas

Majoon

107. Majoon-E-Aqrab
108. Majoon-E-Arad Khurma
109. Majoon-E-Azaraqi
110. Majoon-E-Chobchini
111. Majoon-E-Dabeed-ul-ward
112. Majoon-E-Falasifa
113. Majoon-E-Hajr-Ul-Yahood
114. Majoon-E-Hamal Ambari Alwi Khani
115. Majoon-E-Ispand Sokhtani
116. Majoon-E-Jalali
117. Majoon-E-Jalinoos Lulvi
118. Majoon-E-Jiryan Khas
119. Majoon-E-Jograj Gugal
120. Majoon-E-Khabs-Ul-Hadeed
121. Majoon-E-Kundur
122. Majoon-E-Masik-Ul-Baul
123. Majoon-E-Mochras
124. Majoon-E-Mughalliz
125. Majoon-E-Mughalliz Jawahar Wali
126. Majoon-E-Muqavvi Mumsik

127. Majoon-E-Muqavvi Meda
128. Majoon-E-Muqawwi-e-reham
129. Majoon-E-Musaffi-e-khoon
130. Majoon-E-Nankhwah
131. Majoon-E-Najah
132. Majoon-E-Nisyan
133. Majoon-E-Piyaz
134. Majoon-E-Ra-Hul Momineen
135. Majoon-E-Salab
136. Majoon-E-Sang Sarmahi
137. Majoon-E-Sangdana Murgh
138. Majoon-E-Seer Alwi Khani
139. Majoon-E-Shabab Awar
140. Majoon-E-Sohag Sonth
141. Majoon-E-Suparipak
142. Majoon-E-Suranjan
143. Majoon-E-Ushba
144. Majoon-E-Zanjabeel

Aqras

145. Qurs Abyaz
146. Qurs Al-ahmar
147. Qurs Alkali
148. Qurs-E-Anjabar
149. Qurs Asfar
150. Qurs-E-Bandish Khoon
151. Qurs-E-Deedan
152. Qurs Fizza
153. Qurs Habis
154. Qurs Hilteet
155. Qurs Hawamil
156. Qurs Iksir Falij Wa Laqwa
157. Qurs Jawahar Mohra
158. Qurs Jiryan
159. Qurs-E-kaknaj
160. Qurs-E-kehruba

161. Qurs Kharateen
162. Qurs-E-Mulaiyyin
163. Qurs-E-Musallas
164. Qurs Pudina
165. Qurs Salajeet
166. Qurs-E-Sartan
167. Qurs Suzak
168. Qurs Tinkar
169. Qurs-E-Ziabetus Khaas
170. Qurs-E-Ziabetus Sada

Raughaniyat

171. Raughan-E-Aamla Sada
172. Raughan-E-Bedanjeer (Arandi)
173. Raughan-E-Babchi
174. Raughan-E-Babuna
175. Raughan-E-Badam Shireen
176. Raughan-E-Baiza-E-Murgh
177. Raughan-E-Banafsha
178. Raughan-E-Beer Bahooti
179. Raughan-E-Kaddu Shireen
180. Raughan-E-Kahu
181. Raughan-E-Khashkhash
182. Raughan-E-Azaraqi
183. Raughan-E-Malkangani
184. Raughan-E-Mom
185. Raughan-E-Qust
186. Raughan-E-Suranjan
187. Raughan-E-Surkh
188. Raughan-E-Turb
189. Raughan-E-Zarareeh

Sufoof

190. Sufoof Bars
191. Sufoof-E-Chutki

192. Sufoof-E-Habis-Ud-Dum
193. Sufoof-E-Masik-Ul Baul
194. Sufoof-E-Muqliyasa
195. Sufoof-E-Mohazzil
196. Sufoof-E-Muallif
197. Sufoof-E-Namak Sulemani
198. Sufoof-E-Sailan
199. Sufoof-E-Salab
200. Sufoof-E-Sheikh-Ur-Rais

Sharbat

201. Sharbat-E-Ahmad Shahi
202. Sharbat-E-Alu Balu
203. Sharbat-E-Anar Shireen
204. Sharbat-E-Anjabar
205. Sharbat-E-Banafsha
206. Sharbat-E-Buzoori Barid
207. Sharbat-E-Buzoori Haar
208. Sharbat-E-Buzoori Motadil
209. Sharbat-E-Bel Giri
210. Sharbat-E-Deenaar
211. Sharbat-E-Ejaz
212. Sharbat-E-Folad
213. Sharbat-E-Gulab
214. Sharbat-E-Habbul-Aas
215. Sharbat-E-Kasni
216. Sharbat-E-Khaksi
217. Sharbat-E-Khashkhash
218. Sharbat-E-Murkkab Musaffi Khoon
219. Sharbat-E-Nilofar
220. Sharbat-E-Sandal
221. Sharbat-E-Salajeet
222. Sharbat-E-Toot Siyah
223. Sharbat-E-Tamar Hindi
224. Sharbat-E-Unnab

225. Sharbat-E-Ustukhuddus
226. Sharbat-E-Zufa Sada
227. Sharbat-E-Zufa Murakkab
228. Shikanjabeen Limoon

Unani System of Books

1. Karabadin Qadri
2. Karabadin Kabir
3. Karabadin Azam
4. Ilaj-ul-Amraz
5. Al Karabadin
6. Biaz Kabir, Vol. II
7. Karabadin Jadid
8. Kitab-Ul-Taklis
9. Sanat-Ul-Taklis
10. Mifta-Ul-Khazain
11. Madan-Ul-Aksir
12. Makhzan-Ul-Murabhat
13. National Formulary of Unani Medicine (Part I)

FDA Role in Food

Object

- To provide safe, hygienic, unadulterated and good quality food items.
- Development and enforcement of GMP, GLP, GHP and SOPs in manufacture, storage and distribution processes.
- Formulation, evaluation and monitoring of policies on safe and unadulterated food products thereof.
- Consumer awareness regarding identification of adulteration in food items.
- Preparation of, minimum safety standards-standard operating procedures. Good manufacturing practice. Hazard analysis of critical control points developing guidelines for effective enforcement.

Acts and Rules Implemented

- The Prevention of Food and Adulteration Act, 1954 and Rules, 1955.
- Maharashtra Prevention of Food Adulteration Rules, 1962
- The Maharashtra Country Liquor Rules, 1973.
- The Infant Milk Substitute, Feeding Bottles and Infant Food (Regulation of the Production Supply and Distribution) Act, 1992 and Rules, 1993.

- The Cigarette Act, 1975.
- The Cigarettes and other Tobacco Products (Prohibition of Advertisement and Regulation of Trade and Commerce, Production, Supply and Distribution) Act, 2003 and Rules, 2004.

Acts and Orders Related

- The fruit products order, 1955.
- The edible oils packaging (regulations) order, 1988.
- Meat and poultry products order, 1973.
- Vanaspati oil products order, 1998.
- Solvent extracted oil, de oiled meal and edible flour order, 1967.
- BIS [ISI]

HISTORY OF FOOD SIDE

Staffing Pattern

Food: What do we Understand by the Food Law?

What do we Understand by the Food Law?

It is right of every human being to get pure and wholesome food. In view of this, the parliament of India enacted the law, 'The Prevention of Food Adulteration Act, 1954' and the rules to this Act are known as 'The Prevention of Food Adulteration and Rules, 1955'. The preamble of the law narrates It is the law to safeguard the interest of public as a consumer of food and beverages, to get it in pure and hygienic way.

"For legal reference the law books are available with all law book sellers."

The main synopsis of the law is briefly given below:

1. Definitions (Sec 2 of the Act)
2. Offences (Sec 7 of the Act)
3. Duties and Powers of enforcing officers (rule 9 and Sec10 of the Act)
4. Penalties (Sec 16 and 17 of the Act)
5. Procedures part provided under rules (rule 14 to rule 22 of the Act)

6. Standardization of food and beverages (Rule, Appendix B and C of the Act)

What is Food? [Sec 2 (v)]

Food is defined as any article solid or liquid, which generally enters in the human system, is an article of food. However, food does not include any drug or water (except packaged drinking water/mineral water). Further any such article as declared by the central government as a food shall be considered as food.

What is an Adulteration? [Sec 2 (ia)]

By a plain meaning of an adulteration, we understand that, mixing and thereby making the substance unwholesome. However, the law has considered that adulteration with wide scope, the definition of adulteration given under Section 2, is narrated for understanding.

1. If the article is not sold as per the nature, quality and substance as it should be.
2. Mixing of inferior or cheaper substance to affect the nature and quality seriously.
3. If ingredients are removed to affect quality and nature of the substance seriously.
4. If the article is unhygenically prepared or stored under unsanitary conditions to affect the health.
5. If the article is composed of any filthy, rotten or insect infested making it unfit for consumption.
6. If article contains any poisons or toxic ingredient harmful to health.
7. If the article contains any non-permitted color or permitted color more than 100 parts per million.
8. If the article is not in accordance with the standards fixed under the law.

What is an Misbranding? [Sec 2 (ix)]

Another important aspect is misbranded food article; the definition of misbranded is given under Section 2. It can be understood briefly as:

a. If the article is imitation or substitute to deceive.

b. If the label claims are not proper, deceptive, false, misleading or exaggerated.

Offences

Offences under the law are given in Section 7 of the act, whereby no person shall manufacture for sale, store for sale or sell any

1. Adulterated food
2. Misbranded food
3. Noncompliance of license conditions.
4. Article which is prohibited by food (health) authority
5. Article in contravention to any provision under the act
6. Any adulterant.

Penalties

The law has been framed to protect the social interest, at large, hence, the offences under this act are considered of serious and of anti-social nature. Therefore, serious penalties are provided to make its effect deterrent; the provisions are made under Sections 16 and 17.

For selling adulterated or misbranded food article and any offence under the act the penalty is:

1. Imprisonment for minimum period of 6 months and fine of minimum ₹1000/-
2. For offences related to license; the penalty is little less.
3. The act considers vicarious liability as the principle. Therefore, for an establishment run by more than single individual, each individual is held liable for the offence. However, the act also gives relief to such establishments by appointing a nominee on behalf of such establishment.
4. Such establishment has to register a nominee before a local (health) authority in those jurisdiction such establishment is located.

Enforcement

The law is enforced by the food inspectors at field level. The food inspectors are empowered to exercise duties entrusted upon them.

Powers of Food Inspectors (Sec 10)

1. Food inspectors can inspect any premises, where sale of food is involved, including transportation.
2. Food inspectors are authorised to draw samples of any food articles meant for sale. It is important to note that the seller cannot oppose for drawing of samples by food inspector.
3. Sale of food article to a food inspector for the purpose of analysis is considered as sale in general terms.
4. Food inspectors are empowered to seize or prohibit any suspicious food article in the interest of public health.
5. While collecting the sample for analysis food inspectors is duty bound to pay reasonable price of such article.
6. The seized or prohibited stocks shall be kept in the possession of the possessor.
7. Food inspector can break open any premises or any package suspected to contain any food article, if refused to do so, by its possessor.
8. Food inspectors is also empowered to arrest any person, on disclosing false name and address.
9. Food inspectors can seize any adulterant and can seize any of the documents or book of accounts, registers concerning it.
10. For any action taken by the food inspector, law requires that it shall be done in presence of one or two persons.
11. The food inspector is liable for penalty, if he takes any vexatious action or does any act without reasonable ground; however action taken in good faith and in the interest of public is protected by law.

Procedure of Collecting Samples (Sec 11 and Rules 14 to 22)

1. The food inspector selects demands and purchases. Food articles to be taken for sampling.
2. The cost of such article is to be paid to the seller and to obtain its receipt.
3. Informs the seller his intention of sampling.

4. Informs the seller to furnish the source of procuring the sample.
5. The purchased article is divided into 3 portions. Each portion is kept in proper suitable container.
6. Such containers are tightly closed and sealed.
7. Further, each portion is wrapped in paper.
8. Paper slip having signature and code of local (health) authority is pasted on each portion on which the seller puts his signature.
9. Each container is tied by a strong twine, and again it is sealed at 4 places.
10. All 3 sealed portions are taken possession by the food inspectors.
11. If the remaining stock is seized or prohibited notice in accordance to that effect is issued to the seller.

Analysis (Sec 8, Sec 13 and Rule 7)

On the same day or next working day one portion is to be sent to public analyst for analysis and two portions are sent in the custody of local [health] authority.

Analytical Laboratories (Sec 8)

The analytical laboratories are in existence in the state under department of public health. They are at following places.

1. *State Public Health Laboratory, Pune*

It is the Apex laboratory of the state and is also declared as Central Food Laboratory for state.

2. *Regional Public Health Laboratories are at*

- Aurangabad
- Nagpur
- Amravati.

3. *District Public Health Laboratories are at*

- New Mumbai
- Satara

- Sangli
- Kolhapur
- Sholapur
- Beed
- Nanded
- Jalgaon
- Ahemadnagar
- Nasik
- Akola

In addition to these MCGB has laboratory in Mumbai.

Public analysts are appointed in these laboratories, who analyses the samples and delivers its report, within 40 days from date of receipt.

1. The public analyst verifies sealed portion and shall cause to analyze the food article.
2. The analysis is done as per the methodologies laid down by Director General of Health Services.
3. The public analyst sends its report to the local (health) authority.

Action on Analytical Reports

1. Where the sample is reported of the genuine quality, no further action is needed to be taken, however, if the report is found erroneous the local (health) authority is empowered to send another portion of sample from his custody to any other public analyst for reanalysis. [Sec 13 to (2-E)]
2. Where the sample is reported to be adulterated or misbranded its duty of food inspector to make necessary inquiry and investigation to detect the offenders (Rule 9).
3. Proposal to be submitted to seek orders regarding action to be taken against the offenders (Sec 20).
4. After receiving the orders from Joint Commissioner of his division, a criminal prosecution is launched against the accused persons.

From 15th Jan 2008 the State Govt. has substituted Sec 20 by which all offences are made cognizable and non-bailable and police inspector or officer of above rank are empowered to arrest any person without warrant, having reasonable grounds.

All offences under this act shall be tried summarily; however as a judicial practice they are being tried by follow up warrant procedure. State government had recently issued notification empowering the judicial magistrates to try the cases summarily. This change will help speedy disposal of cases.

13 Testing of Laboratory Products

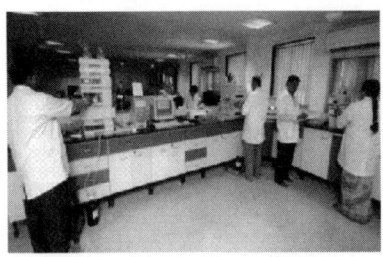

For testing of drugs and cosmetics as stated under Sections 20 and 33 F of Drugs and Cosmetics Act, 1940 and Rules there under, Maharashtra State has established Drugs Control Laboratory at Mumbai and at Aurangabad, under the administrative control of the commissioner, Food and Drug Administration (FDA), Maharashtra State.

History

To give a brief history, till the late sixties, testing of drugs and cosmetics was carried out in Haffkine Institute, Parel, and Mumbai-12. In August 1968, an independent laboratory under the name "Drugs Control Laboratory" was established in Dental College, St. George Hospital, and Mumbai. In March 1970, this laboratory was shifted to MHADA premises at Bandra (East), Mumbai-51. At present from September 1993, this Laboratory is functioning at its own premises at Plot No. 341, Bandra-Kurla Complex, and Bandra (East); Mumbai-51. The laboratory has the capacity to test about 6500 samples of drugs and cosmetics per year. In order to test more number of samples of drugs and cosmetics, Maharashtra Government has established

an additional Drugs Control Laboratory at Aurangabad. The laboratory at Aurangabad is testing about 2500 samples of Drugs and Cosmetics per year.

Organization and Structure

The Laboratory at Mumbai has 9 main divisions namely:

1. Coding
2. Chemical I
3. Chemical II
4. Antibiotics
5. Vitamins
6. Pharmacology
7. Pharmacognosy
8. Cosmetics
9. Central instrument

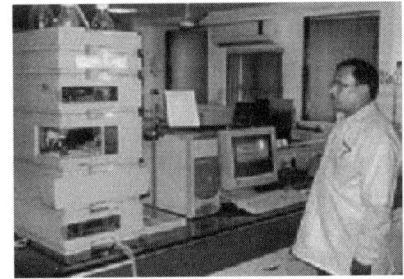

The laboratory at Aurangabad has 7 main divisions as above, except antibiotics and vitamins. Each laboratory is headed by Assistant Director, under the Administrative Control of the Commissioner, Food and Drug Administration, Maharashtra State. The laboratory at Mumbai has 110 number of staffs including both managerial and technical, and at Aurangabad there are around 48 number of staffs, both managerial and technical. The main laboratory divisions are headed by government analyst (Senior Scientific Officer or Notified Scientific Officer). The technical staff such as Senior Technical Assistant, Analytical Chemist, and Scientific Officer is engaged in analytical work. All the technical staff from Assistant Director to lower technical staff is qualified, experienced and trained. The laboratory has the policy to depute the technical staff regularly in reputed institute for training in order to upgrade their knowledge in the areas of drug testing and handling of sophisticated instruments. All the testing divisions including the Central Instrument Division are equipped with modern sophisticated, computerized analytical instruments like IR, GC, HPLC, UV-Visible spectrophotometer, etc. including reference standards required for calibration. All the activities, i.e. from the receipt of sample to final dispatch of the reports are computerized by using the software developed by HCL as per the requirements of FDA and drugs control laboratory.

Brief Function of Each Division

1. *Coding:* Coding of received samples and distribution to other analytical division for analysis.
2. *Chemical I:* Analysis of bulk drug and drug formulations like liquid oral products, ointments, creams, lotions, gels, etc.
3. *Chemical II:* Analysis of drug formulations like tablets and capsules except antibiotics and vitamins.
4. *Antibiotics:* Analysis of antibiotic formulations.
5. *Vitamins:* Analysis of vitamins and nutritional supplement formulations.
6. *Pharmacology:* Analysis of ophthalmic, large volume/small volume parenteral preparations, intramuscular/Intravenous injectables.
7. *Pharmacognosy:* Analysis of ayurvedic drugs and surgical dressings.
8. *Cosmetics:* Analysis of cosmetic products.

Food Laboratory

Food testing laboratory has been started under the control of Commissioner, Food and Drug Administration, from February 2008, both at Mumbai and Aurangabad. Present capacity of testing food samples is 1200 at Mumbai and 720 at Aurangabad. Both the laboratories are well equipped with sophisticated instruments. These laboratories are one of the Hightech Laboratory in State of Maharashtra.

Present Scenario

At present, Drugs Control Laboratory, Mumbai is committed to achieve the excellence in testing of drugs and cosmetics as per IS/ISO/IEC/17025:2005, the international standard for the competence of testing and calibrating laboratories. The laboratory has established its Quality Policy, Quality Objectives and prepared Quality Manual to comply with the requirements of IS/ISO/IEC/17025:2005 for getting accreditation from

National Accreditation Board for Testing and Calibration Laboratories. After compliance with the requirements with this International standards, the Laboratory has been assessed by the assessment team sent by NABL. The assessment team has recommended this laboratory for NABL Accreditation both in chemical and biological testing for the recommended scope as per ISO/IEC/17025:2005. Recently Drugs Control Laboratory, Mumbai has achieved prestigious NABL accreditation certificate for both biological and chemical field. Also, DCL is taking part in Inter Laboratory Comparison Testing Programme.

14   *Adulteration, Spurious, Misbranded 'Products' or 'Drugs'*

ADULTERATED DRUGS

For the purposes of this chapter, an Ayurvedic, Siddha or Unani drug shall be deemed to be adulterated:

a. If it consists, in whole or in part, of any filthy, putrid or decomposed substance; or

b. If it has been prepared, packed or stored under insanitary conditions whereby, it may have been contaminated with filth or whereby, it may have been rendered injurious to health; or

c. If its container is composed, in whole or in part, of any poisonous or deleterious substance which may render the contents injurious to health; or

d. If it bears or contains, for purposes of coloring only, a color other than one which is prescribed; or

e. If it contains any harmful or toxic substance which may render it injurious to health; or

f. If any substance has been mixed therewith so as to reduce its quality or strength.

Explanation

For the purpose of clause (a), a drug shall not be deemed to consist, in whole or in part, of any discomposed substance only by reason of the fact that such decomposed substance is the result of any natural decomposition of the drug: Provided that such decomposition is not due to any negligence on the part of the manufacturer of the drug of the dealer thereof and that it does not render the drug injurious to health.

SPURIOUS DRUGS

For the purposes of this chapter, an Ayurvedic, Siddha or Unani drug shall be deemed to be spurious:

a. If it is sold, or offered or exhibited for sale, under a name which belongs to another drug; or

b. If it is an imitation of, or is a substitute for, another drug or resembles another drug in a manner likely to deceive, or bears upon it or upon its label or container the name of another drug, unless it is plainly and conspicuously marked so as to reveal its true character and its lack identity with such other drug; or

c. If the label or container bears the name of an individual or company purporting to be the manufacturer of the drug, which individual or company is fictitious or does not exist; or

d. If it has been substituted wholly or in part by any other drug or substance; or

e. If it purports to be the product of a manufacture of whom it is not truly a product.

MISBRANDED DRUGS

For the purposes of this chapter, an Ayurvedic, Siddha or Unani drug shall be deemed to be misbranded:

a. If it is so colored, coated, powdered or polished that damage is concealed, or if it is made to appear of better or greater therapeutic value than it really is; or

b. If it is not labelled in the prescribed manner; or

c. If its label or container or anything accompanying the drug bears any statement, design or device which makes any false claim for the drug or which is false or misleading in any particular.

15 Government Licensing Authority

In the beginning of the current century drug Industry was practically non-existent in India and pharmaceuticals were being important from abroad. The First World War changed the situation and not only were finished and cheap drugs imported in increasing volume, the demand for an indigenous product also was voiced from all sides. With the clamor for swadeshi goods manufacturing concerns, both Indian and Foreign, sprang up to produce pharmaceuticals at cheaper rates to compete with imported products. Naturally some of these were of inferior quality and harmful for public health. The government was, therefore, called upon to take notice of the situation and consider the matter of introducing legislation to control the manufacture, distribution and sale of drugs and medicines. Two of the laws, the Poisons Act and the Dangerous Drugs Act were passed in 1919 and 1930 respectively. The Opium Act was quite old having being adopted as early as 1878. But to have a comprehensive legislation, which the rapid expansion of the pharmaceutical production and drug market required by the end of the second decade for its control, the Indian Government appointed in 1931, a Drugs Enquiry Committee under the Chairmanship Lt. Col. RN Chopra which was asked to make sifting enquiries into the whole matter of drug production, distribution and sale by inviting opinions and meeting concerned people. The Committee was asked to make recommendations about the ways and means of controlling the production and sale of drugs and pharmaceuticals in the interest of public health. The Chopra Committee toured all over the country and after carefully examining the data placed before it, submitted a voluminous report to government suggesting creation of drug control machinery at the centre with branches in all provinces. For an efficient and speedy working of the controlling department the committee also recommended the establishment of a well-equipped central drugs laboratory with competent staff and experts in various branches for data standardization work. Under the guidance of the central laboratory, it was suggested, small laboratories would work, in the provinces. For the training of young men and women, the committee recommended the permission of Central Pharmacy Council, and the Provincial Pharmacy Councils, with registrars who would maintain the lists containing names and addresses of the licensed pharmacists.the outbreak of the Second World War in 1939 delayed the introduction of legislation on the lines suggested by the Chopra Committee which the Indian government contemplated and considered as urgent. However, the Drugs Act was passed in 1940 partly implementing the Chopra recommendations. With the achievement of independence in 1947 the rest of the required laws were put on the Statute book. In 1985, the Narcotic Drugs and Psychotropic Substances Act were enacted repealing the Dangerous Drugs Act, 1930 and the Opium Act of 1878. At present the following Acts and Rules made there under that govern the manufacture, sale, import, export and clinical research of drugs and cosmetics in India.

- The drugs and cosmetics act, 1940
- The Pharmacy Act, 1948.
- The Drugs and Magic Remedies (Objectionable Advertisement) Act, 1954.
- The Narcotic Drugs and Psychotropic Substances Act, 1985.
- The Medicinal and Toilet Preparations (Excise Duties) Act, 1956.
- The Drugs (Prices Control) Order 1995 (under the Essential Commodities Act).

SOME OTHER LAWS

There are some other laws which have a bearing on pharmaceutical manufacture, distribution and sale in India. The important ones being:

1. The Industries (development and regulation) Act, 1951.

2. The Trade and Merchandise Marks Act, 1958.
3. The Indian Patent and Design Act, 1970.
4. Factories Act.

THE DRUGS AND COSMETICS ACT, 1940

The object of the act is to regulate the import, manufacture, distribution and sale of drugs. Under the provisions of this act, the central government appoints the Drugs Technical Advisory Board to advise the central government and the state governments on technical matters arising out of the administration of this act. The board can constitute subcommittees for the consideration of a particular matter.

THE PHARMACY ACT, 1948

The Pharmacy Act was passed in 1948 and was amended in 1959, 1976 and 1984. The aim of this law is to regulate the profession of pharmacy in India. Under the provisions of this act the central government constitutes a Central Pharmacy Council of India consisting of following members:

a. Six members from the teachers of pharmacy.
b. Six members from practicing pharmacists or pharmaceutical chemists holding degree of diploma.
c. One member elected by the Medical Council of India.
d. The Director-General of Health Services.
e. The Direct or of the Central Drugs Laboratory.
f. The Chief Chemist, Central Revenues.
g. One member to represent each state elected by members of State Councils who shall be a registered pharmacist.
h. One member to represent each state government who shall be either registered medical practitioner or a registered pharmacist.

The president and vice-president of the central council of pharmacy are elected by the members of the council among themselves, hold office for five years and are eligible for re-election. The conducting of courses of study for pharmacists, and the examinations in pharmacy in the states are subject to the approval of the central council. Besides the council has the responsibility to supervise the education of pharmacy in the states. Where it is found that the course of study is not in conformity with the education regulations, the council may withdraw approval accorded to the course or the examination. The Central Council can approve qualifications granted by an outside authority for qualifying for registration under this act.

State Pharmacy Councils

The act makes it incumbent upon the state governments to constitute State Pharmacy Councils with the following members:
a. Six members elected from amongst themselves by registered pharmacists of the state.
b. Five members of whom at least two shall be persons possessing a prescribed degree or diploma in pharmacy or pharmaceutical chemistry or members of the pharmaceutical profession nominated by the state government.
c. One member elected by the state medical council.
d. The Chief Medical Officer of the State.
e. The State Drug Controller.
f. The Government Analyst.

Registration of Pharmacists

The state government has under the provisions of the pharmacy act to get a register of the state pharmacists prepared and it is the State Pharmacy Council which has to maintain the register. The register shall contain the name and residential address of pharmacist, the date of his first admission to the register, qualifications for registration, his professional address, the name of his employer and prescribed particulars.

THE DRUGS AND MAGIC REMEDIES (OBJECTIONABLE ADVERTISEMENTS) ACT, 1954

This act is meant to control the advertisements regarding drugs; it prohibits the advertising of remedies alleged to possess magic qualities and to provide for matters connected therewith. The Drugs and Magic Remedies Act prohibits a person from taking part in publication of any advertisement referring to any drug which suggests use of the drug for:

a. The procurement of miscarriage in women or prevention of conception in women; and

b. The maintenance or improvement of the capacity of the human being for sexual pleasure;

c. The correction of menstrual disorders in women;

d. The diagnosis, cure, mitigation, treatment or prevention of any venereal disease.

It is prohibited to directly or indirectly give a false impression regarding the true character of a drug or make false claim for it or to convey any false or misleading information in any material particular about it. No person shall import into or export from India any document containing advertisement of this nature.Whoever contravenes the provisions of this act shall, on conviction, be punishable with imprisonment which may extend to six months, with or without fine. In case of subsequent convictions the imprisonment can be extended to one year. The document, article or thing which contains the offending advertisement can be seized and confiscated. If the person contravening any of the provisions of the act is a company, every person who at the time the offence was committed was in charge of the business of the company shall be deemed guilty. The prohibition under this act does not apply to:

a. Any signboard or notice displayed by a registered medical practitioner including the treatment for any of the disease,

b. Any treaties or book dealing with any of the matters from a confide scientific standpoint,

c. Any advertisement related to any drug sent confidentially to any registered medical practitioners or to chemists for distribution among registered medical practitioners or to a hospital or laboratory, and

d. Government advertisements.

THE NARCOTIC DRUGS AND PSYCHOTROPIC SUBSTANCES ACT, 1985

This is an act to consolidate and amend the law relating to narcotic drugs, to make stringent provisions for the control and regulation of operations relating to narcotic drugs and psychotropic substances and for matters connected therewith.

16

Loan Licenses

Applications for the grant or renewal of loan [licenses for the manufacture for sale or for distribution] of drugs specified in Schedules C and C (1) [excluding those specified in Part X-B and Schedule X] shall be made in Form 27-A to the licensing authority and [shall be made up to ten items for each category of drugs categorized in Schedule M and Schedule M-III and shall be accompanied by a fee of rupees six thousand and an inspection fee of rupees one thousand and five hundred for every inspection or for the purpose of renewal of licenses].

Provided that if the applicant applies for the renewal of a license after its expiry but within six months of such expiry the fee payable for renewal of the license shall be 4 (rupees six thousand and an inspection of fee of rupees one thousand five hundred plus an additional fee at the rate of rupees one thousand) per month or a part thereof.

Explanation

For the purpose of this rule a loan license means a license which a licensing authority may issue to an applicant who does not have his own arrangements for manufacture but who intends to avail himself of the manufacturing facilities owned by another licensee in Form 28.

The licensing authority, shall, before the grant of a loan license, satisfy himself that the manufacturing unit has adequate equipment, staff, and capacity for manufacture and facilities for testing to undertake the manufacture on behalf of the applicant for a loan license.

Subject to the provisions of sub-rule (2), the application for manufacture of more than ten items of each category of drugs on a loan license, shall be accompanied by an additional fee at the rate of rupees three hundred for each additional item of drugs.

If the licensing authority is satisfied that a loan license is defaced, damaged or lot, he may, on payment of a fee of rupees one thousand, issue a duplicate copy of loan license.

17

Labeling and Packing

Any drug manufactured for the purpose of examination, test or analysis shall be kept in containers bearing labels indicating the purpose for which it has been manufactured.

If any drug manufactured for the purpose of examination, test or analysis is supplied by the manufacturer to any other person, the container shall bear a label on which shall be stated the name and address of the manufacturer, the accepted scientific name of the substance if known, or if not known a reference which will enable the substance to the identified and the purpose for which it has been manufactured labels on packages or containers of drugs for export shall be adapted to meet the specific requirements of the law of the country to which the drug is to be exported but the following particulars shall appear in a conspicuous position on the innermost container in which the drug is packed and every other covering in which that container is packed:

a. Name of the drug;

b. The name, address of the manufacturer and the number of the license under which the drug has been manufactured;

c. Batch or lot number;

d. Date of expiry, if any.

The medicine is labeled and packed with the following particulars:

a. The name and address of the supplier;

b. The name of the patient and the quantity of the medicine;

c. The number representing serial number of the entry in the prescription register;

d. The dose, if the medicine is for internal use;

e. The words *for externel use only* if the medicine is for external application.
f. Labeled packing must be airtight, free from contamination of sunlight, high temperature and free from dust.

18 Clinical Trials of New Drugs

Application for Permission to Conduct Clinical Trials for New Drug/Investigational New Drug

1. No clinical trial for a new drug, whether for clinical investigation or any clinical experiment by any institution, shall be conducted except under, and in accordance with, the permission, in writing, of the licensing authority defined in clause (b) of Rule 21.

2. An application for grant of permission to conduct.

   a. Human clinical trials (Phase-I) on a new drug shall be made to the licensing authority in Form 44 accompanied by a fee of fifty thousand rupees and such information and data as required under Schedule Y.

   b. Exploratory clinical trials (Phase-II) on a new drug shall be made on the basis of data emerging from Phase I trial, accompanied by a fee of twenty-five thousand rupees;

   c. Confirmatory clinical trials (Phase-III) on a new drug shall be made on the basis of the data emerging from Phase-II and where necessary, data emerging from Phase-I also, and shall be accompanied by a fee of twenty-five thousand rupees,

   Provided that no separate fee shall be required to be paid along with application for import/manufacture of a new drug based on successful completion of phases clinical trials by the applicant.

   Provided further that no fee shall be required to be paid along with the application by Central Government or State Government Institutes involved in clinical research for conducting trials for academic or research purposes.

3. The licensing authority after being satisfied with the clinical trials, shall grant permission in Form 45 or Form 45-A or

Form 46 or Form 46-A, as the case may be, subject to the conditions stated therein.

Provided that the licensing authority shall, where the data provided on the clinical trials is inadequate, intimate the applicant in writing, within six months from the date of such intimation or such extended period, not exceeding a further period of six months, as the licensing authority may, for reasons to be recorded in writing, permit, intimating the conditions which shall be satisfied before permission could be considered.

Explanation

For the purpose of these rules investigational new drug means a new chemical entity or a product having therapeutic indication but which have never been earlier tested on human beings.

19

Blood Bank

Form of application for licence for operation of Blood Bank/ processing of whole human blood for components/ manufacture of blood products for sale or *distribution.* (i) Application for the grant and/or renewal of license for the operation of a Blood Bank/processing of human blood for components/manufacture of blood products shall be made to the Licensing Authority appointed under Part VII in [Form 27-C or Form 27-E, as the case may be], and shall be accompanied by [license fee of rupees six thousand and an inspection fee of rupees one thousand and five hundred for every inspection thereof or for the purpose of renewal of licence].

Provided that if the applicant applies for renewal of license after its expiry but within six months of such expiry the fee payable for the renewal of the license [shall be rupees six thousand and inspection fee of rupees one thousand five hundred plus an additional fee at the rate of rupees one thousand per month or a part thereof in addition to the inspection fee].

Provided further that a licensee holding a license in [Form 28-C or Form 28-E, as the case may be] for operation of Blood Bank/processing of whole human blood for components/ manufacture of blood products shall apply for grant of license under sub rule.

1. Before the expiry of the said license on [Form 27-C or Form 28 E, as the case may be,] and he shall continue to operate the same till the orders on his application are communicated to him. [*Explanation.*— For the purpose of this rule, "Blood Bank" means a place or organizational unit or an institution or other arrangement made by such organizational unit or institution for carrying our all or any of the operations of

manufacture of human blood components, or blood products or whole human blood for its collection, storage, processing, distribution from selected human donors.]

2. A fee of [rupees one thousand] shall be paid for a duplicate copy of a license issued under this rule, if the original is defaced, damaged or lost.

3. Application by a licensee to manufacture additional drugs listed in the application shall be accompanied by a [fee of rupees three hundred] for each drug listed in the application.

4. On receipt of the application for the grant or renewal of such license, the licensing authority shall:

    i. Verify the statements made in the application form;

    ii. Cause the manufacturing the testing establishment to be inspected in accordance with the provision of Rule 122-I and;

    iii. In case the application is for renewal of license, call for information of past performance of the license.

5. If the licensing authority is satisfied that the applicant is in a position to fulfill the requirements laid down in the rules, he shall prepare a report to that effect and forward it [along with the application and the license (in triplicate) to be granted or renewed, duly completed] to the central license approving authority.

    Provided that if the licensing authority is of the opinion that the applicant is not in a position to fulfill the requirements laid down in these rules, he may, by order, for reasons to be recorded in writing, refuse to grant or renew the license, as the case may be.

6. If, on receipt of the application and report of the licensing authority referred to in sub-rule (5) and after taking such measures including inspection of the premises, by the inspector, appointed by the central government under Section 21 of the act, and/or along with the expert in the field concerned if deemed necessary, the central license approving authority is satisfied that the applicant is in a position to fulfill the requirements laid down in these rules, he may grant or renew the license, as the case may be.

Provided that if the central license approving authority is of the opinion that the applicant is not in a position to fulfill the requirements laid down in these rules he may, not withstanding the report of the licensing authority, by order, for reasons to be recorded in writing, reject the application for grant or renewal of licence, as the case may be, and shall supply the applicant with a copy of the inspection report.

Form of Licence for the operation of a Blood Bank/processing of whole human blood for components and manufacture of blood products and the conditions for the grant or renewal of such licence. A licence for the operation of a Blood Bank or for processing whole human blood for components and manufacture of blood products shall be issued in [Form 28-C or Form 28-E or Form 26-G or Form 26-I, as the case may be]. Before a licence in [Form 28-C or Form 28-E or Form 26-G or Form 26-I, as the case may be] is granted or renewed the following conditions shall be complied with by the applicant:

i. The operation of blood bank and/or processing of whole human blood for components shall be conducted under the active direction and personal supervision of competent technical staff consisting of at least one person who is whole-time employee and who is Medical Officer, and possessing:

a. Postgraduate degree in medicine — MD (pathology/ transfusion medicines); or

b. Degree in medicine (MBBS) with diploma in pathology or transfusion medicines having adequate knowledge in blood group serology, blood group methodology and medical principles involved in the procurement of blood and/or preparation of its components; or

c. Degree in Medicine (MBBS) having experience in blood bank for one year during regular service and also has adequate knowledge and experience in blood group serology, blood group methodology and medical principles involved in the procurement of blood and/or preparation of its components. The degree or diploma being from a university recognized by the central government.

Explanation. For the purposes of this conditions, the experience in blood bank for one year shall not apply in the case of persons who are approved by the licensing authority and/or central license approving Authority prior to the commencement of the drugs and cosmetics (Second Amendment) Rules, 1999].

ii. The applicant shall provide adequate space, plant and equipment for any or all the operations of blood collection or blood processing. The space, plant and equipment required for various operation is given in Schedule 'F', Part XII-B and/or XII-C.

iii. The applicant shall provide and maintain adequate technical staff as specified in Schedule F, Part XII-B and/or XII-C.

iv. The applicant shall provide adequate arrangements for storage of whole human blood, human blood components and blood products.

v. The applicant shall furnish to the licensing authority, if required to do so, data on the stability of whole human blood, its components or blood products which are likely to deteriorate, for fixing the date of expiry which shall be printed on the labels of such products on the basis of the data so furnished.

Duration of License

An original license in Form 28-C or Form 28-E or a renewed license in Form 26-G or Form 26-I unless sooner suspended or cancelled shall be valid for a period of five years on and from the date on which, it is granted or renewed.

Inspection before grant or renewal of license for operation of blood bank, processing of whole human blood for components and manufacture of blood products.

Before a license in 1 [Form 28-C or Form 28-E is granted or a renewal of license inform 26-G or Form 26-I is made, as the case may be,] the licensing authority or the central license approving authority, as the case may be, shall cause the establishment in which Blood Bank is proposed to be operated/ whole human blood for components is processed/blood products are manufactured to be inspected by one or more inspectors, appointed under the act and/or along with the expert in the field concerned. The inspector or inspectors shall examine all portions of the premises and appliance/equipment and inspect the process of manufacture intend to be employed or being employed along with the means to be employed or being employed for operation of blood bank/processing of whole human blood for components/manufacture of blood products together with their testing facilities and also enquire into the professional qualification of the expert staff and other technical staff to be employed.

20

Schedule M, MI, MII, MIII

[*See* Rules 71, 74, 76 and 78]

GOOD MANUFACTURING PRACTICES AND REQUIREMENTS OF PREMISES, PLANT AND EQUIPMENT FOR PHARMACEUTICAL PRODUCTS

Note: To achieve the objectives listed below, each licensee shall evolve appropriate methodology, systems and procedures which shall be documented and maintained for inspection and reference; and the manufacturing premises shall be used exclusively for production of drugs and no other manufacturing activity shall be undertaken therein.

PART 1

GOOD MANUFACTURING PRACTICES FOR PREMISES AND MATERIALS

1. General Requirements

1.1. *Location and surroundings:* The factory building(s) for manufacture of drugs shall be so situated and shall have such measures as to avoid risk of contamination from external environmental including open sewage, drain, public lavatory or any factory which product disagreeable or obnoxious odour, fumes, excessive soot, dust, smoke, chemical or biological emissions.

1.2. *Building and premises:* The building(s) used for the factory shall be designed, constructed, adapted and maintained to suit the manufacturing operations so as to permit production of drugs under hygienic conditions. They shall conform to the conditions laid down in the Factories Act, 1948 (63 of 1948).

The premises used for manufacturing, processing, warehousing, packaging labeling and testing purposes shall be .
Omitted by GOI notification no. GSR 462 (E) date 22.06.1982.
Ins.by GOI Notification no GSR 864(E) date 11.12.2001.- applicable to manufacturers licensed to manufacture drugs, for the period upto 31.12.2003.

i. Compatible with other drug manufacturing operations that may be carried out in the same or adjacent area/ section.

ii. Adequately provided with working space to allow orderly and logical placement of equipment, materials and movement of personnel so as to:

   a. Avoid the risk of mix-up between different categories of drugs or with raw materials, intermediates and in-process material;

   b. Avoid the possibilities of contamination and cross-contamination by providing suitable mechanism.

iii. Designed/constructed/maintained to prevent entry of insects, pests, birds, vermins, and rodents. Interior surface (walls, floors and ceilings) shall be smooth and free from cracks, and permit easy cleaning, painting and disinfection.

iv. Air-conditioned, where prescribed for the operations and dosage froms under production. The production and dispensing areas shall be well lighted, effectively ventilated, with air control facilities and may have proper air handling units (wherever applicable) to maintain conditions including temperature and, wherever necessary, humidity, as defined for the relevant product. These conditions shall be appropriate to the category of drugs and nature of the operation. These shall also be suitable to the comforts of the personnel working with protective clothing, products handled, operations undertaken within them in relation to the external environment. These areas shall be regularly monitored for compliance with required specifications.

v. Provided with drainage system, as specified for the various categories of products, which shall be of adequate size and so designed as to prevent back flow and/or prevent insets and rodents entering the premises. Open channels shall be avoided in manufacturing areas and, where provided, these shall be shallow to facilitate cleaning and disinfection.

vi. The walls and floors of the areas where manufacture of drugs is carried out shall be free from cracks and open joints to avoid accumulation of dust. These shall be smooth, washable, covered and shall permit easy and effective cleaning and disinfection. The interior surfaces shall not shed particles. A periodical record of cleaning and painting of the premises shall be maintained.

1.3. *Water system:* There shall be validated system for treatment of water drawn from own or any other source to render it potable in accordance with standards specified by the Bureau of Indian standards or local municipality, as the case may be, so as to produce purified water conforming to pharmacopoeial specification. Purified water so produced shall only be used for all operations except washing and cleaning operations where potable water may be used. Water shall be stored in tanks, which do not adversely affect quality of water and ensure freedom from microbiological growth. The tank shall be cleaned periodically and records maintained by the licensee in this behalf.

1.4. *Disposal of waste:*

i. The disposal of sewage and effluents (solid, liquid and gas) from the manufactory shall be in conformity with the requirements of Environment Pollution Control Board.

ii. All biomedical waste shall be destroyed as per the provisions of the Biomedical Waste (Management and Handling) Rules, 1996.

iii. Additional precautions shall be taken for the storage and disposal of rejected drugs. Records shall be maintained for all disposal of waste.

iv. Provisions shall be made for the proper and safe storage of waste materials awaiting disposal. Hazardous, toxic substances and flammable materials shall be stored in suitably designed and segregated, enclosed areas in conformity with central and state.

LEGISLATIONS

2. Warehousing Area

2.1. *Adequate areas* shall be designed to allow sufficient and orderly warehousing of various categories of materials and products like, starting and packaging materials, intermediates, bulk and finished products, products in quarantine, released, rejected, returned or recalled, machine and equipment spare parts and change items.

2.2. *Warehousing areas* shall be designed and adapted to ensure good storage conditions. They shall be clean, dry and maintained with acceptable temperature limits, where special storage conditions are required (e.g. temperature, humidity), these shall be provided, monitored and recorded. Storage areas shall have appropriate housekeeping and rodent, pests and vermin control procedures and records maintained. Proper racks, bins and platforms shall be provided for the storage of materials.

2.3. *Receiving and dispatch bays* shall protect materials and products from adverse weather conditions.

2.4. *Where quarantine status* is ensured by warehousing in separate earmarked areas in the same warehouse or store, these areas shall be clearly demarcated. Any system replacing the physical quarantine, shall give equivalent assurance of segregation. Access to these areas shall be restricted to authorized persons.

2.5. There shall be a *separate sampling area* in the warehousing area for active raw materials and excipients. If sampling is performed in any other area, it shall be conducted in such a way as to prevent contamination, cross-contamination and mix-up.

2.6. *Segregation* shall be provided for the storage of rejected, recalled or returned materials or products. Such areas, materials or products shall be suitably marked and secured. Access to these areas and materials shall be restricted.

2.7. *Highly hazardous, poisonous and explosive materials* such as narcotics, psychotropic drugs and substances presenting potential risks of abuse, fire or explosion shall be stored in safe and secure areas. Adequate fire protection measures shall be provided in conformity with the rules of the concerned civic authority.

2.8. *Printed packaging materials* shall be stored in safe, separate and secure areas.

2.9. *Separate dispensing* areas for (beta) lactum, sex hormones and cytotoxic substances or any such special categories of product shall be provided with proper supply of filtered air and suitable measures for dust control to avoid contamination. Such areas shall be under differential pressure.

2.10. *Sampling and dispensing* of sterile materials shall be conducted under aseptic conditions conforming to Grade A, which can also be performed in a dedicated area within the manufacturing facility.

2.11. *Regular checks* shall be made to ensure adequate steps are taken against spillage, breakage and leakage of containers.

2.12. *Rodent treatments* (pest control) should be done regularly and at least once in a year and record maintained.

3. Production Area

3.1. *The production area* shall be designed to allow the production preferably in uni-flow and with logical sequence of operations.

3.2. In order to *avoid the risk* of corss-contamination, separate dedicated and self-contained facilities shall be made available for the production of sensitive pharmaceutical products like penicillin or biological preparations with live micro-organisms. Separate dedicated facilities shall be provided for the manufacture of contamination causing and potent products such as beta-lactum, sex hormones and cytotoxic substances.

3.3. *Working and in-process space* shall be adequate to permit orderly and logical positioning of equipment and materials and movement of personnel to avoid cross-contamination and to minimize risk of omission or wrong application of any manufacturing and control measures.

3.4. *Pipe-work, electrical fittings, ventilation openings* and similar services lines shall be designed, fixed and constructed to avoid creation of recesses. Services lines shall preferably be identified by colors and the nature of the supply and direction of the flow shall be marked/indicated.

4. Ancillary Areas

4.1. *Rest and refreshment rooms* shall be separate from other areas. These areas shall not lead directly to the manufacturing and storage areas.

4.2. *Facilities for changing, storing clothes* and for washing and toilet purposes shall be easily accessible and adequate for the number of users. Toilets, separate for males and females, shall not be directly connected with production or storage areas. There shall be written instructions for cleaning and disinfection of such areas.

4.3. *Maintenance workshops* shall be separate and away from production areas. Whenever, spares, changed parts and tools are stored in the production area, these shall be kept in dedicated rooms or lockers. Tools and spare parts for use in sterile areas shall be disinfected before these are carried inside the production areas.

4.4. *Areas housing animals* shall be isolated from other areas. The other requirements regarding animal houses shall be those as prescribed in Rule 150-C (3) of the Drugs and Cosmetics Rules, 1945 which shall be adopted for production purposes.

5. Quality Control Area

5.1. *Quality control laboratories* shall be independent of the production areas. Separate areas shall be provided each for physicochemical, biological, microbiological or radioisotope analysis. Separate instrument room with adequate area shall be provided for sensitive and sophisticated instruments employed for analysis.

5.2. *Quality control laboratories* shall be designed appropriately for the operations to be carried out in them. Adequate space shall be provided to avoid mix-ups and cross-contamination. Sufficient and suitable storage space shall be provided for test samples, retained samples, reference standards, reagents and records.

5.3. *The design of the laboratory* shall take into account the suitability of construction materials and ventilation. Separate air handling units and other requirements shall be provided for biological, microbiological and radioisotopes testing areas. The laboratory shall be provided with regular supply of water of appropriate quality for cleaning and testing purpose.

5.4. *Quality control laboratory* shall be divided into separate sections, i.e. for chemical, microbiological and wherever required, biological testing. These shall have adequate area for basis installation and for ancillary purposes. The microbiology section shall have arrangements such as airlocks and laminar air flow workstation, wherever considered necessary.

6. Personnel

6.1. *The manufacture* shall be conducted under the direct supervision of competent technical staff with prescribed qualifications and practical experience in the relevant dosage and/or active pharmaceutical products.

6.2. *The head of the quality control laboratory* shall be independent of the manufacturing unit. The testing shall be conducted under the direct supervision of competent technical staff who shall be whole time employees of the licensee.

6.3. *Personnel for quality assurance and quality control operations* shall be suitably qualified and experienced.

6.4. *Written duties of technical and quality control personnel* shall be laid and following strictly.

6.5. *Number of personnel employed* shall be adequate and in direct proportion to the workload.

6.6. *The licensee* shall ensure in accordance with a written instruction that all personnel in production area or into quality control laboratories shall receive training appropriate to the duties and responsibility assigned to them. They shall be provided with regular in-service training.

7. Health, Clothing and Sanitation of Workers

7.1. *The personnel handling beta-lactum antibiotics* shall be tested for penicillin sensitivity before employment and those handling sex hormones, cytotoxic substances and other potent drugs shall be periodically examined for adverse effects. These personnel should be moved out of these sections (except in dedicated facilities), by rotation, as a health safeguard.

7.2. *Prior to employment, all personnel,* shall undergo medical examination including eye examination, and shall be free from tuberculosis, skin and other communicable or contagious diseases. Thereafter, they should be medically examined periodically, at least once a year. Records shall be maintained thereof. The licensee shall provide the services of a qualified physician for assessing the health status of personnel involved in different activities.

7.3. *All persons prior to and during employment* shall be trained in practices which ensure personnel hygiene. A high level of personal hygiene shall be observed by all those engaged in the manufacturing processes. Instructions to this effect shall be displayed in change rooms and other strategic locations.

7.4. *No person showing, at any time, apparent illness or open lesions* which may adversely affect the quality of products, shall be allowed to handle starting materials, packing materials, in-process materials, and drug products until his condition is no longer judged to be a risk.

7.5. *All employees* shall be instructed to report about their illness or abnormal health condition to their immediate supervisor so that appropriate action can be taken.

7.6. *Direct contact* shall be avoided between the unprotected hands of personnel and raw materials, intermediate or finished, unpacked products.

7.7. *All personnel* shall wear clean body coverings appropriate to their duties. Before entry into the manufacturing area, there shall be change rooms separate for each sex with adequate facilities for personal cleanliness such as washbasin with running water, clean towels, hand dryers, soaps, disinfectants, etc. The change room shall be provided with cabinets for the storage of personal belongings of the personnel.

7.8. *Smoking, eating, drinking, chewing or keeping plants, food, drink and personal medicines* shall not be permitted in production, laboratory, storage and other areas where they might adversely influence the product quality.

8. Manufacturing Operations and Controls

8.1 *All manufacturing operations* shall be carried out under the supervision of technical staff approved by the licensing authority. Each critical step in the process relating to the selection, weighing and measuring of raw material addition during various stages shall be performed by trained personnel under the direct personal supervision of approved technical staff.

The contents of all vessels and containers used in manufacture and storage during the various manufacturing stages shall be conspicuously labeled with the name of the product, batch number, batch size and stage of manufacture. Each label should be initialed and dated by the auhorised technical staff. Products not prepared under aseptic conditions are required to be free from pathogens like *Salmonella, Escherichia coli, Pyocyanea, etc.*

8.2. *Precautions against mix-up and cross-contamination*

8.2.1. *The licensee* shall prevent mix-up and cross-contamination of drug material and drug product (from environmental dust) by proper air-handling system, pressure differential, segregation, status labeling and cleaning. Proper records and Standard Operating Procedures thereof shall be maintained.

8.2.2. *The licensee* shall ensure processing of sensitive drugs like beta-lactum antibiotics, sex hormones and cytotoxic substances in segregated areas or isolated production areas within the building with independent air-handling unit and proper pressure differential. The effective segregation of these areas shall be demonstrated with adequate records of maintenance and services.

8.2.3. *To prevent mix-ups* during production stages, materials under process shall be conspicuously labeled to demonstrate their status. All equipment used for production shall be labeled with their current status.

8.2.4. *Packaging lines* shall be independent and adequately segregated. It shall be ensured that all left-overs of the previous packaging operations, including labels, cartons and caps are cleared before the closing hour.

8.2.5. *Before packaging operations* are begun, steps shall be taken to ensure that the work area, packaging lines, printing machines, and other equipment are clean and free from any products, materials and spillages. The line clearance shall be performed according to an approximate check-list and recorded.

8.2.6. *The correct details* of any printing (for example, of batch numbers or expiry dates) done separately or in the course of the packaging shall be rechecked at regular intervals. All printing and overprinting shall be authorized in writing.

8.2.7. *The manufacturing environment* shall be maintained at the required levels of temperature, humidity and cleanliness.

8.2.8. *Authorised persons* shall ensure change-over into specific uniforms before undertaking any manufacturing operations including packaging.

8.2.9. There shall be segregated enclosed areas, secured for recalled or rejected material and for such materials which are to be reprocessed or recovered.

9. Sanitation in the Manufacturing Premises

9.1. *The manufacturing premises* shall be cleaned and maintained in an orderly manner, so that it is free from accumulated waste, dust, debris and other similar material. A validated cleaning procedure shall be maintained.

9.2. *The manufacturing areas* shall not be used for storage of materials, except for the material being processed. It shall not be used as a general throughfare.

9.3. *A routine sanitation program* shall be drawn up and observed, which shall be properly recorded and which shall indicate:

a. Specific areas to be cleaned and cleaning intervals;

b. Cleaning procedure to be followed, including equipment and materials to be used for cleaning; and

c. Personnel assigned to and responsible for the cleaning operation.

9.4. *The adequacy* of the working and in-process storage space shall permit the orderly and logical positioning of equipment and materials so as to minimize the risk of mix-up between different pharmaceutical products or their components to avoid cross contamination, and to minimise the risk of omission or wrong application of any of the manufacturing or control steps.

9.5. *Production areas* shall be well lit, particularly where visual on-line controls are carried out.

10. Raw Materials

10.1. *The licensee* shall keep an inventory of all raw materials to be used at any stage of manufacture of drugs and maintain records as per Schedule U.

10.2. *All incoming materials* shall be quarantined immediately after receipt or processing. All materials shall be stored under appropriate conditions and in an orderly fashion to permit batch segregation and stock rotation by a first in/first expiry. .firstout. principle. All incoming materials shall be checked to ensure that the consignment corresponds to the order placed.

10.3. *All incoming materials* shall be purchased from approved sources under valid purchase vouchers. Wherever, possible, raw materials should be purchased directly from the producers.

10.4. *Authorized staff appointed* by the licensee in this behalf, which may include personnel from the quality control department, shall examine each consignment on receipt and shall check each container for integrity of package and seal. Damaged containers shall be identified, recorded and segregated.

10.5. *If a single delivery* of material is made up of different batches, each batch shall be considered as a separate batch for sampling, testing and release.

10.6. *Raw materials* in the storage area shall be appropriately labeled. Labels shall be clearly marked with the following information:

a. Designated name of the product and the internal code reference, where applicable, and analytical reference number;

b. Manufacturer's name, address and batch number;

c. The status of the contents (e.g. quarantine, under test, released, approved, rejected); and

d. The manufacturing date, expiry date and re-test date.

10.7. There shall be *adequate separate areas* for materials under test, approved and rejected with arrangements and equipment to allow dry, clean and orderly placement of stored materials and products, wherever necessary, under controlled temperature and humidity.

10.8. *Containers* from which samples have been drawn shall be identified.

10.9. *Only raw materials* which have been released by the quality control department and which are within their shelf-life shall be used. It shall be ensured that shelf-life of formulation product shall not exceed with that of active raw materials used.

10.10. It shall be ensured that all the *containers of raw materials* are placed on the raised platforms/racks and not placed directly on the floor.

11. Equipment

11.1. *Equipment* shall be located, designed, constructed, adapted and maintained to suit the operations to be carried out. The layout and design of the equipment shall aim to minimise the risk of errors and permit effective cleaning and maintenance in order to avoid cross-contamination, build-up of dust or dirt and, in general any adverse effect on the quality of products. Each equipment shall be provided with a logbook, wherever necessary.

11.2. *Balances and other measuring equipment* of an appropriate range, accuracy and precision shall be available in the raw material stores, production and in process control operations and these shall be calibrated and checked on a scheduled basis in accordance with standard operating procedures and records maintained.

11.3. *The parts of the production equipment* that come into contact with the product shall not be reactive, additive or adsorptive to an extent that would affect the quality of the product.

11.4. *To avoid accidental contamination*, wherever possible, non-toxic/edible grade lubricants shall be used and the equipment shall be maintained in a way that lubricants do not contaminate the products being produced.

11.5. *Defective equipment* shall be removed from production and quality control areas or appropriately labeled.

12. Documentation and Records

Documentation is an essential part of the quality assurance system and, as such, shall be related to all aspects good manufacturing practices (GMP). Its aim is to define the specifications for all materials, method of manufacture and control, to ensure that all personnel concerned with manufacture know the information necessary to decide whether or not to release a bath of drug for sale and to provide an audit trail that shall permit investigation of the history of any suspected defective batch.

12.1. *Documents designed, prepared, reviewed and controlled,* wherever applicable, shall comply with these rules.

12.2. *Documents shall be approved, signed and dated* by appropriate and authorized persons.

12.3. *Documents shall specify the title, nature and purpose.* They shall be laid out in an orderly fashion and be easy to check. Reproduced documents shall be clear and legible. Documents shall be regularly reviewed and kept up to date. Any alteration made in the entry of a document shall be signed and dated.

12.4. *The records* shall be made or completed at the time of each operation in such a way that all significant activities concerning the manufacture of pharmaceutical products are traceable. Records and associated standard operating procedures (SOP) shall be retained for at least one year after the expiry date of the finished product.

12.5. *Data may be recorded* by electronic data processing systems or other reliable means, but master formulae and detailed operating procedures relating to the system in use shall also be available in a hard copy to facilitate checking of the accuracy of the records. Wherever, documentation is handled by electronic data processing methods, authorized persons shall enter modify data in the computer. There shall be record of changed and deletions. Access shall be restricted by passwords or other means and the result of entry of critical data shall be independently checked. Batch records electronically stored shall be protected by a suitable back-up. During the period of retention, all relevant data shall be readily available.

13. Labels and other Printed Materials

Labels are absolutely necessary for identification of the drugs and their use. The Printing shall be done in bright colors and in a legible manner. The label shall carry all the prescribed details about the product.

13.1. *All containers and equipment* shall bear appropriate labels. Different color coded tablets shall be used to indicate the status of a product (for example, under test, approved, passed, rejected).

13.2. *To avoid chance mix-up* of printed packaging materials, product leaflets, relating to different products, shall be stored separately.

13.3. *Prior to release, all labels* for containers, cartons and boxes and all circulars, inserts and leaflets shall be examined by the quality control department of the licensee.

13.4. *Prior to packaging and labeling* of a given batch of a drug, it shall be ensured by the licensee that samples are drawn from the bulk and duly tested, approved and released by the quality control personnel.

13.5. *Records of receipt* of all labeling and packaging materials shall be maintained for each shipment received indicating receipt, control reference numbers and whether accepted or rejected. Unused coded and damaged labels and packaging materials shall be destroyed and recorded.

13.6. *The label or accompanying document* of reference standards and reference culture shall indicate concentration, lot number, potency, date on which containers was first opened and storage conditions, where appropriate.

14. Quality Assurance

This is a wide-ranging concept concerning all matters that individually or collectively influence the quality of a product. It is the totality of the arrangements made with the object of ensuring that products are of the quality required for their intended use.

14.1. *The system of quality assurance appropriate* to the manufacture of pharmaceutical products shall ensure that:

a. The pharmaceutical products are designed and developed in a way that takes account of the requirement of good manufacturing practices (herein referred as GMP) and other associated codes such as those of good laboratory practices (hereinafter referred as GLP) and good clinical practices (herein after referred as GCP).

b. Adequate arrangements are made for manufacture, supply and use of the correct starting and packaging materials.

c. Adequate controls on starting materials, intermediate products, and bulk products and other in-process controls, calibrations, and validations are carried out.

d. The finished product is correctly processed and checked in accordance with established procedures.

e. The pharmaceutical products are not released for sale or supplied before authorized persons have certified that each production batch as been produced and controlled in accordance with the requirements of the label claim and any other provisions relevant to production, control and release of pharmaceutical products.

15. Self-inspection and Quality Audit

It may be useful to constitute a self-inspection team supplemented with a quality audit procedure for assessment of all or part of a system with the specific purpose of improving it.

15.1. *To evaluate the manufacturers compliance* with GMP in all aspects of production and quality control, concept of self-inspection shall be followed. The manufacturer shall constitute a team of independent, experienced, qualified persons from within or outside the company, who can audit objectively the implementation of methodology and procedures evolved. The procedure for self-inspection shall be documented indicating self-inspection results; evaluation, conclusions and recommended corrective actions with effective follow up program. The recommendations for corrective action shall be adopted.

15.2. *The program shall be designed* to detect shortcomings in the implementation of good manufacturing practice and to recommend the necessary corrective actions. Self-inspections shall be performed routinely and on specific occasions, like when product recalls or repeated rejections occur or when an inspection by the licensing authorities is announced. The team responsible for self-inspection shall consist of personnel who can evaluate the implementation of good manufacturing practice objectively; all recommendations for corrective action shall be implemented.

15.3. *Written instructions* for self-inspection shall be drawn up which shall include the following:

a. Personnel

b. Premises including personnel facilities

c. Maintenance of buildings and equipment

d. Storage of starting materials and finished products

e. Equipment

f. Production and in-process controls

g. Quality control

h. Documentation

i. Sanitation and hygiene

j. Validation and revalidation programs

k. Calibration of instruments or measurement systems.

l. Recall procedures

m. Complaints management

n. Labels control

o. Results of previous self-inspections and any corrective steps taken.

16. Quality Control System

Quality control shall be concerned with sampling, specifications, testing, documentation, release procedures which ensure that the necessary and relevant tests are actually carried and that the materials are not released for use, nor products released for sale or supply until their quality has been judged to be satisfactory. It is not confined to laboratory operations but shall be involved in all decisions concerning the quality of the product. It shall be ensured that all quality control arrangements are effectively and reliably carried out the department as a whole shall have other duties such as to establish evaluate, validate and implement all quality control procedures and methods.

16.1. *Every manufacturing establishment* shall establish its own quality control laboratory manner by qualified and experience staff.

16.2. *The area of the quality control laboratory* may be divided into chemical, instrumentation, microbiological and biological testing.

16.3. *Adequate area having the required storage conditions* shall be provided for keeping reference samples. The quality control department shall evaluate, maintain and store reference samples.

16.4. *Standard operating procedures* shall be available for sampling, inspecting and testing of raw materials, intermediate bulk finished products and packing materials and, wherever necessary, for monitoring environmental conditions.

16.5. *There shall be authorized and dated specifications* for all materials, products, reagents and solvents including test of identity, content, purity and quality. These shall include specifications for water, solvents and reagents used in analysis.

16.6. *No batch of the product* shall be released for sale or supply until it has been certified by the authorized person(s) that it is in accordance with the requirements of the standards laid down.

16.7. *Reference/retained samples* from each batch of the products manufactured shall be maintained in quantity which is at least twice the quantity of the drug required to conduct all the tests, except sterility and pyrogen/Bacterial Endotoxin Test performed on the active material and the product manufactured. The retained product shall be kept in its final pack or simulated pack for a period of three months after the date of expiry.

16.8. *Assessment of records pertaining* to finished products shall include all relevant factors, including the production conditions, the results of in process testing, the manufacturing (including packaging) documentation, compliance with the specification for the finished product, and an examination of the finished pack. Assessment records should be signed by the in-charge of production and countersigned by the authorised quality control personnel before a product is released for sale or distribution.

16.9. *Quality control personnel* shall have access to production areas for sampling and investigation, as appropriate.

16.10. *The quality control department* shall conduct stability studies of the products to ensure and assign their shell life at the prescribed conditions of storage. All records of such studies shall be maintained.

16.11. *The in-charge of quality assurance* shall investigate all product complaints and records thereof shall be maintained.

16.12. *All instruments* shall be calibrated and testing procedures validated before these are adopted for routine testing. Periodical calibration of instrument and validation of procedures shall be carried out.

16.13. *Each specification for raw materials, intermediates, final products, and packing materials* shall be approved and maintained by the quality control department. Periodic revisions of the specifications shall be carried out wherever changes are necessary.

16.14. *Pharmacopoeiae, reference standards, working standards, references, spectra, other reference materials and technical books, as required,* shall be available in the quality control laboratory of the licensee.

17. Specification

17.1. *For raw materials and packaging materials.* They shall include:

a. The designated name and internal code reference;
b. Reference, if any, to a pharmacopoeial monograph;
c. Qualitative and quantitative requirements with acceptance limits;
d. Name and address of manufacturer or supplier and original manufacturer of the material;
e. Specimen of printed material;
f. Directions for sampling and testing or reference to procedures;
g. Storage conditions; and
h. Maximum period of storage before re-testing.

17.2. *For product containers and closures*

17.2.1. *All containers and closures intended for use* shall comply with the pharmacopoeial requirements. Suitable validated test methods, sample sizes, specifications, cleaning procedure and sterilization procedure, wherever indicated, shall be strictly followed to ensure that these are not reactive, additive, absorptive, or leach to an extent that significantly affects the quality or purity of the drug. No second hand or used containers and closures shall be used.

17.2.2. *Whenever bottles are being used,* the written schedule of cleaning shall be laid down and followed. Where bottles are not dried after washing, they should be rinsed with de-ionised water or distilled water, as the case may be.

17.3. *For in-process and bulk products:* Specifications for in-process material, intermediate and bulk products shall be available. The specifications should be authenticated.

17.4. *For finished products:* Appropriate specifications for finished products shall include:

a. The designated name of the product and the code reference;

b. The formula or a reference to the formula and the pharmacopoeial reference;

c. Directions for sampling and testing or a reference to procedures;

d. A description of the dosage form and package details;

e. The qualitative and quantitative requirements, with the acceptance limits for release;

f. The storage conditions and precautions, where applicable, and

g. The shelf-life.

17.5. *For preparation of containers and closures:* The requirements mentioned in the Schedule do not include requirements of machinery, equipment and premises required for preparation of containers and closures for different dosage forms and categories of drugs. The suitability and adequacy of the machinery, equipment and premises shall be examined taking into consideration the requirements of each licensee in this respect.

18. Master Formula Records

There shall be Master Formula records relating to all manufacturing procedures for each product and batch size to be manufactured. These shall be prepared and endorsed by the competent technical staff, i.e. head of production and quality control. The master formula shall include:

a. The name of the product together with product reference, code, relating to its specifications;

b. The patent or proprietary name of the product along with the generic name, a description of the dosage form, strength, composition of the product and batch size;

c. Name, quantity, and reference number of all the starting materials to be used. Mention shall be made of any substance that may disappear in the courts of processing;

d. A statement of the expected final yield with the acceptable limits, and of relevant intermediate yields, where applicable;

e. A statement of the processing location and the principal equipment to be used;

f. The methods, or reference to the methods, to be used for preparing the critical equipment including cleaning, assembling, calibrating, sterilizing;

g. Detailed stepwise processing instructions and the time taken for each step;

h. The instructions for in-process control with their limits;

i. The requirements for storage conditions of the products, including the container, labeling and special storage conditions where applicable;

j. Any special precautions to be observed; and

k. Packing details and specimen labels.

19. Packing Records

There shall be authorised packaging instructions for each product, pack size and type. These shall include or have a reference to the following :

a. Name of the product;

b. Description of the dosage form, strength and composition;

c. The pack size expressed in terms of the number of doses, weight or volume of the product in the final container;

d. Complete list of all the packaging materials required for a standard batch size, including quantities, sizes and types with the code of reference number relating to the specifications of each packaging material;

e. Reproduction of the relevant printed packaging materials and specimens indicating where batch number and expiry date of the product have been applied;

f. Special precautions to be observed, including a careful examination of the area and equipment in order to ascertain the line clearance before the operations begin;

g. Description of the packaging operation, including any significant subsidiary operations and equipment to be used;

h. Details of in-process controls with instructions for sampling and acceptance; and

i. Upon completion of the packing and labeling operation, a reconciliation shall be made between number of labeling and packaging units issued, number of units labeled, packed and excess returned or destroyed. Any significant or unusual discrepancy in the numbers shall be carefully investigated before releasing the final batch.

20. Batch Packaging Records

20.1. *A batch packaging record* shall be kept for each batch or part batch processed. It shall be based on the relevant parts of the packaging instructions, and the method of preparation of such records shall be designed to avoid transcription errors.

20.2. *Before any packaging operation begins, check* shall be made and recorded that the equipment and the workstations are clear of the previous products, documents or materials not required for the planned packaging operations, and that the equipment is clean and suitable for use.

21. Batch Processing Records

21.1. *There shall be batch processing record* for each product. It shall be based on the relevant parts of the currently approved Master Formula. The method of preparation of such records included in the master formula shall be designed to avoid transcription errors.

21.2. *Before any processing begins, check* shall be performed and recorded to ensure that the equipment and workstation are clear of previous products, documents or materials not required for the planned process are removed and the equipment is clean and suitable for use.

21.3. *During processing, the following information* shall be recorded at the time each action is taken and the record shall be dated and signed by the person responsible for the processing operations:

a. The name of the product;

b. The number of the batch being manufactured;

c. Dates and time of commencement, of significant intermediate stages and of completion of production;

d. Initials of the operator of different significant steps of production and where appropriate, of the person who checked each of these operations;

e. The batch number and/or analytical control number as well as the quantities of each starting material actually weighed;

f. Any relevant processing operation or event and major equipment used;

g. A record of the in-process controls and the initials of the person(s) carrying them out, and the results obtained;

h. The amount of product obtained after different and critical stages of manufacture (yield);

i. Comments or explanations for significant deviations from the expected yield limits shall be given;

j. Notes on special problems including details, with signed authorization, for any deviation from the Master Formula;

k. Addition of any recovered or reprocessed material with reference to recovery or reprocessing stages.

22. Standard Operating Procedures (SOPs) and Records, Regarding

22.1 *Receipt of materials:*

22.1.1. There shall be written *standard operating procedures and records* for the receipt of each delivery of raw, primary and printed packaging material.

22.1.2. *The records of the receipts* shall include;

a. The name of the material on the delivery note and the number of containers;

b. The date of receipt;

c. The manufacturers and/or suppliers name;

d. The manufacturers batch or reference number;

e. The total quantity, and number of containers, quantity in each container received;

f. The control reference number assigned after receipt and

g. Any other relevant comment or information.

22.1.3. There shall be *written standard operating procedures* for the internal labeling, quarantine and storage of starting materials, packaging materials and other materials, as appropriate.

22.1.4. There shall be *standard operating procedures* available for each instrument and equipment and these shall be placed in close proximity to the related instrument and equipment.

22.2. *Sampling:*

22.2.1. There shall be written *standard operating procedures* for sampling, which include the person(s) authorized to take the samples.

22.2.2. The *sampling instruction* shall include:

a. The method of sampling and the sampling plan;

b. The equipment to be used;

c. Any precautions to be observed to avoid contamination of the material or any deterioration in its quality;

d. The quantity of samples to be taken;

e. Instructions for any required sub-division or poling of the samples;

f. The types of sample containers to be used and

g. Any specific precautions to be observed, especially in regard to sampling of sterile and hazardous materials.

22.3. *Batch numbering:*

22.3.1. There shall be standard operating procedures *describing the details* of the batch (lot) numbering set up with the objective of ensuring that each batch of intermediate, bulk or finished product is identified with a specific batch number.

22.3.2. *Batch numbering* standard operating procedures applied to a processing stage and to the respective packaging stage shall be same or traceable to demonstrate that they belong to one homogenous mix.

22.3.3. Batch number *allocation* shall be immediately recorded in a logbook or by electronic data processing system. The record shall include date of allocation, product identity and size of batch.

22.4. *Testing*:

22.4.1. There shall be *written procedures* for testing materials and products at different stages of manufacture, describing the methods and equipment to be used. The tests performed shall be recorded.

22.5 *Records of analysis*:

22.5.1. The records shall include the following data:

a. Name of the material or product and the dosage form;

b. Batch number and, where appropriate the manufacturer and/or supplier;

c. Reference to the relevant specifications and testing procedures;

d. Test results, including observations and calculations, and reference to any specifications (limits);

e. Dates of testing;

f. Initials of the persons who performed the testing;

g. Initials of the persons who verified the testing and the detailed calculations;

h. A statement of release or rejection, and

i. Signature and date of the designated responsible person.

22.5.2. There shall be written standard operating procedures and the associated records of actions taken for:

a. Equipment assembly and validation;

b. Analytical apparatus and calibration;

c. Maintenance, cleaning and sanitation;

d. Personnel matters including qualification, training, clothing, hygiene;

e. Environmental monitoring;

f. Pest control;

g. Complaints;

h. Recalls made; and

i. Returns received.

23. Reference Samples

23.1. Each *lot of every active ingredient*, in a quality sufficient to carryout all the tests, except sterility and pyrogens/bacterial endotoxin test, shall be retained for a period of 3 months after the date of expiry of the last batch produced from that active ingredient.

23.2. *Samples of finished formulations* shall be stored in the same or simulated containers in which the drug has been actually marketed.

24. Reprocessing and Recoveries

24.1. Where *reprocessing is necessary*, written procedures shall be established and approved by the quality assurance department that shall specify the conditions and limitations of repeating chemical reactions. Such reprocessing shall be validated.

24.2. If the *product batch has to be reprocessed,* the procedure shall be authorized and recorded. An investigation shall be carried out into the causes necessitating re-processing and appropriate corrective measures shall be taken for prevention of recurrence. Re-processed batch shall be subjected to stability evaluation.

24.3. *Recovery of the product residue* may be carried out, if permitted, in the master production and control records by incorporating it in subsequent batches of the product.

25. Distribution Records

25.1. *Prior to distribution or dispatch* of given batch of a drug, it shall be ensure that the batch has been duly tested, approved and released by the quality control personnel. Pre-dispatch inspection shall be performed on each consignment on a random basis to ensure that only the correct goods are dispatched. Detailed instructions for warehousing and stocking of large volume parenterals, if stocked, shall be in existence and shall be complied with after the batch is released for distribution. Periodic audits of warehousing practices followed at distribution centers shall be carried out and records thereof shall be maintained. Standard operating procedures shall be developed for warehousing of products.

25.2. *Records for distribution* shall be maintained in a manner such that finished batch of a drug can be traced to the retain level to facilitate prompt and complete recall of the batch, if and when necessary.

26. Validation and Process Validation

26.1. *Validation studies* shall be an essential part of good manufacturing practices and shall be conducted as per the pre-defined protocols. These shall include validation of processing, testing and cleaning procedures.

26.2. *A written report* summarizing recorded results and conclusions shall be prepared, documented and maintained.

26.3. *Processes and procedures* shall be established on the basis of validation study and undergo periodic revalidation to ensure that they remain capable of achieving the intended results. Critical processes shall be validated, prospectively for retrospectively.

26.4. *When any new Master Formula* or method of preparation is adopted, steps shall be taken to demonstrate its suitability for routine processing. The defined process, using the materials and equipment specified shall be demonstrated to yield a product consistently of the required quality.

26.5. *Significant changes* to the manufacturing process, including any changes in equipment or materials that may affect product quality and/or the reproducibility of the process, shall be validated.

27. Product Recalls

27.1. *A prompt and effective product* recall system of defective products shall be devised for timely information of all concerned stockists, wholesalers, suppliers, up to the retail level within the shortest period. The licensee may make use of both print and electronic media in this regard.

27.2. There shall be *an established written procedure* in the form of standard operating procedure for effective recall of products distributed by the licensee. Recall operations shall be capable of being initiated promptly so as to effectively reach at the level of each distribution channel.

27.3. The *distribution records* shall be readily made available to the persons designated for recalls.

27.4. The *designated person* shall record a final report issued, including reconciliation between the delivered and the recovered quantities of the products.

27.5. The *effectiveness of the arrangements* for recalls shall be evaluated from time to time.

27.6. The *recalled products* shall be stored separately in a secured segregated area pending final decision on them.

28. Complaints and Adverse Reactions

28.1. All *complaints* thereof concerning product quality shall be carefully reviewed and recorded according to written procedures. Each complaint shall be investigated/valuated by the designated personnel of the company and records of investigation and remedial action taken thereof shall be maintained.

28.2. Reports of *serious adverse drug reactions* resulting from the use of a drug along with comments and documents shall be forthwith reported to the concerned licensing authority.

28.3. There shall be *written procedure describing* the action to be taken, recall to be made of the defective product.

29. Site Master File

The licensee shall prepare a succinct document in the form of site master file containing specific and factual good manufacturing practices about the production and/or control of pharmaceutical manufacturing preparations carried out at the licensed premises. It shall contain the following:

29.1. *General information*
a. Brief information of the firm;

b. Pharmaceutical manufacturing activities as permitted by the licensing authority;

c. Other manufacturing activities, if any, carried out on the premises;

d. Type of product licensed for manufacture with flow charts mentioning procedure and process flow;

e. Number of employees engaged in the production, quality control, storage and distribution;

f. Use of outside scientific, analytical or other technical assistance in relation to manufacture and analysis;

g. Short description of the quality management system of the firm; and

h. Products details registered with foreign countries.

29.2. *Personnel*

a. Organisational chart showing the arrangement for quality assurance including production and quality control;

b. Qualification, experience and responsibilities of key personnel;

c. Outline for arrangements for basic and in-service training and how the records are maintained;

d. Health requirements for personnel engaged in production; and

e. Personal hygiene requirements, including clothing.

29.3. *Premises*

a. Simple plan or description of manufacturing areas drawn to scale;

b. Nature of construction and fixtures/fittings;

c. Brief description of ventilation systems. More details should be given for critical areas with potential risk of airborne contamination (schematic drawing of systems). Classification of the rooms used for the manufacture of sterile products should be mentioned;

d. Special areas for the handling of the highly toxic, hazardous and sensitizing materials;

e. Brief description of water system (schematic drawings of systems), including sanitation; and

f. Description of planned preventive maintenance programs for premises and of the recording system.

29.4. *Equipment*:

a. Brief description of major equipment used in production and quality control laboratories (a list of equipment required);

b. Description of planned preventive maintenance programs for equipment and of the recording system; and

c. Qualification and calibration including the recording systems and arrangements for computerized systems validation.

29.5. *Sanitation* *a*vailability of written specifications and procedures for cleaning manufacturing areas and equipment.

29.6. *Documentation*:

a. Arrangements for the preparation, revision and distribution of;

b. Necessary documentation for the manufacture;

c. Any other documentation related to product quality that is not mentioned elsewhere (e.g. microbiological controls about air and water).

29.7. *Production*:

a. Brief description of production operations using, wherever possible, flow sheets and charts specifying important parameters;

b. Arrangements for the handling of starting materials, packaging materials, bulk and finished products, including sampling, quarantine, release and storage;

c. Arrangements for the handling of rejected materials and products; and

d. Brief description of general policy for process validation.

29.8. *Quality control*

Description of the quality control system and of the activities of the quality control department. Procedures for the release of the finished products.

29.9. *Loan licence manufacture and licensee*:

Description of the way in which compliance of good manufacturing practices by the loan licensee shall be assessed.

29.10. *Distribution, complaints and product recall:*

a. Arrangements and recording system for distribution; and

b. Arrangements for handling of complaints and product recalls.

29.11. *Self-inspection:* Short description of the self-inspection system indicating whether an outside, independent and experienced external export was involved in evaluating the manufacturer.s compliance with good manufacturing practices in all aspects of production.

29.12 *Export of drugs*

a. Products exported to different countries; and

b. Complaints and product recall, if any.

PART I-A

Specific Requirements for Manufacture of Sterile Products, Parenteral Preparations (Small Volume Injectables and Large Volume Parenterals) and Sterile Ophthalmic Preparations

Note. The general requirements as given in Part-1 of this schedule relating to requirements of good manufacturing practices for premises and materials for pharmaceutical products shall be complied with, *mutatis mutandis*, for the manufacture of sterile products, parenteral preparations (small volume injectables and large volume parenterals) and sterile ophthalmic preparations. In addition to these requirements, the following specific requirements shall also be followed, namely.

1. General

Sterile products, being very critical and sensitive in nature, a very high degree of precautions, prevention and preparations and needed. Dampness, dirt and darkness are to be avoided to ensure aseptic conditions in all areas. There shall be strict compliance in the prescribed standards especially in the matter of supply of water, air, active materials and in the maintenance of hygienic environment.

2. Building and Civil Works

2.1. *The building* shall be built on proper foundation with standardized materials to avoid cracks in critical areas like aseptic solution preparation, filling and sealing rooms.

2.2. *Location of services* like water, steam, gases etc. shall be such that their servicing or repair shall not pose any threat to the integrity of the facility. Water lines shall not pose any threat of leakage to aseptic area.

2.3. The *manufacturing areas* shall be clearly separated into support areas (e.g. washing and component preparation areas, storage areas, etc.), preparation areas (e.g. bulk manufacturing area, non-aseptic blending areas etc.) change areas and aseptic areas. Operations like removal of outer cardboard wrappings of primary packaging materials shall be done in the de-cartoning areas which are segregated from the washing areas. Wooden pallets, fiberboard drugs, cardboard and other particle shedding materials shall not be taken inside the preparation areas.

2.4. *In aseptic areas*

a. Walls, floors and ceiling should be impervious, non-shedding, non-flaking and non-cracking. Flooring should be unbroken and provided with a cove both at the junction between the wall and the floor as well as the wall and ceiling.

b. Walls shall be flat, and ledges and recesses shall be avoided. Wherever other surfaces join the wall (e.g., sterilizers, electric sockets, gas points, etc.) these shall flush the walls. Walls shall be provided with a cove at the joint between the ceiling and floor.

c. Ceiling shall be solid and joints shall be sealed. Light-fittings and air-grills shall flush with the walls and not hanging from the ceiling, so as to prevent contamination.

d. There shall be no sinks and drains in Grade-A and Grade-B areas.

e. Doors shall be made of non-shedding material. These may be made preferably of Aluminium or Steel material. Wooden doors shall not be used. Doors shall open towards the higher-pressure area so that they close automatically due to air pressure.

f. Windows shall be made of similar material as the doors, preferably with double panel and shall be flush with the walls. If fire escapes are to be provided, these shall be suitably fastened to the walls without any gaps.

g. The furniture used shall be smooth, washable and made of stainless steel or any other appropriate material other than wood.

2.5. *The manufacturing and support areas* shall have the same quality of civil structure described above for aseptic areas, except the environmental standards which may vary in the critical areas.

2.6. *Change rooms with entrance* in the form of airlocks shall be provided before entry into the sterile product manufacturing areas and then to the aseptic area. Separate exit space from the aseptic areas is advisable. Change rooms to the aseptic areas shall be clearly demarcated into black, gray, and white rooms with different levels of activity and air cleanliness. The black change room shall be provided with a handwashing sink. The sink and its drain in the un-classified (first) change rooms may be kept clean all the time. The specially designed drain shall be periodically monitored to avoid presence of pathogenic microorganisms. Change room doors shall not be opened simultaneously. An appropriate interlocking system and a visual and/or audible warning system may be installed to prevent the opening of more than one door at a time.

2.7. *For communication* between aseptic areas and non-aseptic areas, intercom telephones or speak-phones shall be used. These shall be minimum in number.

2.8. *Material transfer* between aseptic areas and outside shall be through suitable airlocks or pass-boxes. Doors of such airlocks and pass-boxes shall have suitable interlocking arrangements.

2.9. *Personal welfare areas* like rest rooms, tea room, canteen and toilets shall be outside and separated from the sterile product manufacturing area.

2.10. *Animal houses* shall be away from the sterile product manufacturing area and shall not share a common entrance or air handling system with the manufacturing area.

3. Air Handling System (Central Air-conditioning)

3.1. *Air handling units* for sterile product manufacturing areas shall be different from those for other areas. Critical areas, such as the aseptic filling area, sterilized components unloading area and change room conforming to Grades-B, C and D respectively shall have separate air handling units. The filter configuration in the air handling system shall be suitably designed to achieve the grade of air as given in Tables 20.1. Typical operational activities for clean areas are highlighted in Tables 20.2 and 20.3.

3.2. *For products* which are filled aseptically, the filling room shall meet Grade-B conditions at rest unmanned. This condition shall also be obtained within a period of about 30 minutes of the personnel leaving the room after completion of operations.

3.3. The *filling operations* shall take place under Grade-A conditions which shall be demonstrated under working of simulated conditions which shall be achieved by providing laminar air flow workstations with suitable HEPA filters or isolator technology.

3.4. *For products*, which are terminally sterilized, the filling room shall meet Grade-C conditions at rest. This condition shall be obtainable within a period of about 30 minutes of the personnel leaving the rook after completion of operations.

3.5. *Manufacturing and component* preparation areas shall meet Grade-C conditions.

3.6. *After completion of preparation*, washed components and vessels shall be protected with Grade-C background and if necessary, under laminar air flow workstation.

3.7. The *minimum air changes* for Grade B and Grade-C areas shall not be less than 20 air changes per hour in a room with god air flow pattern and appropriate HEPA filters. For Grade A laminar air flow workstations, the air flow rate shall be 0.3 meter per second ± 20% (for vertical flows) and 0.45 meter per second ± 20% (for horizontal flows).

3.8. *Differential pressure* between areas of different environmental standards shall be at least 15 Pascal (0.06 inches or 1.5 mm water gauge). Suitable manometers or gauges shall be installed to measure and verify pressure differential.

3.9. *The final change room* shall have the same class or air as specified for the aseptic area. The pressure differentials in the change roods shall be in the descending order from white to black.

3.10. Unless there are *product specific requirements*, temperature and humidity in the aseptic areas shall not exceed 27 degree centigrade and relative humidity 55%, respectively.

Table 20.1
Airborne particulate classification for manufacture of sterile products

Grade at rest (b) In operation (a)

Maximum number of permitted particles per cubic metre equal to or above.

0.5 µm 5 µm 0.5 µm 5 µm

A   3520 29 3500 29

B (a) 35,200 293 3,52,000 2,930

C (a) 3,52,000 2,930 35,20,000 29,300

D (a) 35,20,000 29,300 Not defined (c) Not defined (c)

Notes

a. *In order to reach the B, C and D air grades, the number of air changes shall be* related to the size of the room and the equipment and personnel present in the room. The air system shall be provided with the appropriate filters such as HEPA for Grade A, B and C. the maximum permitted number of particles in the "at rest" condition shall approximately be as under: Grade A corresponds with Class 100 or M 3.5 or ISO Class 5; Grade B with Class 1000 or M 4.5 ISO Class 6; Grade C with Class 10,000 or M 5.5 or ISO Class 7; Grade D with Class 100,000 or M 6.5 or ISO Class 8.

b. *The requirement and limit for the area shall depend on the nature of the operation* carried out.

c. *Type of operations to be carried out in the various grades are given in Tables 20.2 and 20.3 as under.*

Table 20.2: Types of operations to be carried out in the various grades for aseptic preparations

Grade types of operations for aseptic preparations

A   Aseptic preparation and filling

B   Background room conditions for activities requiring Grade A

C   Preparation of solution to be filtered

D   Handling of components after washing.

Table 20.3: Types of operations to be carried out in the various grades for terminally sterilized products

Grade types of operations for terminally sterilized products.

A   Filling of products, which are usually at risk

C   Placement of filling and sealing machines, preparation of solutions when usually at risk. Filling of product when unusually at risk.

D   Moulding, blowing (pre-forming) operations of plastic containers, preparations of solutions and components for subsequent filling.

4. Environmental Monitoring

4.1. *All environmental parameters* listed under para 3.1 to 3.10 shall be verified and established at the time of installation and thereafter monitored at periodic intervals. The recommended frequencies of periodic monitoring shall be as follows:

a. Particulate monitoring in air—6 monthly.

b. HEPA filter integrity testing (smoke testing)—yearly

c. Air change rates—6 monthly.

d. Air pressure differentials—daily.

e. Temperature and humidity—daily

f. Microbiological monitoring by settle plates and/or swabs in aseptic areas—daily, and at decreased frequency in other areas.

Note: The above frequencies of monitoring shall be changed as per the requirements and load in individual cases.

4.2. There shall be a *written environmental monitoring program* and microbiological results shall be recorded. Recommended limits for microbiological monitoring of clean areas in operation are as given in Table below 20.4:

Table 20.4: Recommended limits for microbiological monitoring of clean areas in operation

Grade	air sample cfu/m²	settle plates (dia. 90 mm— cfu/2 hrs 55 mm)	contact plates (dia. cfu per plate (five fingers)	glove points cfu per glove
A	< 1	< 1	< 1	< 1
B	10	5	5	5
C	100	50	25	—
D	500	100	50	—

Notes:

a. These are average values.

b. Individual settle plates may be exposed for not less than two hours in Grade B, C and D areas and for not less than thirty minutes in Grade A area.

4.3. *Appropriate action* shall be taken immediately if the result of particulate and microbiological monitoring indicates that the counts exceed the limits. The standard operating procedures shall contain corrective action. After major engineering modification to the HVAC system of any area, all monitoring shall be re-performed before production commences.

5. Garments

5.1. This section covers *garments required* for use by personnel working only in aseptic area. Outdoor clothing shall not be brought into the sterile areas.

5.2. The *garments* shall be made of non-shedding and tight weave material. Cotton garments shall not be used. The garments shall shed virtually no fibres or particulate matter.

5.3. The *clothing and its quality* shall be adopted to the process and the workplace and worn in such a way as to protect the product from contamination. Garments shall be single piece with fastenings at cuffs, neck and at legs to ensure close fit. Trouser legs shall be tucked inside the cover boots. Suitable design of garments shall either include a hood (head-cover) or a separate hood which can be tucked inside the over-all. Pockets, pleats and belts shall be avoided in garments. Zips (if any) shall be of plastic material. Garments with damaged zips shall not be used.

5.4. *Only clean, sterilized and protective garments* shall be used at each work session where aseptic filtration and filling operations are undertaken and at each work shift for products intended to be sterilized, post-filling. The mask and gloves shall be changed at every work session in both instances.

5.5. *Gloves* shall be made of latex or other suitable plastic materials and shall be powder-free. These shall be long enough to cover wrists completely and allow the over-all cuff to be tucked in.

5.6. The *footwear* shall be of suitable plastic or rubber material and shall be daily cleaned with a bactericide.

5.7. *Safety goggles or numbered glasses* with side extension shall be used inside aseptic areas. These shall be sanitized by a suitable method.

5.8. *Garment changing procedures* shall be documented and operators trained in this respect. A full size mirror shall be provided in the final change room for the operator to verify that he is appropriately attired in the garments. Periodic inspection of the garments shall be done by responsible staff.

6. Sanitation

6.1. There shall be *written procedures* for the sanitation of sterile processing facilities. Employees carrying out sanitation of aseptic areas shall be trained specifically for this purpose.

6.2. *Different sanitizing agent* shall be used in rotation and the concentrations of the same shall be as per the recommendations of the manufacturer. Records of rotational use of sanitizing agents shall be maintained.

6.3. *Distilled water freshly collected directly* from the distilled water plant or water maintained above 70 degree centigrade from the re-circulation loop shall be used for dilution of disinfectants. Alternatively, distilled water sterilized by autoclaving or membrane filtration shall be used. The dilution shall be carried out in the 'white' change room.

6.4. *Where alcohol or isopropyl alcohol* is used for dilution of disinfectants for use as hand sprays, the preparation of the same shall be done in the bulk preparation area and diluted solution membrane filtered into suitable sterile containers held in aseptic area.

6.5. *Diluted disinfectants* shall bear the label 'use before', based on microbiological establishment of the germicidal properties. The solutions shall be adequately labeled and documents maintained.

6.6. *Formaldehyde* or any other equally effective fumigant is recommended for the fumigation of aseptic areas or after major civil modifications. There shall be standard operating procedures for this purpose. Its use for routine purpose shall be discouraged and an equally effective surface cleaning regime shall be followed.

6.7. *Cleaning of sterile processing facilities* shall be undertaken with air suction devices or with non-linting sponges or clothes.

6.8. Air particulate quality shall be evaluated on a regular basis and record maintained.

7. Equipment

7.1. The *special equipment* required for manufacturing sterile products includes component washing machines, steam sterilizers, dry heat sterilizers, membrane filter assemblies, manufacturing vessels, blenders, liquid filling machines, powder filling machines, sealing and labeling machines, vacuum testing chambers, inspection machines, lyophilisers, pressure vessels, etc. suitable and fully integrated washing sterilizing filling lines may be provided, depending upon the type and volume of activity.

7.2. Unit-sterilizers shall be double-ended with suitable interlocking arrangements between the doors. The effectiveness of the sterilization process shall be established initially by biological inactivation studies using microbial spore indicators and then at least once a year by carrying out thermal mapping of the chamber. Various sterilization parameters shall be established based on these studies and documented. For membrane filters used for filtration, appropriate filter integrity tests that ensure sterilization shall be carried out before and after filtration.

7.3. Filling machines shall be challenged initially and then at periodic intervals by simulation trials including sterile media fill. Standard operating procedures and acceptance criteria for media fills shall be established, justified and documented. Special simulation trial procedures shall be developed, validated and documented for special products like ophthalmic ointments.

7.4. The **construction material** used for the parts which are in direct contact with products and the manufacturing vessels may be stainless steel 316 or boro-silicate glass (if glass containers) and the tubing shall be capable of being washed and autoclaved.

7.5. On **procurement, installation qualification** of each of the equipment shall be done by engineers with the support of production and quality assurance personnel. Equipment for critical processes like aseptic filling and sterilizers shall be suitably validated according to a written program before putting them to use.

7.6. Standard operating procedures shall be available for each equipment for its calibration and operation and cleaning. Gauges and other measuring devices attached to equipment shall be calibrated at suitable intervals against a written program. Calibration status of equipment gauges shall be adequately documented and displayed.

8. Water and Steam Systems

8.1. *Potable water meeting microbiological* specification of not more than 500 cfu/ml and indicating absence of individual pathogenic microorganisms, *Escherichia coli, Salmonella, Staphylococcus aureus* and *Pseudomonas aeruginosa* per 100 ml sample shall be used for the preparation of purified water.

8.2. *Purified water* prepared by de-mineralization shall meet the microbiological specification of not more than 100 cfu per ml and indicate absence of pathogenic microorganisms in 100 ml. Purified water shall also meet IP specification for chemical quality. Purified water shall be used for hand washing in change rooms. Containers, closures and machine parts may be washed with potable water followed by suitably filtered purified water. Purified water shall be stored in stainless steel tanks or plastic tanks.

8.3. *Water for injection* (hereinafter as WFI) shall be prepared from potable water or purified water meeting the above specifications by distillation. Water for Injection shall meet microbiological specification of not more than 10 cfu per 100 ml. WFI shall also met IP specification for water for injection and shall have an endotoxin level of not more than 0.25 EU/Ml. bulk solutions of liquid parenterals shall be made in WFI. Final rinse of product containers and machine parts shall be done with WFI. Disinfectant solutions for use in aseptic areas shall be prepared in WFI.

8.4. *Water for injection* for the manufacture of liquid injectables shall be freshly collected from the distillation plant or from a storage or circulation loop where the water has been kept at above 70 degree centigrade. At the point of collection, water may be cooled using suitable heat exchanger.

8.5. *Water for non-injectable sterile* products like eye drops shall meet IP specifications for purified water. In addition, microbiologial specification of not more than 10 cfu per 100 ml and absence of *Pseudomonas aeruginosa* and *Enterobacter coli* in 100 m shall also be met.

8.6. *Water for injection* shall be stored in steam jacketed stainless steel tanks of suitable size and the tanks shall have hydrophobic bacterial retention with 0.2 µ vent filters. The filters shall be suitably sterilized at periodic intervals. The distribution lines for purified water and distilled water shall be of stainless steel 316 construction and shall not shed particles.

8.7. There shall be a *written procedure* and program for the sanitation of different water systems including storage tanks, distribution lines, pumps and other related equipment. Records of sanitation shall be maintained.

8.8. There shall be written *microbiological monitoring program* for different types of water. The results shall justify the frequency of sampling and testing. Investigation shall be carried out and corrective action taken in case of deviation from prescribed limits.

8.9. *Steam coming in contact* with the product, primary containers and other product contact surfaces shall be sterile and pyrogen free. The steam condensate shall meet microbiological specification of not more than 10 cfu per 100 ml. the condensate shall also meet IP specification for water for Injection and shall have an endotoxin levels of not more than 0.25 EU/ml. there shall be a suitable schedule for the monitoring of steam quality.

9. Manufacturing Process

9.1. *Manufacture of sterile products* shall be carried out only in areas under defined conditions.

9.2. *Bulk raw materials* shall be monitored for bio-burden periodically. Bioburden of bulk solution prior to membrane filtration shall be monitored periodically and a limit of not more than 100 cfu per ml is recommended.

9.3. The time between the *start of the preparation* of the solution and its sterilization or filtration through a micro-organism retaining filter shall be minimized. There shall be a set maximum permissible time for each product that takes into account its composition and method of storage mentioned in the master formula record.

9.4. *Gases coming in contact* with the sterile product shall be filtered through two 0.22 µ hydrophobic filters connected in-series. These filters shall be tested for integrity. Gas cylinders shall not be taken inside aseptic areas.

9.5. *Washed containers* shall be sterilized immediately before use. Sterilized containers, if not used within an established time, shall be rinsed with distilled or filtered purified water and re-sterilized.

9.6. Each lot of *finished product* shall be filled in one continuous operation. In each case, where one batch is filled in using more than one operation, each lot shall be tested separately for sterility and held separately till sterility test results are known.

9.7. *Special care* shall be exercised while filling products in powder form so as not to contaminate the environment during transfer of powder to filling machine-hopper.

10. Form-Fill-Seal Technology or Blow, Fill-Seal Technology

10.1. *Form-Fill-Seal units* are specially built automated machines in which through one continuous operation, containers are formed from thermoplastic granules, filled and then sealed. Blow, fill-seal units are machines in which containers are moulded/blown (pre-formed) in separate clean rooms, by non-continuous operations.

Note:
  i. These shall be installed in at least Grade C environment.
  ii. These shall comply with the limits as recommended in Table 20.4 at item 4.2.

10.2. *Form-Fill-Seal/Blow, Fill-Seal machines* used for the manufacture of products for terminal sterilization shall be installed in at least Grade C environment and the filling zone within the machine shall fulfill Grade A requirements.

10.3. *Terminally sterilized products.*

10.3.1. Preparation of *primary packaging* material such as glass bottles, ampoules and rubber stoppers shall be done in at least Grade-D environment. Where there is unusual risk to the product from microbial contamination, the above operation shall be done in Grade-C environment. All the process used for component preparation shall be validated.

10.3.2. *Filling of products* requiring terminal sterilization shall be done under Grade-A environment with a Grade-C background.

10.4. *Preparation of solutions,* which are to be sterilized by filtration, shall be done in Grade-C environment, and if not to be filtered, the preparation of materials and products shall be in a Grade-A environment with Grade-B in background.

10.5. *Filtration (membrane)*

   i. Solutions for large volume parenterals shall be filtered through a non-fiber releasing, sterilizing grade cartridge/membrane filter of nominal pore size of 0.22 µ for aseptic filling whereas, 0.45 µ porosity shall be used for terminally sterilized products.

  ii. A second filtration using another 0.22 µ sterilizing grade cartridge/membrane filter shall be performed immediately prior to filling. Process specifications shall indicate the maximum time during which a filtration system may be used with a view to precluding microbial build-up to levels that may affect the microbiological quality of the large volume parenterals.

 iii. The integrity of the sterilized filter shall be verified and confirmed immediately after use by an appropriate method such as Bubble Point, Diffusive Flow or Pressure Hold Test.

10.6. *Sterilization (autoclaving)*

10.6.1. Before any *sterilization process* is adopted, its suitability for the product and its efficacy in achieving the desired sterilizing conditions in all parts of each type of load pattern to be processed, shall be demonstrated by physical measurements and by biological indicators, where appropriate.

10.6.2. All the *sterilization process* shall be appropriately validated. The validity of the process shall be verified at regular intervals, but at least annually. Whenever, significant modifications have been made to the equipment and product, records shall be maintained thereof.

10.6.3. The *sterilizer* shall be double ended to prevent mix-ups.

10.6.4. *Periodic bio-burden monitoring* of products before terminal sterilization shall be carried out and controlled to limits specified for the product in the master formula.

10.6.5. The *use of biological indicators* shall be considered as an additional method of monitoring the sterilization. These shall be stored and used according to the manufacturer's instructions. Their quality shall be checked by positive controls. If biological indicators used, strict precautions shall be taken to avoid transferring microbial contamination from them.

10.6.6. There shall be *clear means of differentiating* sterilized. and 'unsterilized' products. Each basket, tray or other carrier of products or components shall be clearly labeled with the name of the material, its batch number, and sterilization status. Indicators shall be used, where appropriate, to indicate whether a batch (or sub-batch) has passed through the sterilization process.

10.6.7. *Sterilization records* shall be available for each sterilization run and may also include thermographs and sterilization monitoring strips. They shall be maintained as part of the batch release procedure.

10.7. *Sterilization (by dry heat)*

10.7.1. Each *heat sterilization cycle* shall be recorded on a time/temperature chart of a suitable size by appropriate equipment of the required accuracy and precision. The position of temperature probes used for controlling and/or recording shall be determined during the validation and, where applicable, shall also be checked against a second independent temperature probe located in the same position. The chart shall form a part of the batch record. Container mapping may also be carried out in the case of large volume parenterals.

10.7.2. *Chemical or biological indicators* may also be used, but shall take the place of physical validation.

10.7.3. *Sufficient time* shall be allowed for the load to reach the required temperature before measurement of sterilization time commences. This time shall be separately determined for each type of load to be processed.

10.7.4. After the *high temperature phase* of a heat sterilization cycle, precautions shall be taken against contamination of sterilized load during cooling. Any cooling fluid or gas in contact with the product shall be sterilized unless it can be shown that any leaking container would not be approved for use. Air inlet and outlets shall be provided with bacterial retaining filters.

10.7.5. The *process used for sterilization* by dry heat shall include aircirculation within the chamber and the maintenance of a positive pressure to prevent the entry of non-sterile air. Air inlets and outlets should be provided with microorganism retaining filters. Where this process of sterilization by dry heat is also intended to remove pyrogens, challenge tests using endotoxins would be required as part of the validation process.

10.8. *Sterilization (by moist heat)*

10.8.1. Both the *temperature and pressure* shall be used to monitor the process. Control instrumentation shall normally be independent of monitoring instrumentation and recording charts. Where automated control and monitoring systems are used for these applications, these shall be validated to ensure that critical process requirements are met. System and cycle faults shall be registered by the system and observed by the operator. The reading of the independent temperature indicator shall be routinely checked against the chart-recorder during the sterilization period. For sterilizers fitted with a drain at the bottom of the chamber, it may also be necessary to record the temperature at this position throughout the sterilization period. There shall be frequent leak tests done on the chamber during the vacuum phase of the cycle.

10.8.2. The *items to be sterilized,* other than products in sealed containers, shall be wrapped in a material which allows removal of air and penetration of steam but which prevents re-contamination after sterilization. All parts of the load shall be in contact with the sterilizing agent at the required temperature of the required time.

10.8.3. *No large volume parenteral* shall be subjected to steam sterilization cycle until it has been filled and sealed.

10.8.4. *Care* shall be taken to ensure that the steam used for sterilization is of a suitable quality and does not contain additives at a level which could cause contamination of the product or equipment.

10.9. *Completion/finalisation of sterile products*

10.9.1. All *unit operations and processes* in the manufacture of a batch shall have a minimum time specified and the shortest validated time shall be used from the start of a batch to its ultimate release for distribution.

10.9.2. *Containers* shall be closed by appropriately validated methods. Containers closed by fusion, e.g. glass or plastic ampoules shall be subjected to 100% integrity testing. Samples of other containers shall be checked for integrity according to appropriate procedures.

10.9.3. *Containers sealed under vacuum* shall be tested for required vacuum conditions.

10.9.4. *Filled containers parenteral products* shall be inspected individually for extraneous contamination or other defects. When inspection is done visually, it shall be done under suitably controlled conditions of illumination and background. Operators doing the inspection shall pass regular eye-sight checks with spectacles, if worn, and be allowed frequent rest from inspection. Where other methods of inspection are used, the process shall be validated and the performance of the equipment checked at suitable intervals. Results shall be recorded.

11. Product Containers and Closures

11.1. *All containers and closures intended* for use shall comply with the pharmacopoeial and other specified requirements. Suitable samples sizes, specifications, test methods, cleaning procedures and sterilization procedures, shall be used to assure that containers, closures and other component parts of drug packages are suitable and are not reactive, additive, adsorptive or leachable or presents the risk of toxicity to an extent that significantly affects the quality or purity of the drug. No second hand or used containers and closures shall be used.

11.2. *Plastic granules* shall also comply with the pharmaco-poeial requirements including physio-chemical and biological tests.

11.3. *All containers and closures* shall be rinsed prior to sterilization with water for injection according to written procedure.

11.4. *The design of closures, containers and stoppers* shall be such as to make cleaning, easy and also to make airtight seal when fitted to the bottles.

11.5. It shall be *ensured that containers and closures* chosen for a particular product are such that when coming into contact they are not absorbed into the product and they do not affect the product adversely. The closures and stoppers should be of such quality substances as not to affect the quality of the product and avoid the risk of toxicity.

11.6. Whenever *glass bottles* are used, the written schedule of cleaning shall be laid down and followed. Where bottles are not dried after washing, these shall be finally rinsed with distilled water or pyrogen free water, as the case may be, according to written procedure.

11.7. *Individual containers* of parenteral preparations, ophthalmic preparations shall be examined against black/white background fitted with diffused light after filling so as to ensure freedom from foreign matters.

11.8 *Glass bottles*

11.8.1. *Shape and design of the glass bottle* shall be rational and standardized. Glass bottles made of USP Type-I and USP Type-II glass shall only be used. Glass bottles shall not be reused. Before use, USP Type-II bottles shall be validated for the absence of particulate matter generated over a period of the shelf-life of the product and shall be regularly monitored after the production, following statistical sampling methods. USP Type-III glass containers may be used for non-parenteral sterile products such as otic solutions.

11.9. *Plastic containers*:

11.9.1. *Pre-formed plastic containers* intended to be used for packing of large volume parenteral shall be moulded in-house by one-continuous operation through an automatic machine.

11.9.2. *Blowing, filling and sealing (plugging) operation* shall be conducted in room(s) conforming to requirements as mentioned in Table 20.3 of item 3.10. Entry to the area where such operations are undertaken, shall be through a series of airlocks. Blowers shall have an air supply which is filtered through 0.22 µ filters. Removal of runners and plugging operations shall be conducted under a laminar airflow workstation.

11.10 *Rubber stoppers*: The *tuber stoppers* used for large volume parenterals shall comply with specifications prescribed in the current edition of the Indian Pharmacopoeia.

12. Documentation

12.1. The *manufacturing records* relating to manufacture of sterile products shall indicate the following details:
1. Serial number of the batch manufacturing record.
2. Name of the product.
3. Reference to master rormula record.
4. Batch/Lot number.
5. Batch/Lot size.
6. Date of commencement of manufacture and date of completion of manufacture.
7. Date of manufacture and assigned date of expiry.
8. Date of each step in manufacturing.
9. Names of all ingredients with the grade given by the quality control department.
10. Quality of all ingredients.
11. Control reference numbers for all ingredients.
12. Time and duration of blending, mixing, etc., whenever applicable.
13. pH of solution whenever applicable.
14. Filter integrity testing records.
15. Temperature and humidity records whenever applicable
16. Records of plate-counts whenever applicable.
17. Results of pyrogen and/or bacterial endotoxin and toxicity.

18. Results of weight or volume of drug filled in containers.
19. Bulk sterility in case of aseptically filled products.
20. Leak test records.
21. Inspection records.
22. Sterilization records including autoclave leakage test records, load details, date, duration, temperature, pressure, etc.
23. Container washing records.
24. Total number of containers filled.
25. Total numbers of containers rejected at each stage
26. Theoretical yield, permissible yield, actual yield and variation thereof.
27. Clarification for variation in yield beyond permissible yield.
28. Reference numbers of relevant analytical reports.
29. Details of reprocessing, if any.
30. Name of all operators carrying out different activities.
31. Environmental monitoring records.
32. Specimens of printed packaging materials.
33. Records of destruction of rejected containers printed packaging and testing.
34. Signature of competent technical staff responsible for manufacture and testing.

Note:
1. Products shall be released only after complete filling and testing.
2. Result of the tests relating to sterility, pyrogens, and bacterial endotoxins shall be maintained in the analytical records.
3. Validation details and simulation trail records shall be maintained separately.
4. Records of environmental monitoring like temperature, humidity, microbilogical data, etc. shall be maintained. Records of periodic servicing of HEPA filters, sterilizers and other periodic maintenance of facilities and equipment carried out also be maintained.
5. Separate facilities shall be provided for filling-cum-sealing of small volume parenterals in glass containers and/or plastic containers.

6. It is advisable to provide separate facilities for manufacture of large volume parenterals in glass containers and/or plastic containers.

7. For manufacture of large volume parenterals in plastic containers, it is advisable to install automatic (with all operations) Form-Fill-Seal machines having one continuous operation.

PART I-B

Specific Requirements for Manufacture of Oral Solid Dosage Forms (Tablets and Capsules)

Note: The general requirements as given in Part 1 of this schedule relating to requirements of good manufacturing practices for Premises and materials for pharmaceutical products shall be complied with, mutates mutandis, for the manufacture of oral solid dosage forms (tablets and capsules). In addition to these requirements, the following specific requirement shall also be followed, namely:

1. General

1.1. The *processing of dry materials* and products creates problems of dust control and cross-contamination. Special attention is therefore, needed in the design, maintenance and use of premises and equipment in order to overcome these problems. Wherever required, enclosed dust control manufacturing systems shall be employed.

1.2. *Suitable environmental conditions* for the products handled shall be maintained by installation of air-conditioning wherever necessary. Effective airextraction systems, with discharge points situated to avoid contamination of other products and professes shall be provided. Filters shall be installed to retain dust and protect the factory and local environment.

1.3. *Special care* shall be taken to protect against subsequent contamination of the product by particles of metal or wood. The use of metal detector is recommended. Wooden equipment should be avoided. Screens, sieves, punches and dies shall be examined for wear and tear or for breakage before and after each use.

1.4. All *ingredients for a dry product* shall be sifted before use unless the quality of the input material can be assured. Such sifting shall normally be carried out at dedicated areas.

1.5. Where the *facilities* are designed to provide special environmental conditions of pressure differentials between rooms, these conditions shall be regularly monitored and any specification results brought to the immediate attention of the production and quality assurance department which shall be immediately attended to.

1.6. *Care* shall be taken to guard against any material lodging and remaining undetected in any processing or packaging equipment. Particular care shall be taken to ensure that any vacuum, compressed air or air-extraction nozzles are kept clean and that there is no evidence lubricants leaking into the product from any part of the equipment.

2. Sifting, Mixing and Granulation

2.1. *Unless operated as a closed system,* mixing, sifting and blending equipment shall be fitted with dust extractors.

2.2. *Residues from sieving operations* shall be examined periodically for evidence of the presence of unwanted materials.

2.3. *Critical operating parameters* like time and temperature for each mixing, blending and drying operation shall be specified in a Master Formula, monitored during processing, and recorded in the batch records.

2.4. *Filter bags fitted to fluid-bed drier* shall not be used for different products, without being washed in-between use. With certain highly potent or sensitizing products, bags specific to one product only shall be used. Air entering the drier shall be filtered. Steps shall be taken to prevent contamination of the site and local environment by dust in the air leaving the drier due to close positioning of the air-inlets and exhaust.

2.5. *Granulation and coating solutions* shall be made, stored and used in a manner which minimizes the risk of contamination or microbial growth.

3. Compressions (Tablets)

3.1. *Each tablets compressing machine* shall be provided with effective dust control facilities to avoid cross-contamination. Unless the same product is being made on each machine, or unless the compression machine itself provides its own enclosed air controlled environment, the machine shall be installed in separate cubicles.

3.2. *Suitable physical, procedural and labeling arrangements* shall be made to prevent mix up of materials, granules and tables on compression machinery.

3.3. *Accurate and calibrated weighting equipment* shall be readily available and used for in-process monitoring of tablet weight variation. Procedures used shall be capable of detecting out-of-limits tablets.

3.4. At the *commencement* of each compression run and in case of multiple compression points in a compression machine, sufficient individual tablets shall be examined at fixed intervals to ensure that a tablet from each compression station or from each compression point has been inspected for suitable pharmacopoeial parameters like appearance, weight variation, disintegration, hardness, friability and thickness. The results shall be recorded as part of the batch documentation.

3.5. *Tablets* shall be de-dusted, preferably by automatic device and shall be monitored for the presence of foreign materials besides any other defects.

3.6. Tablets shall be collected into clean, *labeled containers.*

3.7. *Rejected or discarded tablets* shall be isolated in identified containers and their quality recorded in the Batch manufacturing record.

3.8. *In-process control* shall be employed to ensure that the products remain within specification. During compression, samples of tablets shall be taken at regular intervals of not greater than 30 minutes to ensure that they are being produced in compliance with specified in-process specification. The tablets shall also be periodically checked for additional parameters such as appearance, weight variation, disintegration, hardness, friability and thickness and contamination by lubricating oil.

4. Coating (Tablets)

4.1. *Air supplied to coating pans* for drying purposes shall be filtered air and of suitable quality. The area shall be provided with suitable exhaust system and environmental control (temperature, humidity) measures.

4.2. *Coating solutions and suspensions* shall be made afresh and used in a manner, which shall minimize the risk of microbial growth. Their preparation and use shall be documented and recorded.

5. Filling of Hard Gelatin Capsule

Empty capsules shells shall be regarded as drug component and treated accordingly. They shall be stored under conditions which shall ensure their safety from the effects of excessive heat and moisture.

6. Printing (Tablets and Capsules)

6.1. *Special care* shall be taken to avoid product mix-up during any printing of tablets and capsules. Where different products, or different batches of the same product, are printed simultaneously, the operations shall adequately be segregated. Edible grade colors and suitable printing ink shall be used for such printing.

6.2. *After printing, tablets and capsules* shall be approved by quality control before release for packaging or sale.

7. Packaging (Strip and Blister)

7.1. *Care* shall be taken when using automatic tablet and capsule counting, strip and blister packaging equipment to ensure that all 'rogue' tablets, capsules or foils from packaging operation are removed before a new packaging operation is commenced. There shall be an independent recorded check of the equipment before a new batch of tablets or capsules is handled.

7.2. *Uncoated tablets* shall be packed on equipment designed to minimize the risk of cross-contamination. Such packaging shall be carried out in an isolated area when potent tablets or beta-iactum containing tablets are being packed.

7.3. *The strips* coming out of the machine shall be inspected for defects such as misprint, cuts on the foil, missing tablets and improper sealing.

7.4. *Integrity* of individual packaging strips and blisters shall be subjected to vacuum test periodically to ensure leak proofness of each pocket strip and blister and records maintained.

PART I-C

Specific Requirements for Manufacture of Oral Liquids (Syrups, Elixirs, Emulsions and Suspensions)

Note: The general requirements as given in Part-I of this schedule relating to requirements of good manufacturing practices for premises and materials for pharmaceutical products shall be complied with, mutates mutandis, for the manufacture of (syrups, elixirs, emulsions and suspensions). In addition to these requirement, the following specific requirements shall also be followed, namely:

1. Building and Equipment

1.1. The *premises and equipment* shall be designed, constructed and maintained to suit the manufacturing of oral liquids. The layout and design of the manufacturing area shall strive to minimize the risk of cross-contamination and mix-ups.

1.2. *Manufacturing area* shall have entry through double door airlock facility. It shall be fly proof by use of fly catcher and/or air curtain.

1.3. *Drainage* shall be of adequate size and have adequate traps, without open channels and design shall be such as to prevent back flow. Drains shall be shallow to facilitate cleaning and disinfecting.

1.4. The *production area* shall be cleaned and sanitized at the end of every production process.

1.5. *Tanks, containers, pipe work and pumps* shall be designed and installed so that they can be easily cleaned and sanitized. Equipment design shall be such as to prevent accumulation of residual microbial growth or cross-contamination.

1.6. *Stainless steel* or any other appropriate material shall be used for parts of equipment coming in direct contact with the products. The use of glass apparatus shall be minimum.

1.7. *Arrangements for cleaning* of containers, closures and droppers shall be made with the help of suitable machines/ devices equipped with the high pressure air, water and steam jets.

1.8. The *furniture* used shall be smooth, washable and made of stainless steel.

2. Purified Water

2.1. The *chemical and microbiological quality* of purified water used shall be specified and monitored routinely. The microbiological evaluation shall include testing for absence of pathogens and shall not exceed 100 cfu/ml (as per Appendix 12.5 of IP 1996.)

2.2. There shall be a *written procedure* for operation and maintenance of the purified water system. Care shall be taken to avoid the risk of microbial proliferation with appropriate methods like re-circulation, use of UV treatment, treatment with heat and sanitizing agent. After any chemical sanitization of the water systems, a flushing shall be done to ensure that the sanitizing agent has been effectively removed.

3. Manufacturing

3.1. *Manufacturing personnel* shall wear non-fiber shedding clothing to prevent contamination of the product.

3.2. *Materials* likely to shed fiber like gunny bags, or wooden pallets shall not be carried into the area where products or cleaned-containers are exposed.

3.3. *Care* shall be taken to maintain the homogenicity of emulsion by use of appropriate emulsifier and suspensions by use of appropriate stirrer during filling. Mixing and filling processes shall be specified and monitored. Special care shall be taken at the beginning of the filling process, after stoppage due to any interruption and at the end of the process to ensure that the product is uniformly homogenous during the filling process.

3.4. The *primary packaging area* shall have an air supply which is filtered through 5 micron filters. The temperature of the area shall not exceed 30°C.

3.5. When the *bulk product* is not immediately packed, the maximum period of storage and storage conditions shall be specified in the master formula. The maximum period of storage time of a product in the bulk stage shall be validated.

PART I-D

Specific Requirements for Manufacture of Topical Products, i.e. External Preparations (Creams, Ointments, Pastes, Mulsions, Lotions, Solutions, Dusting Powders and Identical Products)

Note: The general requirements as given in part-I of this schedule relating to requirements of good manufacturing practices for premises and materials for pharmaceutical products shall be complied with, mutates mutandis, for the manufacture of topical products i.e. external preparations (creams, ointments, pastes, emulsions, lotions, solutions, dusting powders and identical products used for external applications).

In addition to these requirements, following specific requirements shall also be followed, namely:
1. The entrance to the area where topical products are manufactured should be through a suitable airlock. Outside the airlock, insectocutors shall be installed.
2. The air to this manufacturing area shall be filtered through at least 20 μ air filters and shall be air-conditioned. The area shall be ventilated.

3. The area shall be fitted with an exhaust system of suitable capacity to effectively remove vapours, fumes, smoke, floating dust particles.

4. The equipment used shall be designed and maintained to prevent the product from being accidentally contaminated with any foreign matter or lubricant.

5. No rags or dusters shall be used in the process of cleaning or drying the process equipment or accessories used.

6. Water used in compounding shall be purified water IP.

7. Powders, wherever used, shall be suitably sieved before use.

8. Heating vehicles and a base like petroleum jelly shall be done in separate mixing area in suitable stainless steel vessels, using steam, gas, electricity, solar energy, etc.

9. A separate packing section may be provided for primary packaging of the products.

PART I-E

Specific Requirements for Manufacture of Metered-Dose-Inhalers (MDI)

Note: The general requirements as given in part-I of this schedule relating to requirements of good manufacturing practices for premises and materials for pharmaceutical products shall be complied with, mutates mutandis, for the manufacture of metered-dose-inhalers (MDI). In addition to these requirements, the following specific requirements shall also be followed, namely:

1. General

Manufacture of metered-dose-inhalers shall be done under conditions which shall ensure minimum microbial and particulate contamination. Assurance of the quality of components and the bulk product is very important. Where medicaments are in suspended state, uniformity of suspension shall be established.

2. Building and Civil Works

2.1. The *building* shall be located on a solid foundation to reduce risk of cracking walls and floor due to the movement of equipment and machinery.

2.2. All *building surfaces* shall be impervious, smooth and non-shedding. Flooring shall be continuous and provided with a cove between the floor and the wall as well as the wall to the ceiling. Ceiling shall be solid, continuous and covered to walls. Light fittings and air-grills shall be flush with the ceiling. All service lines requiring maintenance shall be erected in such a manner that these accessible from outside the production area.

2.3. The *manufacturing area* shall be segregated into change rooms for personnel, container preparation area, bulk preparation and filling area, quarantine area and spray testing and packing areas.

2.4. *Secondary change rooms* shall be provided for operators to change from factory clothing to special departmental clothing before entering the manufacturing and filling area.

2.5. *Separate area* shall be provided for de-cartoning of components before they are air washed.

2.6. The *propellants* used for manufacture shall be delivered to the manufacturing area distribution system by filtering them through 2 μ filters. The bulk containers of propellants shall be stored, suitably identified, away from the manufacturing facilities.

3. Environmental Conditions

3.1. Where *products or clean components* are exposed, the area shall be supplied with filtered air of Grade-C.

3.2. The requirements of *temperature and humidity* in the manufacturing area shall be decided depending on the type of product and propellants handled in the facility. Other support area shall have comfort levels of temperature and humidity.

3.3. There shall be a *difference in room pressure* between the manufacturing area and the support areas and the differential pressure shall be not less than 15 Pascals (0.06 inches or 1.5 mm water gauge).

3.4. There shall be a *written schedule* for the monitoring of environmental conditions. Temperature and humidity shall be monitored daily.

4. Garments

4.1. Personnel in the *manufacturing and filling section* shall wear suitable single-piece-garment made out of non-shedding, tight weave material. Personnel in support areas shall wear clean factory uniforms.

4.2. *Gloves made of suitable material* having no interaction with the propellants shall be used by the operators in the manufacturing and filling areas. Preferably, disposable gloves shall be used.

4.3. *Suitable department* specific personnel protective equipment like footwear and safety glasses shall be used wherever hazard exists.

5. Sanitation

5.1. There shall be *written procedures for the sanitation* of the MDI manufacturing facility. Special care should be taken to handle residues and rinses of propellants.

5.2. *Use of water for cleaning* shall be restricted and controlled. Routinely used disinfectants are suitable for sanitizing the different areas. Records of sanitation shall be maintained.

6. Equipment

6.1. *Manufacturing equipment* shall be of closed system. The vessels and supply lines shall be of stainless steel.

6.2. *Suitable check* weights, spray testing machines and labeling machines shall be provided in the department.

6.3. All the *equipment* shall be suitably calibrated and their performance validated on receipt and thereafter periodically.

7. Manufacture

7.1. There shall be *approved Master Formula Records* for the manufacture of metered close inhalers. All propellants, liquids and gases shall be filtered through 2 μ filters to remove particles.

7.2. The *primary packing material* shall be appropriately cleaned by compressed air suitably filtered through 0.2 μ filter. The humidity of compressed air shall be controlled as applicable.

7.3. The *valves* shall be carefully handled and after de-cartoning, there shall be kept in clean, closed containers in the filling room.

7.4. *For suspensions, the bulk* shall be kept stirred continuously.

7.5. *In-process controls* shall include periodical checking of weight of bulk formulation filled in the containers. In a two-shot-filling process (liquid filling followed by gaseous filling), it shall be ensured that 100% check on weight is carried out.

7.6. *Filled containers* shall be quarantined for a suitable period established by the manufacturer to detect leaking containers prior to testing, labeling and packing.

8. Documentation

8.1. In addition to the *routine good manufacturing* practices documentation, manufacturing records shall show the following additional information:
1. Temperature and humidity in the manufacturing area.
2. Periodic filled weights of the formulation.
3. Records of rejections during on line check weighing.
4. Records of rejection during spray testing.

PART I-F

Specific Requirements of Premises, Plant and Materials for Manufacture of Active Pharmaceutical Ingredients (Bulk Drugs)

Note: The general requirements as given in Part-I of this schedule relating to requirements of good manufacturing practices for premises and materials for pharmaceutical products shall be complied with, mutates mutandis, for the manufacture of active pharmaceutical ingredients (bulk drugs). In addition to these requirements, the following specific requirements shall also be followed, namely:

1. Building and Civil Works

1.1. Apart from the *building requirements contained* Part-I, general note, the active pharmaceutical ingredients facilities for manufacture of hazardous reactions, beta-lactum antibiotics. Steroids and steroidal hormones/cytotoxic substances shall be provided in confined areas to prevent contamination of the other drugs manufactured.

1.2. The *final stage of preparation of a drug,* like isolation/filtration/drying/milling/sieving and packing operations shall be provided with air filtration systems including pre-filters and finally with a 5 micron filter. Air handling systems with adequate number of air changes per hour or any other suitable system to control the air borne contamination shall be provided. Humidity/temperature shall also be controlled for all the operations wherever required.

1.3. *Air filtration systems* including pre-filters and particulate matter retention air filters shall be used, where appropriate, for air supplies to production areas. If air is recirculated to production areas, measures shall be taken to control re-circulation of floating dust particles from production. In areas where air contamination occurs during production, there shall be adequate exhaust system to control contaminants.

1.4. *Ancillary area* shall be provided for boiler-house. Utility areas like heat exchangers, chilling workshop, store and supply of gases shall also be provided.

1.5. For *specified preparation* like manufacture of sterile products and for certain antibiotics, sex hormones, cytotoxic and oncology products, separate enclosed areas shall be designed. The requirements for the sterile active pharmaceutical ingredient shall be in line with the facilities required for formulation to be filled aseptically.

2. Sterile Products

Sterile active pharmaceutical ingredient filled aseptically shall be treated as formulation from the stage wherever the process demands like crystallization, lyophilization, filtration, etc. all conditions applicable to formulations that are required to be filled aseptically shall apply *mutates mutandis* for the manufacture of sterile active pharmaceutical ingredients involving stages like filtration crystallization and lyophilization.

3. Utilities/Services

Equipment like chilling plant, boiler, heat exchangers, vacuum and gas storage vessels shall be serviced, cleaned, sanitized and maintained at appropriate intervals to prevent malfunctions or contamination that may interfere with safety, identity, strength, quality or purity of the drug product.

4. Equipment Design, Size and Location

4.1. *Equipment* used in the manufacture, processing, packing or holding of an active pharmaceutical ingredient shall be of appropriate design, adequate size and suitably located to facilitate operations for its intended use and for its cleaning and maintenance.

4.2. If the equipment is used for *different intermediates* and active pharmaceutical ingredients, proper cleaning before switching from one product to another becomes particularly important. If cleaning of a specific type of equipment is difficult, the equipment may need to be dedicated to a particular intermediate or active pharmaceutical ingredient.

4.3. The *choice of cleaning methods*, detergents and levels of cleaning shall be defined and justified. Selection of cleaning agents, (e.g. solvents) should depend on:

a. The suitability of the cleaning agent to remove residues of raw materials, intermediates, precursors, degradation products and isomers, as appropriate;
b. Whether the cleaning agent leaves a residue itself,
c. Compatibility with equipment construction materials like centrifuge/filtration, dryer/fluid bed dryer, rotocone proton

dryer, vacuum dryer, frit mill, multimill/jet mills/sewetters cut sizing;

d. Test for absence of intermediate or active pharmaceutical ingredient in the final rinse.

4.4. *Written procedures* shall be established and followed for cleaning and maintenance of equipment, including utensils used in the manufacture, processing, packing or holding of active pharmaceutical ingredients. These procedures shall include but should not be limited to the following:

a. Assignment of responsibility for cleaning and maintaining equipment;

b. Maintenance and cleaning program schedules, including where appropriate, sanitizing schedules;

c. A complete description of the methods and materials used to clean and maintain equipment, including instructions for de-assembling and reassembling each article of equipment to ensure proper cleaning and maintenance;

d. Removal or obliteration of previous batch identification;

e. Protection of clean equipment from contamination prior to use;

f. Inspection of equipment for cleanliness immediately before use;

g. Establishing the maximum time that may elapse between completion of processing and equipment cleaning as well as between cleaning and equipment reuse.

4.5. *Equipment* shall be cleaned between successive batches to prevent contamination and carry-over of degraded material or contaminants unless otherwise established by validation.

4.6. As *processing approaches* the final purified active pharmaceutical ingredient, it is important to ensure that incidental carry over between batches does not have adverse impact on the established impurity profile. However, this does not generally hold good for any biological, active pharmaceutical ingredient where many of the processing steps are accomplished aseptically and where it is necessary to clean and sterilize equipment between batches.

5. In-process Controls

5.1. In-process control for *chemical reactions* may include the following:

a. Reaction time or reaction completion;

b. Reaction mass appearance, clarity, completeness or pH solutions;

c. Reaction temperature;

d. Concentration of a reactant;

e. Assay or purity of the product;

f. Process completion check by TLC/any other means.

5.2. In-process control for *physical operations* may include the following:

a. Appearance and color;

b. Uniformity of the blend;

c. Temperature of a process;

d. Concentration of a solution;

e. Processing rate or time;

f. Particle size analysis;

g. Bulk/tap density;

h. pH determination;

i. Moisture content.

6. Product Containers and Closures

6.1. *All containers and closures* shall comply with the pharmacopoeial or any other requirement, suitable sampling methods, sample sizes, specifications, test methods, cleaning procedures and sterilization procedures, when indicated, shall be used to assure that containers, closures and other component parts of drug packages are suitable and are not reactive, additive, adsorptive or leachable to an extent that significantly affects the quality or purity of the drug.

6.2. The *drug product container* shall be tested or re-examined as appropriate and approved or rejected and shall be identified and controlled under a quarantine system designed to prevent their use in manufacturing or processing operations for which these are unsuitable.

6.3. *Container closure system* shall provide adequate protection against foreseeable external factors in storage/transportation and use that may cause deterioration or contamination of the active pharmaceutical ingredient.

6.4. *Bulk containers and closures* shall be cleaned and, where indicated by the nature of the active pharmaceutical ingredient, sterilized to ensure that they are suitable for their intended use.

6.5. The container shall be *conspicuously marked* with the name of the product and the following additional information concerning:

a. Quality and standards, if specified;
b. Manufacturing licence number/drug master file number (whichever applicable), batch number;
c. Date of manufacture and date of expiry;
d. Method for container disposal (label shall give the methodology, if required);
e. Storage conditions, if specified and name and address of the manufacturer, if available.

6.6. *Areas for different operation* of active pharmaceutical ingredients (bulk drugs) section shall have appropriate area which may be suitably partitioned for different operations.

PART- II

REQUIREMENTS OF PLANT AND EQUIPMENT

1. External Preparations

The following equipments are recommended for the manufacture of external preparations, i.e. ointments, emulsion, lotions, solutions, pastes, creams, dusting powders and such identical products used for external applications whichever is applicable, namely:

1. Mixing and storage tanks (stainless steel);
2. Jacketted kettle (steam, gas or electrically heated);
3. Mixer (electrically operated);
4. Planetary mixer;
5. A colloid mill or a suitable emulsifier;
6. A triple roller mill or an ointment mill;

7. Liquid filling equipment (electrically operated);

8. Jar or tube filling equipment (electrically operated);

Area

1. A minmum area of thirty square meters for basic installation of ten square meters for ancillary area is recommended.
2. Areas for formulations meant for external use and internal use shall be separately provided to avoid mix-up.

2. Oral Liquid Preparations

The following equipment are commended for the manufacture of oral/internal use preparations, i.e. syrups, elixirs, emulsions and suspensions, whichever is applicable, namely:

1. Mixing and storage tanks (stainless steel);
2. Jacketted kettle/stainless steel tank (steam, gas or electrically heated).
3. Portable stirrer (electrically operated);
4. A colloid mill or suitable emulsifier (electrically operated);
5. Suitable filtration equipment (electrically operated);
6. Semi-automatic/automatic bottle filling machine;
7. Pilfer proof cap sealing machine;
8. Water distillation unit or deioniser;
9. Clarity testing inspection units.

Area

A minimum area of thirty square meters for basic installation and ten square meters for ancillary area is recommended.

3. Tablets

The Tableting section shall be free from dust and floating particles and may be air-conditioned. For this purpose, each tablet machine shall be isolated into cubicles and connected to a vacuum dust collector or an exhaust system. For effective operations, the tablet production department shall be divided into four distinct and separate sections as follows:

a. Mixing, granulation and drying section;
b. Tablet compression section;
c. Packaging section (strip/blister machine wherever required);
d. Coating section (wherever required).

3.1. The following *electrically operated equipment* are recommended for the manufacture of compressed tablets and hypodermic tablets, in each of the above sections, namely:
a. Granulation-cum-drying section;
   1. Disintegrator and sifter;
   2. Powder mixer;
   3. Mass mixer/Planetary mixer/Rapid mixer granulator;
   4. Granulator;
   5. Thermostatically controlled hot air oven with trays (preferably mounted on a trolley)/Fluid bed dryer;
   6. Weighing machines;
b. Compression section.
   1. Tablet compression machine, single/multi-punch/rotatory;
   2. Punch and dies storage cabinets;
   3. Tablet de-duster;
   4. Tablet Inspection unit/belt;
   5. Dissolution test apparatus;
   6. In-process testing equipment like single pan electronic balance, hardness tester, friability and disintegration test apparatus;
   7. Air-conditioning and dehumidification arrangement (wherever necessary);
c. Packaging section.
   1. Strip/blister packaging machine;
   2. Leak test apparatus (vacuum system);
   3. Tablet counters (wherever applicable);
   4. Air-conditioning and dehumidification arrangement (whereever applicable).

Area

A minimum area of sixty square meters for basic installation and twenty square meters for ancillary area is recommended for un-coated tablets.

d. Coating section,

1. Jacketted kettle (steam, gas or electrically heated for preparing coating suspension).
2. Coating pan (stainless steel).
3. Polishing pan (where applicable).
4. Exhaust system (including vacuum dust collector).
5. Air-conditioning and dehumidification arrangement.
6. Weighing balance.

3.2. The *coating section* shall be made dust free with suitable exhaust system to remove excess powder and fumes resulting from solvent evaporation. It shall be air-conditioned and dehumidified wherever, considered necessary. Area — A minimum additional area of thirty square meters for coating section for basic installation and ten square meters for ancillary area is recommended. Separate area and equipment for mixing, granulation, drying, tablet compression, coating and packing shall be provided for Penicillin group of drugs on the lines indicated above. In case of operations involving dust and floating particles, care shall be exercised to avoid cross-contamination.

3.3. The *manufacture of hypodermic tablets* shall be conducted under aseptic conditions in a separate air-conditioned room, the walls of which shall be smooth and washable. The granulation, tableting and packing shall be done in this room.

3.4. The *manufacture of effervescent and soluble/dispersible tablets* shall be carried out in air-conditioned and dehumidified areas.

4. Powders

The following equipment is recommended for the manufacture of powders, namely:

1. Disintegrator.
2. Mixer (electrically operated).
3. Sifter.
4. Stainless steel vessels and scoops of suitable sizes.
5. Filling equipment (electrically operated).
6. Weighing balance.

In the case of operation involving floating particles of fine powder, suitable exhaust system shall be provided. Workers should be provided with suitable masks during operation.

Area

A minimum area of thirty square meters is recommended to allow for the basic installations. Where the actual blending is to be done on the premises, an additional room shall be provided for the purpose.

5. Capsules

For the manufacture of capsules, separate enclosed area suitably air-conditioned and dehumidified with an airlock arrangement shall be provided. The following equipment is recommended for filling hard gelatin capsules, namely:

1. Mixing and blending equipment (electrically or power driven);
2. Capsules filling units (preferably semi-automatic or automatic filling machines).
3. Capsules counters (wherever applicable).
4. Weighing balance.
5. Disintegration test apparatus.
6. Capsule polishing equipment.

Separate equipment and, filling and packaging area shall be provided in penicillin and non-penicillin sections. In case of operations involving floating particles of fine powder, a suitable exhaust system shall be provided. Manufacture and filling shall be carried out in air-conditioned area. The room shall be dehumidified. Area—A minimum area of twenty-five square meters for basic installation and ten square meters for ancillary area each for penicillin and non-penicillin sections is recommended.

6. Surgical Dressing

The following equipment is recommended for the manufacture of surgical dressings other than absorbent cotton wool, namely:

1. Rolling machine.
2. Trimming machine.
3. Cutting equipment.
4. Folding and pressing machine for gauze.
5. Mixing tanks for processing medicated dressing.
6. Hot air dry oven.
7. Steam sterilizer or dry heat sterilizer or other suitable equipment.
8. Work tables/benches for different operations.

Area

A minimum area of thirty square meters is recommended to allow for the basic installations. In case medicated dressings are to be manufactured, another room with a minimum area of thirty square meters shall be provided.

7. Ophthalmic Preparations

For the manufacture of ophthalmic preparations, separate enclosed areas with airlock arrangement shall be provided. The following equipment is recommended for the manufacture under aseptic conditions of eye-ointment, eye-lotions and other preparations for external use, namely;

1. Thermostatically controlled hot air ovens (preferably double ended).
2. Jacketted kettle/stainless steel tanks (steam, gas or electrically heated).
3. Mixing and storage tanks of stainless steel/planetary mixer.
4. Colloid mill or ointment mill.
5. Tube filling and crimping equipment (semi-automatic or automatic filling machines).
6. Tube cleaning equipment (air jet type).
7. Tube washing and drying equipment, if required.
8. Automatic vial washing machine.
9. Vial drying oven.
10. Rubber bung washing machine.

11. Sintered glass funnel, Seitz filter and filter candle (preferably cartridge and membrane filters).
12. Liquid filling equipment (semi-automatic or automatic filling machines).
13. Autoclave (preferably ventilator autoclave).
14. Air-conditioning and dehumidification arrangement (preferably centrally air-conditioned and dehumidification system).
15. Laminar airflow units.

Area

1. A minimum area of twenty-five square meters for basic installation and ten square meters for ancillary area is recommended. Manufacture and filling shall be carried out in air-conditioned areas under aseptic conditions. The rooms shall be further dehumidified as considered necessary if, preparations containing antibiotics are manufactured.
2. Areas for formulations meant for external use and internal use shall be separately provided to avoid mix-up.

8. Pessaries and Suppositories

i. The following equipment is recommended for manufacture of pessaries and suppositories, namely:
   1. Mixing and pouring equipment.
   2. Moulding equipment.
   3. Weighing devices.

Area

A minimum area of twenty square meters is recommended to allow for the basic installation.

ii. In the case of pessaries manufactured by granulation and compression, the requirements as indicated under "Item 3 of Tablet." shall be provided.

9. Inhalers and Vitralle

The following equipment is recommended for manufacture of inhalers and vitrallae, namely:

1. Mixing equipment.
2. Graduated delivery equipment for measurement of the medicament during filling.
3. Sealing equipment.

Area

An area of minimum twenty square meters is recommended for the basic installations.

10. Repacking of Drugs and Pharmaceutical Chemicals

The following equipment is recommended for repacking of drugs and pharmaceuticals chemicals, namely:
1. Powder disintegrator.
2. Powder sifter (electrically operated).
3. Stainless steel scoops and vessels of suitable sizes.
4. Weighing and measuring equipment.
5. Filling equipment (semi-automatic/automatic machines).
6. Electric sealing machine.

Area

An area of minimum thirty square meters is recommended for the basic installation. In case of operations involving floating particles of fine powder, a suitable exhaust system shall be provided.

11. Parenteral Preparations

The whole operation of manufacture of parenteral preparations (small volume injectables and large volume parenterals) in glass and plastic containers may be divided into the following separate areas/rooms, namely:

11.1. *Parenteral preparations in glass containers*:
1. *Water management area:* This includes water treatment and storage.
2. *Containers and closures preparation area:* This includes washing and drying of ampoules, vials, bottles and closures.

3. *Solution preparation area:* This includes preparation and filtration of solution.

4. *Filling, capping and sealing area:* This includes filling and sealing of ampoules and/or filling, capping and sealing of vials and bottles.

5. *Sterilization area.*

6. *Quarantine area.*

7. *Visual inspection area.*

8. *Packaging area.*

The following equipment is recommended for different above mentioned areas, namely:

a. Water management area.

1. De-ionised water treatment unit.
2. Distillation (multi-column with heat exchangers) unit.
3. Thermostatically controlled water storage tank.
4. Transfer pumps.
5. Stainless steel service lines for carrying water into user areas.

b. Containers and closures preparation area

1. Automatic rotary ampoule/vial/bottle washing machine having separate air, water distilled water jets.
2. Automatic closures washing machine.
3. Storage equipment for ampoules, vials, bottles and closures.
4. Dryer/sterilizer (double ended)
5. Dust proof storage cabinets.
6. Stainless steel benches/stools.

c. Solution preparation area

1. Solution preparation and mixing stainless steel tanks and other containers.
2. Portable stirrer.
3. Filtration equipment with cartridge and membrane filters/bacteriological filters.
4. Transfer pumps.
5. Stainless steel benches/stools.

d. Filling, capping and sealing area

1. Automatic ampoule/vial/bottle filling, sealing and capping machine under laminar air flow workstation.

  2. Gas line (nitrogen, oxygen, carbon dioxide) wherever required.
  3. Stainless steel benches/stools.
e. Sterilization area
  1. Steam sterilizer preferably with computer control for sterilization cycle along with trolley sets for loading/ unloading containers before and after sterilization.
  2. Hot air sterilizer (preferably double ended).
  3. Pressure leak test apparatus.
f. Quarantine area
  1. Storage cabinets.
  2. Raised platforms/steel racks.
g. Visual inspection area
  1. Visual inspection units (preferably conveyor belt type and composite white and black assembly supported with illumination).
  2. Stainless steel benches/stools.
h. Packaging area
  1. Batch coding machine (preferably automatic).
  2. Labelling unit (preferably conveyor belt type).
  3. Benches/stools.

Area

1. A minimum area of one hundred and fifty square meters for the basic installation and an ancillary area of one hundred square meters for small volume injectables are recommended. For large volume parenterals, an area of one hundred and fifty square meters each for the basic installation and for ancillary area is recommended. These areas shall be partitioned into suitable enclosures with airlock arrangements.
2. Areas for formulations meant for external use and internal use shall be separately provided to avoid mix up.
3. Packaging materials for large volume parenteral shall have a minimum area of 100 square meters.

11.2. *Parenteral preparations in plastic containers by form-fill-seal/blow, fill-seal technology.* The whole operation of manufacture of large volume parenteral preparations in plastic containers including plastic pouches by automatic (all operations in one station) Form-Fill-Seal machine or by semi-automatic blow moulding, filling-cumsealing machine may be divided into following separate areas/rooms, namely:

1. Water management area.
2. Solution preparation area.
3. Containers moulding-cum filling and sealing area.
4. Sterilization area.
5. Quarantine area.
6. Visual inspection area.
7. Packing area.

The following equipment is recommended for different above mentioned areas namely:

Water Management Area

1. De-ionised water treatment unit.
2. Distillation unit (multi column with heat exchangers).
3. Thermostatically controlled water storage tank.
4. Transfer pumps.
5. Stainless steel service lines for carrying water into user areas.

Solution Preparation Area

1. Solution preparation and storage tanks.
2. Transfer pumps.
3. Cartridge and membrane filters.

Container Moulding-cum-Filling and Sealing Area

1. Sterile form-fill-seal machine (all operations in one station with built-in laminar air flow workstation having integrated container output conveyor belt through pass box).
2. Arrangement for feeding plastic granules through feeding-cum-filling tank into the machine.

Sterilization Area

Super heated steam sterilizer (with computer control for sterilization cycle along with trolley sets for loading/unloading containers for sterilization).

Quarantine Area

Adequate number of platforms/racks with storage system. Visual inspection area, visual inspection unit (with conveyor belt and composite.

Packaging Area

1. Pressure leak test apparatus (pressure belt or rotating disc type)
2. Batch coding machine (preferably automatic).
3. Labelling unit (preferably conveyor belt type).

Area

1. A minimum area of two hundred and fifty square meters for the basic installation of an Ancillary area of one hundred and fifty square meters for large volume parenteral preparations in plastic containers by form-fill-seal technology is recommended. These areas shall be partitioned into suitable enclosures with airlock arrangements.
2. Areas for formulations meant for external use and internal use shall be separately provided to avoid mix up.
3. Packaging materials for large volume parenteral shall have a minimum area of 100 square meters.

*SCHEDUE M-I (*see* RULE 85-E (2))

1. Requirements of Factory Premises for Manufacture of Homeopathic Preparations

a. *Location and surroundings*: The factory shall be situated in a place which shall not be adjacent to an open sewage drain, public lavatory or any factory which produces a disagreeable

---

* Ins. by GOI Notification G.S.R. No. 507(E) dated 12-06-1987 w.e.f. 12.06.1987

or obnoxious odor or fumes or large quantities of soot, dust or smoke. The factory shall be located in a sanitary place, remove from filthy surroundings.

b. *Buildings*: The part of the building used for manufacturing shall not be used for a sleeping place and no sleeping place adjoining to it shall communicate therewith except through open air or through an intervening open space. The walls of the room in which manufacturing operations are carried out shall, up to a height of six feet from the floor, be smooth, waterproof and shall be capable of being kept clean. The flooring shall be smooth, even and washable and shall be such as not to permit retention or accumulation of dust. There shall be no chinks or crevices in the walls or floor.

c. The building used for the factory shall be constructed so as to permit production under hygienic conditions laid down in the Factories Act, 1948 (63 of 1948).

d. *Water supply*: The water used in manufacture shall be pure and drinkable quality, free from pathogenic microorganisms.

e. *Disposal of waste*: There should be adequate arrangement for disposal of waste water and other residues from the laboratory.

f. The rooms should be airy and clean and the temperature of the room should be moderately comfortable.

g. *Health, clothing and sanitary requirement of the staff*: All workers shall be free from contagious or obnoxious disease. Their clothing shall consist of a white or colored uniform suitable to the nature of the work and the climate, and shall be clean. Adequate facilities for personal cleanliness, such as clean towels, soap and hand scrubbing brushes, shall be provided separately for each sex. The workers shall be required to wash and change into clean footwear before entering the rooms where the manufacturing operations are carried on. Workers shall be required to wear either a clean cap or a suitable headgear so as to avoid any possibility of contamination by air or perspiration.

h. *Medical services*: The manufacturer shall provide adequate facilities for first aid, medical inspection of workers at the time of employment and periodically check-up thereafter at least once a year.

i. *Working benches*: Working benches shall be provided for carrying out operations such as filling, labeling, packing, etc. such benches shall be fitted with smooth, impervious tops capable of being washed.

j. *Container management*: Where operations involving use of containers such as bottles, phials and jars are conducted, there shall be adequate arrangements separated from potentisation chamber for washing, cleaning and drying such containers, with suitable equipment for the purpose. Wherever, these are attended manually adequate precaution of perfection in respect of cleanliness and avoidance of pollutants shall be taken.

2. Requirements of Plant and Equipment

a. *Mother tinctures: External tinctures and other solution section.* The following plant and equipment shall be provided namely:

   i. Disintegrator.

   ii. Sieved Separator.

   iii. Balances and fluid measures.

   iv. Chopping boards and knives.

   v. Macerators with lids.

   vi. Percolators with lids and regulated discharge.

   vii. Moisture determination apparatus or other suitable arrangement.

   viii. Filtering arrangement.

   ix. Mixing vessels and suitable non-metallic storage containers.

   x. Portable stirrers.

   xi. Water still.

Note:

1. As for as possible metal contacts may be avoided once the drug is processed.

2. An area of 55 square meters is recommended for basic installations.

3. Adequate separate storage facility should be provided for raw material quarantine, storage and bonded room for alcohol were applicable.

4. Separate and suitable storage facility should be provided for fresh herbs and odorous raw materials.
5. Adequate laboratory facility shall be provided for testing of raw material and finished products.

b. *Potentisation section*:

1. The following arrangements are recommended for container for closure preparation section namely:
   i. Washing tanks with suitable brushing arrangement manual or mechanical.
   ii. Purified water rinsing tank.
   iii. Closure macerating or washing tanks.
   iv. Drying chambers.
   An area of 20 square meters is recommended for basic installation.

2. The following arrangements are recommended for potency preparation section, namely:
   i. Working tables with washable top.
   ii. Facilities for separate storage of different grades of back potencies.
   iii. Suitable measuring devices for discharge of drug and diluent in potentisation vial.
   iv. Potentiser with counter or suitable manual arrangement.

Note:

1. Different droppers shall be used for different drugs potencies.
2. All measuring devices shall be of metric system and be made of glass and shall be free from metallic contents.
3. It is desired that glass droppers, etc. intended for re-use after cleaning should be sterilized by autoclave or heating in a hot air oven.
4. Plastics, rubber tubes, bulks, etc. coming in contact with tinctures or back potencies should not be re-used for other tincture and potencies.
5. Method of potentisation will be adopted as specified in Homoeopathic Pharmacopoeia of India Vol. I (3) Triturating, Tableting and Pill/Globules section.

3. The following Arrangement are Recommended

i. Triturating machine for suitable device.

ii. Disintegrator.

iii. Mass mixer.

iv. Granulator.

v. Oven.

vi. Tableting punches or machines.

vii. Kettle (Steam/gas/electrically heated) for preparation solution.

viii. Dryers.

ix. Sieved separator, tablet counters and balances.

Note: Tablet section shall be free from dust and floating particles. An area of 55 square meters is recommended for basis installations

4. Ointments and Lotion Section

The following arrangements are recommended namely:

i. Mixing tank.

ii. Kettle (Steam, gas or electrically heated).

iii. Suitable powder mixer.

iv. Ointment mill.

v. Filling equipment or arrangement.

An area of 20 square meters is recommended for basic installation.

5. Syrups and Tonics

The following arrangements are recommended namely:

i. Mixing and storage tank.

ii. Potable mixer.

iii. Filtering equipment.

iv. Water still/Deioniser.

v. Filling and sealing equipment.

An area of 20 square meters is recommended for basic installations.

6. Ophthalmic Preparations

The following equipment is recommended for manufacture under aseptic conditions of eye-ointments, eye-drops, eye-lotion and other preparations for external use, namely:

i. Hot air even electrically heated with thermostatic control.

ii. Colloid mill or ointment mill.

iii. Kettle (gas or electrically heated) with suitable mixing arrangement.

iv. Tube filling equipment.

v. Mixing and storage tanks of stainless steel or of other suitable material.

vi. Sintered glass funnel, seitz filter or filter candle.

vii. Liquid filling equipment.

viii. Autoclaves.

Adequate precaution should be taken to ensure that the finished product is sterile. An area of 20 sqaure meters is recommended for basic installations.

7. Adequate Arrangements for Space and Equipment should made for Labeling and Packing

*(SCHEDULE M-II (*SEE* RULE 139)

Requirement of Factory Premises for Manufacture of Cosmetics

1. General Requirements

a. *Location and surroundings.* The factory shall be located in a sanitary place and hygienic conditions shall be maintained in the premises. Premises shall not be used for residence or be interconnected with residential area. It shall be well ventilated and clean

b. *Buildings.* The buildings used for the factory shall be constructed so as to permit production under hygienic conditions and not to permit entry of insects, rodents, files, etc. The walls of the room in which manufacturing operations

---

* Ins. by GOI Notification No. GSR 723(E) dt 11-8-1992.

are carried out, shall up to a height of six feet from the floor, be smooth, waterproof and capable of being kept clean. The flooring shall be smooth, even and washable and shall be such as not to permit retention or accumulation of dust.

c. *Water supply*: The water used in manufacture shall be of potable quality.

d. *Disposal of water.* Suitable arrangements shall be made for disposal of wastewater.

e. *Health, clothing and sanitary requirements of the staff.* All workers shall be free from contagious or infectious diseases. They shall be provided with clean uniforms, masks, headgears, and gloves wherever required. Washing facilities shall also be provided.

f. *Medical services.* Adequate facilities for first aid shall be provided.

g. Working benches shall be provided for carrying out operations such as filling, labeling, packing, etc. such benches shall be fitted with smooth, impervious tops capable of being washed.

h. Adequate facilities shall be provided for washing and drying of glass containers if the same are to be used for packing the product.

Requirements of Plant and Equipment

The following equipment, area and other requirements are recommended for the manufacture of:

A. Powders

Face powder, cake make-up, compacts, face packs, masks and rouges, etc.

1. Equipment.
   a. Powder mixer of suitable type provided with a dust collector.
   b. Perfume and color blender.
   c. Sifter with sieves of suitable mesh size.
   d. Ball mill or suitable grinder.
   e. Trays and scoops (stainless steel).
   f. Filling and sealing equipment provided with dust extractor.

g. For compacts:
  i. A separate mixer,
  ii. Compact pressing machine.
h. Weighing and measuring devices
i. Storage tanks.

An area of 15 square meters is recommended. The section is to be provided with adequate exhaust fans.

B. *Creams, Lotions, Emulsions, Pastes, Cleansing Milks, Shampoos, Pomade, Brilliantine, Shaving Creams and Hair-oils, etc.*

a. Mixing and storage tanks of suitable materials.
b. Heating kettle, steam, gas or electrically heated.
c. Suitable agitator.
d. Colloidal mill or homogeniser (wherever necessary).
e. Triple roller mill (wherever necessary).
f. Filling and sealing equipment.
g. Weighing and measuring devices.

An area of 25 square meters is recommended.

C. *Nail Polishes and Nail Lacquers*

1. *Equipment:*
  a. A suitable mixer.
  b. Storage tanks.
  c. Filling machine hand operated or power driven.
  d. Weighing and measuring devices.

An area of 15 square meters is recommended. The section shall be provided with flameproof exhaust system.

2. *Premises:* The following are the special requirements related to nail polishes and nail lacquers:
  a. It shall be suited in an industrial area.
  b. It shall be separate from other cosmetic-manufacturing areas by metal/brick partition up to ceiling.
  c. Floors, walls, ceiling and doors shall be fireproof.
  d. Smoking, cooking and dwelling shall not be permitted and no naked flame shall be brought in the premises.

    e. All electrical writing and connections shall be concealed and main electric switch shall be outside the manufacturing area.

    f. All equipment, furniture and light fittings in the section shall be flameproof.

    g. Fire extinguisher like foam and dry powder and sufficient number of buckets containing sand shall be provided.

    h. All doors of the section shall open outwards.

3. *Storage:* All explosive solvents and ingredients shall be stored in metal cupboards or in a separate enclosed area.

4. *Manufacture:*

    a. Manufacture of lacquer shall not be undertaken unless the above conditions are complied with.

    b. Workers shall be asked to wear shoes with rubber soles in the section.

5. *Other requirements:* No objection certificate from the local fire brigade authorities shall be furnished.

D. Lipsticks and Lip-gloss, etc.

1. *Equipment:*

    a. Vertical mixer.

    b. Jacketted kettle steam, gas or electrically heated.

    c. Mixing vessel (stainless steel)

    d. Triple roller mill/ball mill.

    e. Moulds with refrigeration facility.

    f. Weighing and measuring devices.

    An area of 15 square meters is recommended.

E. Depilatories

1. *Equipment:*

    a. Mixing tanks.

    b. Mixer.

    c. Triple roller mill or homogeniser (where necessary).

    d. Filling and sealing equipment.

    e. Weighing and measuring devices.

    f. Moulds (where necessary).

    An area of 10 square meters is recommended.

F. Preparations used for Eyes

Such preparations shall be manufactured under strict hygienic conditions to ensure that these are safe for use.

1. Eyebrows, Eyelashes, Eyeliners, etc.

Equipment:

a. Mixing tanks.

b. A suitable mixer.

c. Homogeniser (where necessary).

d. Filling and sealing equipment.

e. Weighing and measuring devices.

An area of 10 square meters is recommended.

2. Kajal and Surma

Equipment:

a. Base sterilizer.

b. Powder sterilizer (dry heat oven).

c. Stainless steel tanks.

d. A suitable mixer.

e. Stainless steel sieves.

f. Filling and sealing arrangements.

g. Weighing and measuring devices.

h. Homogeniser (where necessary).

i. Pestle and Mortar (for Surma).

An area of 10 square meters with a separate area of 5 square meters for base sterilization is recommended. Other requirements for 1 and 2:

a. False ceiling shall be provided wherever required.

b. Manufacturing area shall be made fly proof. An airlock or an air curtain shall be provided.

c. Base used for Kajal shall be sterilized by heating the base at 150°centigrate for required time in a separate enclosed area.

d. The vegetable carbon black powder shall be sterilized in a drying oven at 120°centigrate for required time.

e. All utensils used for manufacture shall be of stainless steel and shall be washed with detergent water, antiseptic liquid and again with distilled water.

f. Containers employed for 'Kajal' shall be cleaned properly with bactericidal solution and dried.

g. Workers shall put on clean overalls and use hand gloves wherever necessary.

G. Aerosol

Equipment:

a. Air-compressor (wherever necessary).

b. Mixing tanks.

c. Suitable propellant filling and crimping equipment.

d. Liquid filling unit.

e. Leak testing equipment.

f. Fire extinguisher (wherever necessary).

g. Suitable filtration equipment.

h. Weighing and measuring devices.

An area of 15 square meters is recommended.

Other requirements: No objection certificate from the local fire brigade authorities shall be furnished.

H. Alcoholic Fragrance Solutions

Equipment:

a. Mixing tanks with stirrer.

b. Filtering equipment.

c. Filling and sealing equipment.

d. Weighing and measuring devices.

An area of 15 square meters is recommended.

I. Hair Dyes

Equipment:

a. Stainless steel tanks.

b. Mixer.

c. Filling unit

d. Weighing and measuring devices.

e. Masks, gloves and goggles.

An area of 15 square meters with proper exhaust is recommended.

J. Tooth-Powders and Toothpastes, etc.

1. Tooth-powder in general
Equipment:
a. Weighing and measuring devices.
b. Dry mixer (powder blender).
c. Stainless steel sieves.
d. Powder filling and sealing equipment.

An area of 15 square meters with proper exhaust is recommended.

2. Toothpastes
Equipment:
a. Weighing and measuring devices.
b. Kettle steam, gas or electrically heated (where necessary).
c. Planetory mixer with de-aerator system.
d. Stainless steel tanks.
e. Tube filling equipment.
f. Crimping machine.

An additional area of 15 square meters with proper exhaust is recommended.

3. Tooth-powder (Black)
Equipment:
a. Weighing and measuring devices.
b. Dry mixer powder blender.
c. Stainless steel sieves.
d. Powder filling arrangements.

An area of 15 square meters with proper exhaust is recommended. Areas for manufacturing black and white tooth-powders should be separate.

K. Toilet Soaps

Equipment:
a. Kettles/pans for saponification.
b. Boiler or any other suitable heating arrangement.
c. Suitable stirring arrangement.
d. Storage tanks or trays.

e. Driers.

f. Amalgamator/chipping machine.

g. Mixer.

h. Triple roller mill.

i. Granulator.

j. Plodder.

k. Cutter.

l. Pressing, stamping and embossing machine.

m. Weighing and measuring devices.

A minimum area of 100 square meters is recommended for the small-scale manufacture of toilet soaps. The areas recommended above are for basic manufacturing of different categories of cosmetics. In addition to that separate adequate space for storage of raw materials, finished products, packing materials shall be provided in factory premises.

Note No. I. The above requirements of the schedule are made subject to modification at the direction of the licensing authority, if he is of the opinion that having regard to the nature and extent of the manufacturing operations it is necessary to relax or alter them in the circumstances of a particular case.

Note No. II. The above requirements do not include requirements of machinery, equipment and premises required for preparation of containers and closers of different categories of cosmetics. The licensing authority shall have the discretion to examine the suitability and adequacy of the machinery, equipment and premises for the purpose of taking into consideration of the requirements of the licence.

Note No. III. Schedule M-II specifies equipment and space required for certain categories of cosmetics only. There are other cosmetics items, viz. attars, perfumes, etc. which are not covered in the above categories. The licensing authority shall, in respect of such items or the words 'A testing laboratory shall also be provided' were omitted by GOI Notification No. GSR 285 (E) dt 16.07.1996. categories of cosmetics have the discretion to examine the adequacy of factory premises, space, plant and machinery and other requisites having regard to the nature and extent of the manufacturing operations involved and direct the licensee to carry on necessary modification in them.

Note No. IV. [Areas for formulations meant for external use and areas for formulations meant for internal use shall be separately provided to avoid mix-up even though they are from the same category of formulations.]

***(SCHEDULE M-III (*SEE RULE 76*)

Requirements of Factory Premises for Manufacture of Medical Devices

1. General Requirements

1.1.1. *Location and surroundings:* The factory building(s) shall be located in a sanitary place and hygienic conditions shall be maintained in the premises. Premises shall be not used for residence or be interconnected with residence. It shall be well ventilated and clean.

1.1.2. *Buildings:* The buildings used for the factory shall be constructed so as to permit production under hygienic conditions and not to permit entry of insets, rodents, flies, etc. The walls of the rooms in which manufacturing operations are carried out, shall be up to a height of six feet from the floor, be smooth, waterproof and capable of being kept clean. The floor shall be smooth, even and washable and shall be such as not to permit retention or accumulation of dust.

1.1.3. *Water supply:* The water used in manufacture shall be of potable quality.

1.1.4. *Disposal of waste:* Suitable arrangements shall be made for disposal of wastewater.

1.1.5. *Health, clothing and sanitation of workers:* All workers shall be free from contagious or infectious diseases. They shall be provided with clean uniforms, masks, headgears and gloves wherever required. Washing facilities shall also be provided.

1.1.6. *Medical services:* Adequate facilities for first-aid shall be provided.

1.1.7. Workbenches shall be provided for carrying out operations such as moulding, assembling, labeling, packing,

---

*** *Ins. by GOI Notification No. GSR 109(E), w.e.f. 22.2.1994.*

etc. such benches shall be fitted with smooth impervious tops capable of being washed.

1.1.8. Adequate facilities shall be provided wherever required for cleaning, washing, drying of different containers of devices.

1.1.9. The premises shall be kept under controlled conditions of temperature and humidity so as to prevent any deterioration in the properties of materials and products due to storage and process conditions.

2. Requirements for Manufacture of Medical Devices

The process of manufacture of medical devices shall be conducted at the licensed premises, wherever required, and shall be divided into the following separate operations/sections:

1. Moulding (wherever manufacture of medical devices is to start from granules).
2. Assembling (include cutting, washing and drying, sealing, packing, labeling, etc.)
3. Raw materials.
4. Storage area.
5. Washing, drying and sealing area (wherever required).
6. Sterilization.
7. Testing facilities.

The following equipment and space are recommended for the basic manufacture of different categories of medical devices.

A. *Sterile Disposable Perfusion and Blood Collection Sets*

1. *Moulding:*
   a. Injection moulding machine.
   b. Extruder machine.
   c. PVC resin compounding machine.
2. *Assembling:*
   a. Hand pressing machine for filter fixing a drip chamber.
   b. Bag sealing machine.
   c. Compressor machine.
   d. Leak testing bench.

e. PVC tube cutting machine.

f. Tube winding machine (wherever necessary).

g. Welding machine (wherever necessary).

An area of 30 square meters for moulding and 15 square meters for assembling are recommended for basic installation. The assembling area shall be air-conditioned provided with HEPA filters. The moulding section shall, if necessary, have proper exhaust system.

Note: An additional area of 20 square meters is recommended for any extra category.

B. *Sterile Disposable Hypodermic Syringes*

1. *Moulding:*
   a. Granulator.
   b. Injection moulding machine.
   c. Weighing devices.
2. *Assembling:*
   a. Blister pack machine.
   b. Vacuum dust cleaner.
   c. Rubber-tip washing machine.
   d. Foil stamping or screen printing equipment.

An area of 30 square meters for moulding and 15 square meters for assembling are recommended for basic installation. The assembling area shall be air-conditioned provided with HEPA filters. The moulding section, shall, if necessary, have proper exhaust system.

Note: An additional area of 20 square meters is recommended for any extra category.

C. *Sterile Disposable Hypodermic Needles*

1. *Moulding:*
   a. Needle grinding and leveling machine.
   b. Electro polishing machine.
   c. Cutting machine
   d. Injection moulding machine.
   e. Needle pointing deburrine machine.
   f. Air-compressor.

2. *Assembling:*

a. Needle cleaning machine with magnetic separator.

b. Blister packing machine.

c. Needle inspection unit.

An area of 30 square meters for moulding and 15 square meters for assembling are recommended for basic installation. The assembling area shall be air-conditioned provided with HEPA filters. The molding section shall, if necessary, have proper exhaust system.

Note: An additional area of 20 square meters is recommended for any extra category.

3. Raw Materials

The licensee shall keep an inventory of all raw materials to be used at any stage of manufacture of devices and shall maintain records as per Schedule U. All such raw materials shall be identified and assigned control reference umber. They shall be conspicuously labeled indicating the name of the material, control reference number, name of the manufacturer and be specially labeled 'Under Test' or 'Approved' or 'Rejected'. The under test, approved or rejected materials shall appropriately be segregated. These shall be tested for compliance with required standards of quality. A minimum area of 10 square meters shall be provided for storage of raw materials.

4. Storage Area

The licensee shall provide separate storage facilities for quarantine and sterilized products. An area not less than 10 square meters shall be provided for each of them.

5. Washing, Drying and Sealing Area

The licensee shall provide wherever required adequate equipments like water distillation still, deionizer, washing machine. Dying oven with trays for washing, drying and sealing of medical device. An area not less than 10 square meters shall be provided.

6. Sterilization

The licensee shall provide requisite equipment with required controls and recording device for sterilization of medical devices by ethylene oxide gas in his own premises or may make arrangements with some institution approved by the licensing authority for sterilization. The products sterilized in this manner shall be monitored to assure acceptable levels of residual gas and its degradation products. An area of 10 square meters is recommended for basic installation of such facility. Provided that the above equipment may not be required in case the licensee opts for sterilization of medical devices by ionising radiation.

7. Testing Facilities

The licensee shall provide testing laboratory for carrying out chemical and physio-chemical testing of medical devices and of raw materials used in its own premises: Provided that the licensing authority shall permit the licensee in the initial stage to carry out testing of sterility, pyrogens, toxicity on their products from the approved testing institutions but after one renewal period of licensee shall provide testing facilities of all such tests in their own premises.

8. Records

The licensee shall maintain records of different manufacturing activities with regard to each stage of manufacture in-process control, assembling, packing, batch records for the quantity of devices manufactured from each lot of blended granules, duration of work, hourly quantum of production in respect of each item as well as record of each sterilizing cycle of the gaseous method employed.

Note: The above requirements of machinery, equipments, space, qualifications are made subject to the modification at the discretion of the licensing authority, if he is of the opinion that having regard to the nature and extent of the manufacturing operations it is necessary to relax or alter them in the circumstances of a particular case.

21

Drug and Cosmetic Rules Schedules: 1945 A to Y

Schedule A: Applications for licenses for import, mfg., and sale of drug and cosmetics, the forms in which the licenses are granted and renewed and other forms.

Schedule B: Fees for analysis of drug and cosmetics that have to be paid to the central drug laboratories or other government laboratories.

Schedule C: List of biological and immunological products, antibiotics and ophthalmic lotions and ointments and all products for parenteral use (Injections).

Schedule C (I): List of drugs, from biological origin, namely alkaloids, hormones, vitamins and antibiotics for oral use.

Schedule D: Exemptions that have been granted to drugs and importers of drugs from complying with the requirements of import of drugs and also the conditions for such exemptions.

Schedule E: List of poisons for which labeling and other requirements were to be complied with. This schedule has been deleted.

Schedule E (I): List of poisonous substances under the Ayurveda, Siddha and Unani systems of medicines.

Schedule F: Special provisions to be complied with, for the manufacture, testing and labeling of biological products for human use like sera and vaccines. These provisions have now been deleted. The requirements for running blood banks and other requirements are now includes in this schedule.

Schedule F (I): Special provisions to be complied with for the manufacture, testing and labelling of veterinary biological Products.

Schedule F (II): Standards for surgical dressings.

Schedule F (III): Standards for umbilical tapes.

Schedule FF: Additional standards for ophthalmic preparations.

Schedule G: List of drugs which should be used by patient under medical supervision and which shall be labeled with the words "Caution – It is dangerous to take this preparation except under medical supervision".

Schedule H: List of drugs which are to be sold by retail against the prescription of registered medical practitioner and which shall be labeled with words "Schedule H Drug—Warning: to be sold by retail on the prescription of a registered medical practitioner only."

Schedule I: List of poisons of particulars about the proportion of poison in certain cases. Schedule I was linked with schedule E. When schedule E was deleted in 1982, schedule I was also deleted.

Schedule J: Names of diseases and ailments (by whatever name described) which a drug may not purpose to prevent or cure by means of claims made on the label of the container of the drug.

Schedule K: Names of drugs or classes of drugs which are exempted from complying with the provisions for manufacture, sale and standards of drugs and the conditions of such exemption.

Schedule L: List of drugs which were required to be sold by retail against the prescription of registered medical practitioner. Subsequently the drugs listed in Schedule L were transferred to Schedule H. Schedule L was deleted in 1982.

ScheduleL1: Good laboratory practices.

Schedule M: Good manufacturing practices (GMP) and the requirements of premises, plant and equipment for manufacture of drugs.

Schedule M(I): Requirements for factory premises of homeopathic medicines.

Schedule M(II): Requirements for factory premises of cosmetics.

Schedule M(III): Requirements of factory premises for manufacture of medical devices.

Schedule N: List of minimum equipment, requirements of premises for the effective running of a pharmacy.

Schedule O: Standards for disinfectant fluids.

Schedule P: Life period and conditions of storage of drugs.

Schedule P(I): Pack sizes of drugs.

Schedule Q: List of coal tar colors permitted to be used in cosmetics.

Schedule R: Standards and labeling requirements of condoms, copper t and contraceptive tube rings.

Schedule R(I): Standards to be complied with by medical devices.

Schedule S: Standards for cosmetics.

Schedule T: Requirements of factory premises and hygienic conditions to be complied with by the manufacturer of Ayurvedic, Siddha and Unani drugs.

Schedule U: Particulars to be shown in the manufacturing records, record of raw materials and in the analytical records of drugs.

Schedule V: Standards for patient and proprietary medicines and the maximum and minimum quantities of vitamins that are permitted to be added in such preparations for oral use.

Schedule W: Names of drugs which shall be marketed under generic names only.

Schedule X: Names of psychotropic drugs for which special control measures have been laid down.

Schedule Y: Requirements and guidelines on clinical trials for import and manufacture of new drugs.

22

Banned Drugs in India

List of Drugs Prohibited for Manufacture and Sale through Gazette Notifications under Section 26a of Drugs and Cosmetics Act, 1940 by the Ministry of Health and Family Welfare

1. Amidopyrine.
2. Fixed dose combinations of vitamins with anti-inflammatory agents and tranquilizers.
3. Fixed dose combinations of atropine in analgesics and antipyretics.
4. Fixed dose combinations of strychnine and caffeine in tonics.
5. Fixed dose combinations of yohimbine and strychnine with testosterone and vitamins.
6. Fixed dose combinations of Iron with strychnine, arsenic and yohimbine.
7. Fixed dose combinations of sodium bromide/chloral-hydrate with other drugs.
8. Phenacetin.
9. Fixed dose combinations of antihistaminic with anti-diarrheals.
10. Fixed dose combinations of penicillin with sulphonamides.
11. Fixed dose combinations of vitamins with analgesics.
12. Fixed dose combinations of any other tetracycline with vitamin c.
13. Fixed dose combinations of hydroxyquinoline group of drugs with any other drug except for preparations meant for external use.
14. Fixed dose combinations of corticosteroids with any other drug for internal use.

15. Fixed dose combinations of chloramphenicol with any other drug for internal use.
16. Fixed dose combinations of crude ergot preparations except those containing ergotamine, caffeine, analgesics, antihistamines for the treatment of migraine, headaches.
17. Fixed dose combinations of vitamins with anti TB drugs except combination of isoniazid with pyridoxine hydrochloride (vitamin B_6).
18. Penicillin skin/eye ointment.
19. Tetracycline liquid oral preparations.
20. Nialamide.
21. Practolol.
22. Methapyrilene, its salts.
23. Methaqualone.
24. Oxytetracycline liquid oral preparations.
25. Demeclocycline liquid oral preparations.
26. Combination of anabolic steroids with other drugs.
27. Fixed dose combination of oestrogen and progestin (other than oral contraceptive) containing per tablet estrogen content of more than 50 mcg (equivalent to Ethinyl estradiol) and progestin content of more than 3 mg (equivalent to norethisterone acetate) and all fixed dose combination injectable preparations containing synthetic Oestrogen and progesterone. (Subs. By Notification numbers 743 (E) dt 10-08-1989)
28. Fixed dose combination of substitution sedatives/hypnotics/anxiolytics with analgesics-antipyretics.
29. Fixed dose combination of rifampicin, isoniazid and pyrazinamide, except those which provide daily adult dose given below:

Drugs	Minimum	Maximum
Rifampicin	450 mg	600 mg
Isoniazid	300 mg	400 mg
Pyrazinamide	1000 mg	1500 mg

*30. Fixed dose combination of histamine H-2 receptor antagonists with antacids except for those combinations approved by drugs controller, India.

*31. The patent and proprietary medicines of fixed dose combinations of essential oils with alcohol having percentage higher than 20% proof except preparations given in the Indian Pharmacopoeia.

*32. All pharmaceutical preparations containing chloroform exceeding 0.5% w/w or v/v whichever is appropriate.

**33. Fixed dose combination of ethambutol with INH other than the following: INH ethambutol 200 mg 600 mg 300 mg 800 mg.

**34. Fixed dose combination containing more than one antihistamine.

35. Fixed dose combination of any anthelmintic with cathartic/purgative except for piperazine/santonim.

36. Fixed dose combination of salbutamol or any other drug having primarily bronchodilatory activity with centrally acting anti-tussive and/or antihistamine.

**37. Fixed dose combination of laxatives and/or anti-spasmodic drugs in enzyme preparations.

**38. Fixed dose combination of metoclopramide with systemically absorbed drugs except fixed dose combination of metoclopramide with aspirin/paracetamol

**39. Fixed dose combination of centrally acting, antitussive with antihistamine, having high atropine like activity in expectorants.

**40. Preparations claiming to combat cough associated with asthma containing centrally acting antitussive and/or an antihistamine.

**41. Liquid oral tonic preparations containing glycerophosphates and/or other phosphates and/or central nervous system stimulant and such preparations containing alcohol more than 20% proof.

**42. Fixed dose combination containing pectin and/or kaolin with any drug which is systemically absorbed from GI tract except for combinations of pectin and/or kaolin with drugs not systemically absorbed.

***43. Chloral hydrate as a drug.

44. Dovers powder IP
45. Dover's powder tablets IP.
46. Antidiarrheal formulations containing kaolin or pectin or attapulgite or activated charcoal.
47. Antidiarrhoeal formulations containing phthalyl sulphathiazole or sulphaguanidine or succinyl sulphathiazole.
48. Antidiarrhoeal formulations containing neomycin or streptomycin or dihydrostreptomycin including their respective salts or esters.
49. Liquid oral antidiarrhoeals or any other dosage form for pediatric use containing diphenoxylate lorloperamide or atropine or belladona including their salts or esters or metabolites hyoscyamine or their extracts or their alkaloids.
50. Liquid oral antidiarrheals or any other dosage form for pediatric use containing halogenated hydroxyquinolines.
51. Fixed dose combination of antidiarrhoeals with electrolytes.
52. Patent and proprietary oral rehydration salts other than those conforming to the
53. Fixed dose combination of oxyphenbutazone or phenylbutazone with any other drug.
54. Fixed dose combination of analgin with any other drug.
55. Fixed dose combination of dextropropoxyphene with any other drug other than anti-spasmodics and/or non-steriodal anti-inflammatory drugs (NSAIDs).
56. Fixed dose combination of a drug, standards of which are prescribed in the second schedule to the said act with an Ayurvedic, Siddha or Unani drug.
57. Mepacrine hydrochloride (quinacrine and its salts) in any dosage form for use for female sterilization or contraception.
58. Fenfluramine and dexfenfluramine.
59. Fixed dose combination of diazepam and diphenhydramine hydrochloride.
60. Rimonabant.

61. Rosiglitazone.
62. Nimesulide formulations for human use in children below 12 years of age.
63. Cisapride and its formulations for human use.
64. Phenylpropanolamine and its formulation for human use.
65. Human placental extract and its formulations for human use.
66. Sibutramine and its formulations for human use.
67. R-sibutramine and its formulations for human use.
68. Gatifloxacin formulation for systemic use in human by any route including oral and injectable.
69. Tegaserod and its formulation for human use.

23

Drug Price Control

THE FIRST SCHEDULE

List of Price Controlled Drugs (DPCO 1995)

BULK DRUGS

1. Sulphamethoxazole
2. Penicillins
3. Tetracycline
4. Rifampicin
5. Streptomycin
6. Ranitidine
7. Vitamin C
8. Betamethasone
9. Metronidazole
10. Chloroquine
11. Insulin
12. Erythromycin
13. Vitamin A
14. Oxytetracycline
15. Prednisolone
16. Cephazolin
17. Methyldopa
18. Aspirin
19. Trimethoprim
20. Cloxacillin
21. Sulphadimidine
22. Salbutamol
23. Famotidine
24. Ibuprofen
25. Metamizol (analgin)

26. Doxycycline
27. Ciprofloxacin
28. Cefotaxime
29. Dexamethasone
30. Ephedrine
31. Vitamin B_1 (thiamine)
32. Carbamazepine
33. Vitamin B_2 (riboflavin)
34. Theophylline
35. Levodopa
36. Tolnaftate
37. Vitamin E
38. Nalidixic acid
39. Griseofulvin
40. Gentamicin
41. Dextropropoxyphene
42. Halogenated hydroxyquinoline
43. Pentazocine
44. Captopril
45. Naproxen
46. Pyrental
47. Sulphadoxine
48. Norfloxacin
49. Cefadroxyl
50. Panthonates and panthenols
51. Furazolidone
52. Pyrithioxine
53. Sulphadiazine
54. Framycetin
55. Verapamil
56. Amikacin sulphate
*57. Glipizide
58. Spironolactone
59. Pentoxyfylline
60. Amodiaquin

61. Sulphamoxole
62. Frusemide
63. Pheniramine maleate
64. Chloroxylenols
65. Becampicillin
66. Lincomycin
67. Chlorpropamide
68. Mebhydroline
69. Chlorpromazine
70. Methendienone
71. Phenyl butazone
72. Lynestranol
73. Salazosulphapyrine
74. Diosmine
75. Trimipramine
76. Mefenamic acid

Drugs (Prices Control) Order, 1995

- Definitions
- Fixation of sale prices of bulk drugs
- Bulk drug manufacturers
- Calculation of retail price
- Power to fix formulation prices
- Power to fix ceiling price
- Power to recover dues
- Power to recover overcharged amt.
- Issue of price list
- Power to review
- List of price controlled drugs
- Application for bulk drug prices: form I
- Information for non-scheduled bulk drugs: Form II
- Application for formulation prices: Form III
- Forms IV, V, VI
- The third schedule

THE SECOND SCHEDULE FORMS: FORM I

(To be submitted in duplicate) form of information/application for fixation or revision of prices of scheduled bulk drugs.

1. Name of the bulk drug.
2. Name of the manufacturer.
3. Address of the registered/head office of the manufacturer.
4. Address of the factory.
5. Capacity under industrial licence/small scale industry registration/industrial entrepreneure memorandum acknowledgement:
   - Number and date of industrial licence/small scale industry registration/industrial entrepreneure memorandum acknowledgement;
   - Production capacity (Tonnes/kgs/litres, etc.).
6. Installed capacity:
   - Number of shifts per day;
   - Number of operating days per year;
   - Maximum production per shift (tonnes/kgs/litres, etc.);
   - Date of commissioning;
   - Annual installed capacity.
7. Date of commencement of commercial production.
8. Actual production achieved during the last accounting year (preferably monthwise) and also monthly production during the current year (tonnes/kgs/litres, etc.).
9. Brief note on the manufacturing process adopted by you indicating all stages including recovery of by-products, if any, solvents, etc. and sagewise overall yield for each bulk drug.
10. Average hourly rate of production for each of the bulk drug since the commencement of the commercial production.
11. Maximum hourly rate of production achievable.
12. Estimated production of the bulk drug during the next three years.

13. If the production is proposed to be captively consumed for manufacturer of the formulation, please furnish the quantity to be so consumed out of the production given against serial number 8 and serial number 12.
14. Capital employed for the manufacture of the bulk drug(s):
    • Net fixed assets;
    • Working capital;
    • Total.
15. Please state how the above capital employed is financed by net worth and borrowings. (In the case of multi-purpose plant the capital employed/net worth as above and the share to be allocated to the bulk drug/ intermediate under consideration to be given).
16. Please state the average rate of interest paid by you on your borrowings, supported by figures of the amount of loans, average rate of interest etc. as per latest audited Balance sheet.
17. Please furnish latest c.i.f price of the bulk drug if the same had been imported or is being imported by you or by any other agency known to you.
18. Please furnish the cost of production of the bulk drug as per annexure to this Form duly certified by a practicing cost accountant/chartered accountant.
19. Please furnish number of persons employed/to be employed, gradewise, and their average monthly emoluments including contribution on account of provident fund, etc.
20. Please furnish the total amount of expenses under each of the element of other conversion costs *viz.* stores, factory and administration overheads and depreciation and the basis adopted for allocation to the product in question.
21. If this item is manufactured/to be manufactured in a multi-product plant, the method adopted for allocations to individual drugs for common expenses viz. process hours, equipment hours etc. may be furnished.
22. Please also furnish the following:
    • The types of packing materials used and their average rates;

- Basis and calculations of profit margin;
- Photocopies of invoices of raw materials having substantial consumption and also for power, fuel ofi etc.;
- Details of the fixed assets, method of depreciation, rate of depreciation alongwith working capital required for the product;
- A copy each of audit and balance sheet and profit and loss account for the last three years and in the case of a company copies of the latest cost audit report and annual report.

Notes:
1. Any hold up affecting production to be shown clearly against serial number 8.
2. In case the same plant facilities are used for production of more than one product, the information as per serial number 6 may be given product wise.

Annexure

(See Item Number 18 of the Form I of the First Schedule)

I. Name of the bulk drug.

II. a. Production in tonnes/kgs/litres, etc.

   b. Sales in tonnes/kgs/litres, etc.

   c. Despatches in tonnes/kgs/litres, etc.

III. Details of cost:

   a. Period;

   b. Cost data:

SI. no.	Particulars	Norms of consumption guaranteed by the know how supplier or as per standards developed	Unit	Actual consumption (Per kg/lit, etc. of the product)		
				Quantity (Rs.)	Rate/Unit (Rs.)	Amount
(1)	(2)	(3)	(4)	(5)	(6)	(7)

1. *Raw materials:*
   a. Imported
   1.
   2.
   3. etc.
   b. Indigenous
   1.
   2.
   3. etc.
   Total raw materials cost:
   Less recoveries of solvents:
   Net raw materials cost:

2. *Utilities:*
   a. Power
   b. Water
   c. Fuel (oil/coal)
   d. Others (To be specified) total utilities cost.

3. *Conversion cost:*
   a. Salaries and wages
   b. Operating supplies or consumable stores
   c. Repairs and maintenance
   d. Quality assurance
   e. Effluent treatment other factory overheads
   f. Administration overheads
   g. Research and development expenses
   h. Depreciation total conversion cost.

4. Cost of production (1+2+3).
5. Interest on borrowings.
6. Minimum bonus.
7. Total (4+5+6).
8. Packing:
    a. Materials
    b. Other expenses total packing cost.
9. Selling expenses.
10. Transport charges.
11. Transit insurance charges.
12. Non-recoverable taxes. (please specify and submit details along with supporting documents).
13. Total cost of sales.
14. Profit margin. (basis of calculations be submitted).
15. Selling price (13+14).
16. Place notified by the government, if any (please give number and date of notification).
17. Actual sale price, or notional price, if used captively.

Notes:

1. Items of expenses to be excluded from costs
    • Bonus in excess of statutory minimum,
    • Bad debts and provisions
    • Donations and charities
    • Loss/gain on sale of assets
    • Brokerage and commission expenses not recognised by income tax authorities (salary, perquisities, advertisements, etc.)
    • Adjustments relating to previous years.
2. In the case of imported raw materials, please furnish seperately the c.i.f. price, duty of customs and other charges totalling to the landed cost adopted against 8. number 1 (a).
3. Cost of intermediates manufactured for captive use should be on the basis of factory cost of production inclusive of administration overheads and shown separately against 8. number 1(b). A separate cost-sheet in the same proforma may please be appended.
4. Cost of generated utilities like power, steam, etc. should be separately given furnishing the details of purchased utilities consumed, rate and cost with other expenses incurred on generation with reference to Section number 2.
5. Details in respect of factory overheads, administration overheads and selling expenses should be furnished against Section number 3(d), 3(e) and 8.

6. The basis of depreciation adopted in your financial accounts may please be given against Section number 3(f).
7. Please indicate clearly whether the existing price is notified by the government or notional price against Section number 16 and 17.
8. **The information furnished in this form is to be certified by the Authorised signatory of the company and by the cost accountant/ chartered accountant.** This information furnished above is correct and true to the best of my knowledge and belief.

Authorised signatory:
Place:
Name:
Date:
Designation:

24

Supreme Court of India

Purchaser of drug or cosmetic enabled to obtain test or analysis. Any person [(Note: Ins. by Act 71 of 1986, Section 2 (w.e.f. 15-9-1987)) or any recognised consumer association, whether such person is a member of that association or not] shall, on application in the prescribed manner and on payment of the prescribed fee, be entitled to submit for test or analysis to a government analyst any drug [(Note: ins. by Act 21 of 1962, Section 15 (w.e.f. 27-7-1964)) or cosmetic] [(Note: Subsection by Act 71 of 1986, Section 2) purchased by him or it] and to receive a report of such test or analysis signed by the government analyst.
[(Note: Added by Act 71 of 1986, Section 2)

Explanation. For the purposes of this section and section 32, "recognised consumer association" means a voluntary consumer association registered under the Companies Act, 1956 or any other law for the time being in force.

26A. *Powers of Central Government to prohibit manufacture, etc. of drug and cosmetic in public interest:* Without prejudice to any other provision contained in this chapter, if the central government is satisfied, that the use of any drug or cosmetic is likely to involve any risk to human beings or animals or that any drug does not have the therapeutic value claimed or purported to be claimed for it or contains ingredients and in such quantity for which there is no therapeutic justification and that in the public interest it is necessary or expedient so to do, then, that Government may, by notification in the official gazette, prohibit the manufacture, sale or distribution of such drug or cosmetic.

Comment

The State's obligation of enforce production of qualitative drugs and elimination of the injurious ones from the market must take within its sweep an obligation to make useful drugs available at reasonable price so as to be within the common man's reach; Vincent Panikurlangara v. Union of India; AIR 1987 SC 990.

27. Penalty for manufacture, sale,of drugs in contravention of this chapter. Whoever, himself or by any other person on his behalf, manufacturers for sale or for distribution, or sells, or stocks or exhibits or offers for sale or distributes:

a. Any drug deemed to be adulterated under section 17A or spurious under section 17 B or which when used by any person for or in the diagnosis, treatment, mitigation, or prevention of any disease or disorder is likely to cause his death or is likely to cause such harm on his body as would amount to grievous hurt within the meaning of Section 320 of the Indian Penal Code solely on account of such drug being adulterated or spurious or not of standard quality, as the case may be, shall be punishable with imprisonment for a term which shall not be less than five years but which may extend to a term of life and with fine which shall not be less than ten thousand rupees;

b. Any drug

   i. Deemed to be adulterated under Section 17A, but not being a drug referred to in clause (a), or

   ii. Without a valid licence as required under clause (c) of Section 18, shall be punishable with imprisonment for a term which shall not be less than one year but which may extend to three years and with fine which shall not be less than five thousand rupees.

   Provided that the Court may, for any adequate and special reasons to be recorded in the judgment, impose a sentence of imprisonment for a term of less than one year and of fine of less than five thousand rupees.

c. Any drug deemed to be spurious under Section 17 B, but not being a drug referred to in clause (a) shall be punishable with imprisonment for a term which shall not be less than three years but which may extend to five years and with fine which shall not be less than five thousand rupees.

Provided that the court may, for any adequate and special reasons, to be recorded in the judgement, impose a sentence of imprisonment for a term of less than three years but not less than one year,

d. Any drug, other than a drug referred to in clause (a) or clause (b) or clause (c), in contravention of any other provision of this chapter or any rule made there under, shall be punishable with imprisonment for a term which shall not be less than one year but which may extend to two years and with fine :

Provided that the court may for any adequate and special reasons to be recorded in the judgement impose a sentence of imprisonment for a term of less than one year.

Comment

"The absence of any comma after the word "stocks" clearly indicates that the clause "stocks or exhibits for sale" is one indivisible whole and it contemplates not merely stocking the drugs but stocking the drugs for the purposes of sale and unless all the ingredients of this category are satisfied, Section 27 of the act would not be attracted; Mohd Shabir v. State of Maharashtra, (1979) 1 SCC 568.

27A. Penalty for manufacture, sale, etc., of cosmetics in contravention of this chapter. Whoever himself or by any other person on his behalf manufacturers for sale or for distribution, or sells, or stocks or exhibits or offers for sale:

i. Any cosmetic deemed to be spurious under Section 17C shall be punishable with imprisonment for a term, which may extend to three years and with fine;

ii. Any cosmetic other than a cosmetic referred to in clause (I) above in contravention of any provisions of this chapter or any rule made there under shall be punishable with imprisonment for a term which may extend to one year or with fine which may extend to one thousand rupees or with both.

28. Penalty for non-disclosure of the name of the manufacturer. Whoever contravenes the provisions of section 18A [or Section 24] shall be punishable with imprisonment for a term which may extend to one year, or with fine which may extend to [one thousand rupees], or with both.

28A. Penalty for not keeping documents, and for non-disclosure of information. Whoever without reasonable cause or excuse, contravenes the provision of Section 18 B shall be punishable with imprisonment for a term which may extend to one year or with fine which may extend to one thousand rupees or both.

29. Penalty for use of government analyst's report for advertising. Whoever uses any report of a test or analysis made by the central drugs laboratory or by a government analyst, or any extract from such report, for the purpose of advertising any drug [(Note: Ins. by Act 21 of 1962, Section 15 (w.e.f. 27-7-1964)) or cosmetic], shall be punishable with fine which may extend to five hundred rupees.

30. Penalty for subsequent offences. [(1) (Note: Subsection by Act 68 of 1982, Section 25, for sub-Section (1) (w.e.f. 1-2-1983)). Whoever having been convicted of an offence, —

(a) Under clause (b) of Section 27 is again convicted of an offence under that clause, shall be punishable with imprisonment for a term which shall not be less than two years but which may extend to six years and with fine which shall not be less than ten thousand rupees.

Provided that the court may, for any adequate and special reasons to be mentioned in the judgement, impose a sentence of imprisonment for a term of less than two years and of fine of less than ten thousand rupees.

(b) Under clause (c) of Section 27, is again convicted of an offence under that clause shall be punishable with imprisonment for a term which shall not be less than two years but which may extend to four years or with fine which shall not be less than five thousand rupees, or with both.

(c) Under clause (d) of Section 27, is again convicted of an offence under that clause shall be punishable with imprisonment for a term which shall not be less than two years but which may extend to four years or with fine which shall not be less than five thousand rupees, or with both.

[(1A) (Note: Ins. by Act 21 of 1962, Section 20 (w.e.f. 27-7-1964)) Whoever, having been convicted of an offence under Section 27-A is again convicted under that section, shall be punishable with imprisonment for a term which may extend to two years, or with fine which may extend to [(Note: Subsection by Act 68 of 1982, Section 25, for "one thousand rupees" (w.e.f. 1-2-1983)) two thousand rupees], or with both.]

[(2) Whoever, having been convicted of an offence under (Note: The words and figures "Section 28 or" omitted by Act 13 of 1964, Section 20 (w.e.f. 15-9-1964)) Section 29 is again convicted of an offence under the same section, shall be punishable with imprisonment which may extend to [(Note: Subsection by Act 13 of 1964, Section 20, for "two years") ten years], or with fine, or with both.]

Kerala Drug Case

Following the judgments from the Kerala High Court and later on from the Supreme Court of India in favor of the drugs control department of Kerala in the SLPs filed by the Kerala branch of the Qualified Private Medical Practitioners Association (QPMPA), the drugs control sleuths of Haryana last week raided two major private hospital pharmacies in Panchkula and seized huge quantum of medicines for not obtaining pharmacy licence from the department.

The officials registered cases against National Skin Hospital and Alchemist Hospital for violation of Sections 18 a and 18 c of the Drugs and Cosmetics Act. Lalith Goyal, the drugs controller of Haryana said the drug store house of one of the hospitals was also working without licence.

This is the first incident of cases against hospital pharmacies for selling drugs without licence in a state outside of Kerala after the Supreme Court dismissed the SLP (C), number 6877/11 on 18.3.2011 filed by the QPMPA, an association of doctors running private hospitals.

With regard to the reported departmental action by Haryana drugs control department, Dr Kishore Kumar, the secretary of the QPMPA said the drug control officials have no right to raid the pharmacies of hospitals because it is the right to a doctor to keep drugs in his place of work. According to him the doctors' community is exempted from drug licence under Section 5 of Schedule K of the Drug and Cosmetic Act, and it is a constitutional right enjoyed by them for the last 70 years. He said the drug authorities have misinterpreted Section 5 A in Schedule K to impose drug licence on all hospital pharmacies and thereby to bring the hospitals under their control.

After losing the case in the Supreme Court, and before that 21 years of fight in the high court of Kerala, the QPMPA informed the President of India Pratibha Patil and the Chief Justice of India that due to the ignorance of the bureaucracy one clause in item 5 of Schedule K in the Drug and Cosmetic Act, 1940 in and Rules, 1945 is misinterpreted and it needs amendment. Following it, the Central Drugs Standard Control Organisation (CDSCO) invited the QPMPA office-bearers for a detailed discussion and interpretation of the clause in item 5 of the Schedule K of the Drugs and Cosmetics Act (D&C Act).

The Kerala High Court in its order of March 25, 2010 had mandated all pharmacies attached to private hospitals in Kerala, either for dispensing or for stocking drugs, to obtain licences from the drugs control department. Against this verdict, the QPMPA filed a review petition in the high court which was dismissed later. After that, the doctors association approached the Supreme Court which also did not give them a relief.

In Kerala, the drug control officials went one step ahead in enforcing the act properly by strictly insisting the wholesalers not to supply medicines to the hospital pharmacies which have no licences. 'Ten wholesale dealers' licences were cancelled by the department for not following the orders of the department.

But the doctors' body got a severe setback from the high court while dismissing their petition. The court ordered the Association to make a payment of ₹10,000 as legal cost to the Kerala Legal Services Authority.

Andhra Pradesh Case

In a major crack down on pharmacies for operating without registered pharmacists, the Andhra Pradesh Drug Control Administration (AP DCA) conducted raids on the retail and corporate pharmacies in the state and booked as many as 281 cases against the medical shops spread across the state.

In the raid, it has been found by the AP DCA officials that more than 70 percent of the pharmacies in the state are operating without registered pharmacists and do not issue regular bills to consumers.

The raids were conducted by DCA as a part of its special drive to check the functioning of registered pharmacists in the state. The drug inspectors and other DCA officials found various irregularities by many medical stores and issued notices to them especially with regard to the absence of the registered pharmacists and for selling outdated drugs at the stores.

Corporate pharmacies like Apollo, Hetero Pharmacy, Medimart and Medplus were also raided.

When contacted a DCA official said, "We have conducted the raids as per the Drugs and Cosmetics Act, 1940 (DCA), the Drugs and Cosmetics Rules, 1945 (DCR). Many pharmacies are not complying with the rules and acts as mentioned while issuing the license." Based on the complaints, the DCA has acted on the pharma stores and brought to light many irregularities.

About 406 retail medical shops throughout the state were raided and out of these 281 retail medical shops were found selling medicines in the absence of registered pharmacists and without bills.

All the licensing authorities and assistant directors were directed to issue show-cause notices to the violators and appropriate action following the notices would be taken by the licensing authorities.

"We have noticed that registered pharmacists were not available at many retail pharmacies. So, the DCA inspected over 406 retail medical shops, including retail outlets of corporate pharmacies. Out of these, 281 medical shops were found selling medicines without pharmacists or without bill," said RP Thakur, director general of DCA, Andhra Pradesh.

"We have even found that some expired drugs are being sold without bills and we have checked all these aspects while raiding the shops," Thakur said.

"In addition to issuing show-cause notices, the shops will be closed for one week. If the same violation is repeated, we will cancel their license," he said.

New Delhi Case

The Union health ministry will soon withdraw its ban on advertisements on emergency contraceptive pills like Unwanted-72, Option-72 and I-Pill. The ministry had imposed the ban in January last year after experts raised concern that these advertisements may promote the misuse of the pill by the young generation.

According to sources, the Drugs Technical Advisory Board (DTAB) of the union health ministry in its meeting held on October 10 has decided to allow the advertisements on emergency contraceptive pills with some riders. As per the new DTAB guidelines, a committee consisting of the principal of a reputed girls college, representatives from civil society groups and the advertising council should screen the ads and the scripts before they are on air.

Ever since the drug companies launched advertisements on emergency contraceptive pills like, Unwanted-72, Option-72 and I-Pill, experts and public interest groups in the country have been raising concern that these advertisements may promote the misuse of the pill by the young generation who have started looking at the pills as a regular contraceptive method as the advertisements are said to have failed to drive home the message clearly that these pills are emergency contraceptives.

Apart from the civil society organisations, gynecologists in the country have also been expressing concern on the misuse of the pill by the young generation. It triggered a debate in sexually conservative India with critics arguing that the easy availability of such pills would encourage promiscuity among the millions of young people. There was also criticism that the easy availability of these drugs will also promote unsafe sex among younger generation and may result in promotion of diseases like HIV/AIDS in the country.

When the public criticism reached its crescendo after the companies started airing competitive ads on these pills, the Drugs Controller General of India (DCGI) banned the advertisements on these emergency pills and left the matter to the DTAB, which is the highest authority of health experts on technical matters under the union health ministry.

Now that the DTAB has taken a final decision in favor of the pharma companies, they can start advertisements on these pills.

Haryana Case

Following the instructions of the High Court of Punjab and Haryana, the drugs control department of Haryana has initiated a raid against the hooka bars selling nicotine contained products and other intoxicants, throughout the state.

After conducting raids in 66 hooka bars in several parts of the state, the director of drugs control Dr. G.L. singhal said his officials have seized 102 samples of tobacco molasses containing nicotine. The test reports of 92 samples showed presence of the intoxicant.

Apart from sampling, FIR has been registered against the Hooka Bars in Panchkula (five cases), Ambala (two cases), Panipat (two cases) and Faridabad (one case).

The cases were registered under Section IPC 188, 270/272/273/284 and Cigarettes and Other Tobacco Products (Prohibition of Advertisement and Regulation of Trade and Commerce, Production, Supply and Distribution) Act, 2003 (COTPA).

Dr Singhal said action under Cr. PC 144 has also been taken against Hooka bars located in Rohtak, Panchkula, Faridabad, Gurgaon, Panipat, Ambala, Hisar, Kurukshetra and Fatehabad districts.

Investigations at manufacturing premises of tobacco molasses, which are being used at these hooka bars, have been conducted by a two member team of drug control officers along with the officers of concerned from Moradabad (UP), Chandigarh (UT) and Mumbai (Maharashtra). Prosecution permission in 27 cases have been issued to the investigating officers for filing cases against the offenders under Drugs and Cosmetics Act 1940 and Rules 1945. More than 10 cases have been filed in various courts under the Drugs and Cosmetics Act against the violators, Dr Singhal told Pharmabiz.

He said Haryana is the first state in the country which can be termed soon as hookah-bar free state. The efforts of the state government in this regard were appreciated in the state level advocacy workshop held on 27.4.2012 at Panchkula. This advocacy workshop was convened by the World Health Organization and Government of India jointly, wherein states of Haryana, Punjab, Himachal Pradesh and the UT participated.

Lalith Goyal, ADC at Gurgaon said hooka bar is the biggest menace in Haryana against which the drugs control department is initiating actions for years.

Drug Licence Case 2003
Saturday, 4th December 2010—11:29
IN THE HIGH COURT OF KERALA AT ERNAKULAM
WP (C). No. 38494 of 2003(Y)

1. Qualified Private Medical Practitioners'   ... *Petitioner(s)*
2. Dr Babu Vasudevan, Director
3. Dr TA Abdul Jaleel, Managing Partner
4. Dr Muhammad Babu, Dr. Kunhalu's,
5. Dr K Bharathan, Vijayakumara Menon,
6. Dr VV Haridas, Chief Medical Officer

Vs

1. **State of Kerala,** Represented   ... *Respondent(s)*
2. Union of India, Represented
3. The Drugs Controller,

For Petitioner: Sri E Subramani (SR.)
For Respondent: Sri D Kishore, ADDL.CGSC

The Honorable Mr Justice K. Balakrishnan Nair
The Honorable Mr Justice PN Ravindran

Dated : 25/03/2010

W.P. (C) Nos. 38494 of 2003, 3016 of 2004 and 23733 of 2007

JUDGMENT

Balakrishnan Nair, J.

Dismissed

The first petitioner is an association of qualified private medical practitioners. Petitioners 2 to 6 are its members. The members of the first petitioner are running private hospitals/nursing homes. The grievance raised in this writ petition is concerning the insistence of the third respondent that the petitioners' hospitals should take out licence for dispensing medicines/ drugs.

2. The brief facts of the case are the following. The manufacture and sale of drugs and cosmetics in India are governed by the Drugs and Cosmetics Act, 1940 (hereinafter referred to as 'the Act'). Under Section 18 (c) of the Act, for sale of drugs, it is mandatory to obtain licence from the competent authority. The Central Government have been authorised by the act to frame rules, granting exemption from various provisions of the act in chapter IV thereof subject to appropriate conditions. Section 18 (c) comes under the said Chapter. The Central Government have framed Drugs and Cosmetics rules, 1945, invoking its power under the provisions of the Act. Rule 123 of the Drugs and Cosmetics Rules, 1945, deals with the exemption. The said rule states that the drugs specified in Schedule 'K' **shall be exempted from the provisions of Chapter IV of the Act and the Rules** made thereunder, to the extent and subject to the conditions specified in that schedule. Item 5 of Schedule 'K' exempts drugs supplied by a registered medical practitioner to his own patient or any drug specified in Schedule C supplied by a registered medical practitioner, at the request of another such medical practitioner, if it is specifically prepared with reference to the condition and for the use of an individual

patient. The said item also specifies the conditions, subject to which the exemption is granted. Item 5A exempts drugs supplied by a hospital or dispensary maintained or supported by the government or local body. **The petitioners claim that they should also be included under the purview of item 5A of Schedule 'K' of the aforementioned Rules.**

3. When the local Drug Inspectors started inspecting their hospitals and pressed the petitioners to take licence, they moved the Government by filing a representation before the Honorable Chief Minister, on 27.10.1990. The said representation was forwarded by the Government to the third respondent. The third respondent replied to the first petitioner, by issuing Ext.P1 communication dated 6.12.1990. The first petitioner was informed that its members are **not exempted from the liability to take licence.** That order was challenged before this Court, by filing O. P. Number 2179 of 1991. The said original petition was disposed of by Ext.P2 judgment. This court directed the government to consider the matter, as undertaken by the learned government pleader. Later, the government rejected the claim of the petitioners and the Drugs Controller granted time to the members of the first petitioner up to 30.4.1995 to take licence. This is evident from Ext.P3 communication issued by the third respondent to the Secretary of All Kerala Chemists and Druggists Association. By Ext. P3, the Secretary of All Kerala Chemists and Druggists Association was advised to inform its members to quote the drug licence numbers of the hospitals in the invoice/bills issued for supply of medicines/drugs. The petitioners challenged Ext.P3 before this court. The said challenge was repelled by a division bench of this Court, by the decision reported in *Thomas v. Union of India* (2000 (2) KLT 459). Though the original petitions were dismissed, certain directions adverse to the government were also issued in that judgment. So, both sides appealed before the Supreme Court, challenging the said decision. The Apex Court, by Ext. P4 order permitted to withdraw the writ petitions, with liberty to file fresh writ petitions, with proper pleadings. In the light of Ext.P4, the present writ petition is filed, seeking the following reliefs:

a. *Issue a writ of mandamus or other appropriate writs, directions or orders declaring that the petitioners are not obliged to take out a drug licence under Section 18 (c) of the Drugs and Cosmetics Act, 1940 and the Rules framed thereunder;*

b. *Issue writ of mandamus or other appropriate writs, directions or orders declaring that the petitioners are exempted under Rule 123 of the Drugs and Cosmetics Rules, 1945 and Schedule K to the said Rules from the provisions of Chapter IV of the Drugs and Cosmetics Act, 1940;*

c. *Issue a writ of mandamus or other appropriate writs, directions or orders declaring that the provisions of Item 5 and 5A of Schedule K to the Drugs and Cosmetics Rules, 1945 are ultra vires the Act apart from being unconstitutional;*

d. *Issue a writ of certiorari or other appropriate writs, directions or orders calling for the records leading up to Ext.P3 order issued by the 3rd respondent and quash the same;*

e. *Issue a writ of mandamus or other appropriate writs, directions or orders restraining the respondents from insisting the private hospitals/clinics in the State of Kerala from obtaining drug licence under Section 18 (c) of the Drugs and Cosmetics Act, 1940 and Rules framed thereunder;*

f. *Issue a writ of mandamus or other appropriate writs, directions or orders directing the respondents to include private hospitals/clinics for exemption under Schedule K to the Drugs and Cosmetics Rules, 1945;*

g. *To award the costs of the petitioners of these proceedings; and*

h. *To grant such other reliefs as this Hon'ble Court may deem just and proper in the circumstances of the case."*

4. The petitioners contended that their establishments are also liable to be exempted, along with the hospitals covered by item 5-A of Schedule 'K' of the Rules framed by the Central government. According to them, they are similarly placed. Their non-inclusion in item 5-A violates their fundamental rights under Article 14 of the constitution of India. The respondents filed a detailed counter affidavit, resisting the prayers in the Writ Petition.

5. We heard the learned counsel on both sides. The learned counsel for the petitioners pointed out that item 5-A of

Schedule 'K' suffers from the vice of under-inclusiveness. The petitioners' hospitals are similarly placed like the hospitals run or funded by the government or local bodies. Private hospitals do not sell any medicines to their patients. Medicines are administered as part of the treatment, for which a fee is collected. So, there is no reason why their hospitals also should not be exempted. The learned government pleader, on the other hand, submitted that all the hospitals sell medicines to their patients and receive consideration for the same. The sale clearly comes under the definition of **'retail sale' under rule 2 (f)** of the aforementioned Rules. **Item 5 exempts only individual medical practitioners,** subject to the stipulations contained therein. Item 5-A deals with hospitals run out of public funds. They form a different class and cannot be equated with private hospitals. If private hospitals are also included, the classification will be vitiated by over-inclusiveness. The hospitals run with the aid of public funds form a separate class. The classification is based on an intelligible differentia, it is submitted.

6. We considered the rival submissions made at the bar and also went through the relevant statutory provisions. Section 18 (c) of the Drugs and Cosmetics Act reads as follows:

"18. (c) manufacture for sale or for distribution, or sell, or stock or exhibit or offer for sale, or distribute any drug or cosmetic, except under, and in accordance with the conditions of, a licence issued for such purpose under this chapter:

Provided that nothing in this section shall apply to the manufacture, subject to prescribed conditions, of small quantities of any drug for the purpose of examination, test or analysis.

Provided further that the central government may, after consultation with the board, by notification in the official gazette, permit, subject to any conditions specified in the notification, the manufacture for sale or for distribution, sale, stocking or exhibiting or offering for sale or distribution of any drug or class of drugs not being of standard quality."

Section 33 (q) of the act enables the central government to frame rules exempting any specified drug or class of drugs or cosmetic or class of cosmetics from all or any of the provisions of that chapter (Chapter IV). Invoking that power, the central government have framed rule 123 of the drugs and cosmetics Rules, which reads as follows:

"123. The drugs specified in Schedule K shall be exempted from provisions of Chapter IV of the act and the rules made thereunder to the extent and subject to the conditions specified in that schedule."

All drugs specified in Schedule 'K' shall be exempted from the provisions of Chapter IV of the act and the Rules made thereunder, to the extent and subject to the conditions specified in that schedule.

Item 5-A, which is relevant in this case, reads as follows:
"5-A. Drugs supplied by a hospital or dispensary maintained or supported by government or local body."

The provision of Chapter IV of the act and the rules thereunder which require them to be covered by a sale licence, subject to the following conditions:
1. **The dispensing and supply of drugs shall be carried out by or under the supervision of a qualified person;**
2. **The premises where drugs are supplied or stocked shall be open to inspection by an inspector appointed under the drugs and cosmetics act who can, if necessary, take samples for test;**

3. **The drugs shall be stored under proper storage conditions."**

The grievance of the petitioners is that they should also have been included in the said item. But, we think, a private hospital cannot be equated with a hospital maintained or supported by the government or local body. They form different classes and they have been classified separately, on valid grounds. So, the claim of the petitioners that the said classification suffers from the vice of under-inclusiveness cannot be accepted. The learned counsel for the petitioners pointed out various inconveniences that may be caused, if licence is insisted. But, such inconveniences caused to persons are not grounds to interfere with the operation of the rules, especially in the field of drugs. We are of the view that none of the grounds raised in the writ petition is tenable and the petitioners are not entitled to any of the reliefs prayed for. The challenge against Ext.P3 is also untenable.

In the result, the writ petition fails and it is accordingly dismissed.

W.P (C) Nos. 3016 of 2004 and 23733 of 2007

In view of the dismissal of W.P.(C) number 38494 of 2003, these writ petitions are also dismissed.

In the High Court of Delhi at New Delhi

Subject: Section 18(A)(I) Read With Section 27(C),
Drugs and Cosmetics Act, 1940

Crl. M.C. number 5392/2005

Reserved On: 20.08.2007

Date of Decision: 23.08.2007

Nicholas Piramal India Ltd. .... Petitioner

through: Mr Siddharth Luthra, senior advocatedwith

Mr.Sandeep Kapur and Mr.Rachna

Midha, Advocate

Versus

S. Sundaranayagam .... Respondent

through: Mr Anil Soni, advocate for the State.

Pradeep Nandrajog, J.

1. Petitioner, Nicholas Piramal India Limited, arrayed as accused No.5 in the complaint lodged by the respondent under Section 18(a)(i) read with Section 27(c), Drugs and Cosmetics Act, 1940 seeks quashing of the summoning order dated 18.12.2003.

2. Facts in brief are that on 21.9.2000, a sample of drug known as Erythromycin estolate oral suspension USP (60 ml), batch Number 1028, with manufacturing date August, 2000 and expiry date November, 2002 was collected by the drug inspector (complainant) from the premises of Sarvanand Hospital in the presence of the proprietor of the hospital.

3. On 21.9.2000, one sealed sample portion of the said drug was forwarded to the government analyst, Central Indian Pharmacopoeia Laboratoray, Ghaziabad, UP

4. On analysis the sample of the drug was found to be not of standard quality.

5. The manufacturing firm in its letter dated 7.11.2001 stated that it did not accept the government analyst's report and intend to adduce evidence in controversion of Government Analyst's report as provided under Section 25(3) of the Act and requested that sample be sent to Central Drugs Laboratory, Kolkata for retesting.

6. On re-testing by Central Drugs Laboratory, Kolkata, sample was again declared to be not of standard quality.

7. Investigation conducted by the complainant revealed that the said drug was manufactured by M/s Biodeal Laboratories for M/s Rhone-Poulene (India) Ltd.

   Investigation further revealed that pursuant to orders of the Honorable High Court of Bombay, on 27.9.2001, M/s. Rhone-Poulene (India) Ltd. was amalgamated with Nicholas Piramal India Ltd.

8. On completion of the investigation, complainant lodged a complaint with the learned metropolitan magistrate impleading following persons as accused:

   i. Neil Goodes .... Managing Director, M/s Rhone-Poulene India (Ltd.).

   ii. Jayant Chimanlal Jani .... Deputy Managing Director, M/s. Rhone-Poulene (India) Ltd.

   iii. J.P.Pandit .... Supervisory Chemist, M/s Rhone-Poulene (India) Ltd.

   iv. JV Vagle .... Supervisory Chemist, M/s Rhone-Poulene (India) Ltd.

   v. M/s. Nicholas Piramal India Ltd. .... through its Director, Ajay G Piramal

   vi. Thobhan Bhai Kurji Patel .... Managing Director, M/s. Biodeal Laboratories Pvt. Ltd.

   vii. M/s Biodeal Laboratories Pvt. Ltd. .... Through its Managing Director, Thobhan Bhai Kurji Patel.

8. Vide order dated 18.12.03, learned MM summoned the accused persons to face trial in the complaint. Same reads as under: "8.12.2003

Present: DI in person

I have heard DI/Complainant in person and have perused the record. I take cognizance of the offence. Since the complainant is public servant his statement is dispensed with. Issue summons of the complaint to the accused persons for 3.5.2004. MM, Delhi 8.12.2003"

9. Learned senior counsel for the petitioner submitted that the summoning order is based on non-application of judicial mind by the learned metropolitan magistrate. He further submitted that learned Metropolitan Magistrate failed to note that M/s Rhone-Poulene (India) Ltd. and Nicholas Piramal India Ltd. are two different companies. That the effect of amalgamation between the 2 companies is that M/s Rhone-Poulene (India) Ltd. is no longer in existence. That since the offence was committed by M/s Rhone-Poulene (India) Ltd. (transferor company), petitioner which is an entity seperate from transferor company cannot be prosecuted for the said offence.

10. Per contra, learned counsel for the State contended that petitioner is liable to be tried for the offence as it has taken over all the assets and liabilities of the firm M/s Rhone-Poulene (India) Ltd. In support of his contention, counsel relied upon clause 8 of scheme of arrangement between the 2 companies. Said clause reads as under:

8. *Legal Proceedings*

All suits, actions and proceedings of whatsoever nature by or against RPIL, NFL (except in relation to the assets and liabilities specified in Schedule A to the scheme) and SPL pending and/or arising on or before the effective date relating to their respective undertaking (as defined), including the assets and liabilities referred to in 3.1 and 3.2 hereof, shall neither abate nor shall in any way of prejudicially affected by reason of of said undertaking, assets and liabilities of RPIL, NFL and SPL having finally stood transferred and vested in NPIL as provided under this scheme but the same shall be continued and be enforced by and/or against NPIL as effectually as if the same has been pending and/or arising against NPIL."

11. A company which has complied with the requirement relating to incorporation of companies contained in companies act is a legal entity separate and distinct from the individual members of the company as held by the House of Lords in Salomon vs. Salomon and Corporation Limited (1895–1899) All England Reports 33.

12. In the decision reported as In Re: Walker's Settlement (1935) 1 Ch.D.567, 'amalgamation' was defined as under:-
"The word 'amalgamation' has no definite legal meaning. It contemplates a state of things under which 2 companies are so joined as to form a third entity or one company is absorbed into and blended with another company."

13. In the decision reported as Nokes vs. Doncaster (1940) 3 All E.R. 549, it was held that a contract of personal service previously existing between an individual and the transferor company, does not automatically becomes a contract between the individual and the transferee company. With reference to Section 154 of the English Companies Act, 1929, it was opined as under: "Section 154 contemplates or, at any rate, provide for — the dissolution of the transferor company when the transfer of its undertaking has been made, and there appears to be no means of calling back to life the company so dissolved."

14. In the decision reported as In Re: Skinner (1958) 3 All E.R. 273, it was opined as under: "................schemes and orders made by virtue of Section 206 and Section 208 of the Companies Act, 1948 can only transfer such rights, powers, duties and property as are capable of being lawfully transferred by a party to the scheme if no such sections of the companies act existed. It is not necessary in a scheme to exclude specifically from its operation things incapable of such transfer as general words in the scheme and any order in furtherance must be taken to operate in a manner not to repugnant to the general law of England."

15. In the decision reported as Oklahoma Natural Gas Co. vs. State of Oklahoma 273 US 257 (1927), Supreme Court of the United States observed as under: "There is no specific provision in our rules for the substitution as a party litigant of a successor to a dissolved corporation. It is well settled that a common law and in the federal jurisdiction a corporation which is being dissolved is as if it did not exit, and the result of the dissolution cannot be distinguished from the death of the natural person in its effect. .... It follows, therefore, that as the death of natural person abates all pending litigation to which the corporation is appearing either as a plaintiff or defendant. To allow actions to continue would be to continue the existence of the corporation pro hac vice. But corporations exist for specific purposes, and only by legislative act, so that if the life of the corporation is to continue even only for litigating purposes it is necessary that there should be some statutory authority for the prolongation.

16. In the decision reported as American Exch. Bank vs. Mitchell, 179 III. App.612, 615, 616, it was held that after a corporation is dissolved, it is incapable of maintaining an action; and that all such actions pending at the time of dissolution abate, in the absence of a statute to the contrary.

17. In the decision reported as M/s General Radio and Appliances Co. Ltd. vs. M.A.Khader (dead) by LR's (1986) 2 SCC 656, the effect of amalgamation of two companies was considered by the Honorable Supreme Court. It was held that after the amalgamation of the two companies the transferor company ceases to have any entity and the amalgamated company acquires a new status and it is not possible to treat the two companies as partners or jointly liable in respect of their liabilities and assets.

18. In para 6 of the decision reported as Saraswati Industrial Syndicate Limited vs. CIT, Haryana, H.P. and Delhi, AIR 1991 SC 70, Supreme Court observed as under: "The true effect and character of the amalgamation largely depends on the terms and scheme of merger but there can be any

doubt that when two companies amalgamate and merge into one the transferor company loses its entity as it ceases to have its business. However, their respective rights or liabilities are determined under the scheme of amalgamation but the corporate entity of the transferor company ceases to exist with effect from the date the amalgamation is made effective."

19. The legal position which emerges from afore-noted judicial decisions is that upon an amalgamation between two companies, the transferor company dies a civil death and the entity which has evolved upon amalgamation cannot be prosecuted for an offence committed by the transferor company. To the same effect are the observations of the High Court of Himachal Pradesh in the unreported decision in Crl. Rev. Number 150/1994 M/s Brooke Bond Lipton (India) Limited & Anr vs. State of H.P. and Anr. decided on 24.3.1995.

20. So far as clause 8 relied upon by the counsel for the state is concerned, same relates to transfer of legal proceedings. The clause does not contemplate that criminal liability for offence committed by the earlier company would be transferable to the petitioner company.

21. Noting that the petitioner company came into picture on 27.9.2001, after the date of manufacture of the said drug in year 2000, I hold that it cannot be prosecuted for the said offence.

22. Order dated 18.12.2003 summoning the petitioner to face trial in the complaint in question is quashed.

23. No costs.

25

Sunny Allied Industries, Jammu

Business planning for production of essential oils, spice oils and spice powder.

1. **Spice oils and essential oils needs**
   a. Steam distillation machine s.s parts 50 kg capacity ₹5 lacs
   b. Boiler 100 kg capacity ₹4 lacs
   c. Assembly and spare parts ₹2 lacs
   Sub total= 11 lacs

2. **Spice powder**
   a. Grinder machine ₹2 lacs
   b. S.S scoops ₹50 thousand
   c. Sieving machine ₹2 lacs
   d. Sachet filling machine ₹5 lacs
   Sub total = ₹9.5 lacs

3. **Construction rooms: 2000 square feet**
   a. Steam distillation room ₹3 lacs
   b. Boiler room ₹3 lacs
   c. Assembly room ₹3 lacs
   d. Grinder room ₹3 lacs
   e. S.S scoop room ₹3 lacs
   f. Sieving machine room ₹3 lacs
   g. Sachet filling room ₹3 lacs
   h. Bonded room ₹9 lacs
   i. Toilet room ₹3 lacs
   Sub total = 33 lacs

4. **Testing room**
   a. HPLC and acetone ₹15 lacs
   b. Chemicals, apparatus ₹3 lacs
   c. Laboratory room = 3 lacs
   Sub total = 21 lacs

5. Manpower

a. Consultancy charges ₹10,000 per month
b. Manager operation ₹20,000 per month
c. Operator ₹8,000 per month
d. Skilled worker ₹8,000 per month
e. Seed captial for running factory ₹5 lacs

Sub total = 5.5 lacs (approx.)

Total cost price = ₹80 lacs only

26

Project Report

Production Capacity

a. Capacity
  1. Ashkarishta   6000 Bottles
  2. Laxmibilas Ras (N)   400 Kgs
  3. Bhaskar Lavan   12000 Kgs
  4. Sitopaladi Churan   6000 Kgs
  5. Chavan Prash   6000 Kgs
  6. Mritasanjivani   6000 Kgs
  7. Gandhkadi Malham   600 Kgs
b. Value   ₹2,64,36,000

Financial Aspects

A. Fixed Capital

i. Land and building   **(₹)**

	(₹)
Land 1000 sq. mt. @ ₹4,000	40,00,000
Covered Area 600 sq. mtr @ ₹10000	60,00,000
Total	**1,00,00,000**

ii. Machinery and equipments

Sl. No.	Description	Rate (₹)	Qty. (Nos.)	Price (₹)
1.	S.S Vat, 1,500 kg capacity	1,00,000	1	1,00,000
2.	S.S Vat, 750 kg capacity	70,000	1	70,000
3.	Fermenter 500 Lt cap.	60,000	1	60,000
4.	Sintered glass crucible	10,000	10	1,00,000
5.	Disintegrator with 7.5 H.P. size 22" with sieves of different mesh sizes	2,00,000	1	2,00,000
6.	Micro pulverizer with 5 H.P. and 2.5 H.P. motor	1,50,000	1	1,50,000

7.	Tablet making machine	1,00,000	1	1,00,000
8.	Bottle filling machine	5,00,000	1	5,00,000
9.	Bottle sealing machine	20,000	1	20,000
10.	S.S Pastle and motor	20,000	1	20,000
11.	S.S Mixing vessel with motor 200 litre capacity	1,50,000	1	1,50,000
12.	Distillation unit 500 Lt. cap. Electrically heated fitted with pipeline made of stainless steel AISI 316.12 kW	5,00,000	1	5,00,000
13.	Water treatment plant 100 liters cap.	3,00,000	1	3,00,000
14.	Filtering unit fitted with paper and cloth	50,000	1	50,000
15.	Furnace	50,000	2	1,00,000
16.	Weighing scale 100 kg cap.	40,000	1	40,000
17.	Weighing scale 10 kg cap.	35,000	1	35,000
18.	Glass jars with stopper 25 liters cap.	1,000	20	20,000
19.	Glass jars with lid 3 kg cap.	500	20	10,000
20.	Vessel covered 100 litres	10,000	5	50,000
21.	Air oven with 12 trays with 2.5 HP motor	50,000	1	50,000
22.	Bottle washing machine	1,50,000	1	1,50,000
23.	Bottle dryer	1,50,000	1	2,50,000
24.	Aluminium container for storage of powder, etc.	3,000	0	1,50,000
25.	Testing equipments			8,50,000
26.	Water, ETP, clean room, generator		LS	15,00,000
27.	Electrification and installation @ 10%			6,42,000
28.	Furniture and office equipment			5,00,000
29.	Pre-operative expenses			5,00,000
	Total			**71,67,000**

B. Working Capital (per month)

i. Staff and labour

Sl. No.	Description	Nos.	Salary (₹)	Total (₹)
1.	Manager-manufacturing chemist	1	20,000	20,000
2.	Analytical chemist	2	12,000	24,000
3.	Accountant-cum-typist	2	8,000	16,000
4.	Clerk-cum-typist	2	5,000	10,000
5.	Skilled workers	10	4,000	40,000
6.	Unskilled workers	12	3,500	42,000
7.	Watchman	4	4,000	16,000
8.	Sales representative	1	12,000	12,000
	Perquisites @ 15%			40,000
	Total			**2,20,000**

ii. Raw materials (per month)

Particulars	Ind.	Imp.	Qty.	Rate (₹)	Value (₹)
Raw materials, different parts of plants, drugs from animal origin, minerals, sugar, honey, etc. are available indigenously and consumables including packing materials like glass bottles, etc.	Ind.		–	–	10,00,000

iii.

Utilities	(₹)
1. Power	25,000
2. Fuel	15,000
3. Water	5,000
Total	45,000

iv. Other contingent expenses

	(₹)
1. Postage/Stationery	3,000
2. Travelling expenses and transport charges	50,000

3. Repair/Maintenance   12,000
4. Sales expenses   15,000
5. Advertisement/Publicity   25,000
6. Insurance   20,000
7. Consumable stores   15,000
    Total   **1,40,000**

v. Working capital (per month)   **(₹)**

1. Staff and labour   2,20,000
2. Raw material   10,00,000
3. Utilities   45,000
4. Other contingent expenses   1,40,000
    Total   **14,05,000**

vi. Working capital (for 3 months)   **42,15,000**

C. Total Capital Investment

    i. Fixed capital   ₹ 1,71,67,000
    ii. Working capital (for 3 months)   ₹ 42,15,000
    Total   **₹ 2,13,82,000**

Financial Analysis

1. **Cost of production (per year)**   **(₹)**
   - Total recurring expenditure   1,68,60,000
   - Depreciation on machinery and equipment @ 10%   6,67,000
   - Depreciation on furniture office 20%   1,00,000
   - Interest on total investment @ 12%   25,66,000
   - **Total**   **2,01,93,000**

2. **Total sale (per annum)**   **(₹)**

• Ashokarishta	6000 Bottles	750 ml.	@60	36,000
• Lakhibilas Ras (N)	400 kgs	10 gm.	@60	24,00,000
• Bhaskarlavan	12000 kgs	100 gm.	@90	1,08,00,000
• Sitopaladi Churan	6000 kgs	100 gm	@90	54,00,000
• Chyavan Prash	6000 kgs	100 gm	@60	36,00,000

- Mritasanjivani 6000 kgs 300 gm @120 24,00,000
- Gandhkadi 300 kgs 10 gm @60 18,00,000
  Malham
  Total 2,64,36,000

3. Profit (per annum)

$$₹2,64,36,000 - ₹2,01,93,000 = ₹62,43,000$$

4. Rate of return

$$= \frac{\text{Net profit per year}}{\text{Total investment}} \times 100$$

$$= \frac{62,43,000}{2,13,82,000} \times 100 = 29.2\%$$

5. Net profit ratio

$$= \frac{\text{Profit per year}}{\text{Turn over per year}}$$

$$= \frac{62,43,000}{2,64,36,000} \times 100 = 23.6\%$$

6. Break-even point

• Fixed cost	(₹)
Depreciation on machinery and equipment @ 10%	6,67,000
Furniture and office equipment @ 20%	1,00,000
Interest 12% p.a.	25,66,000
Staff and labour @ 40%	10,56,000
Miscellaneous @ 40%	6,72,000
Total	**50,61,000**

$$\text{B.E.P} = \frac{FC \times 100}{FC + \text{Profit}}$$

$$= \frac{50,61,000 \times 100}{50,61,000 + 62,43,000}$$

$$= \frac{50,61,000}{1,13,09,000} \times 100 = 44.7\%$$

27

Technology Transfer

INTRODUCTION

In the pharmaceutical industry, *"technology transfer"* refers to the processes that are needed for successful progress from drug discovery to product development to *clinical trials* to full-scale commercialization or it is the process by which a developer of technology makes its technology available to commercial partner that will exploit the technology.

The importances of technology transfer are:
- To elucidate necessary information to transfer technology from R and D to actual manufacturing by sorting out various information obtained during R and D.
- To elucidate necessary information to transfer technology of existing products between various manufacturing places.
- To exemplify specific procedures and points of concern for the two types of technology transfer in the above to contribute to smooth technology transfer. This is *applicable* to the technology transfer through R and D and production of drug (chemically synthesized drug substances and drug products) and the technology transfer related to post-marketing changes in manufacturing places.

Various *stages* of formulation development are as follows:
1. Preformulation studies
2. Bench scale (1/1000th of X)
3. Lab scale (1/100th of X)
4. Scale up (1/10th of X or 0.1M whichever is maximum)
5. Commercial (X)

Where X is the final *commercial scale* batch size.

Technology transfer process: Technology transfer is both integral and critical to the drug discovery and development process for new medicinal products. The decision to transfer products between manufacturing sites is frequently driven by economics. Key stages of the process include data collection, data review, regulatory impact with particular emphasis on any change approvals, analytical validation, pilot or full-scale process batch, stability set down (if required). Typical technology transfer process is described in Fig. 27.1.

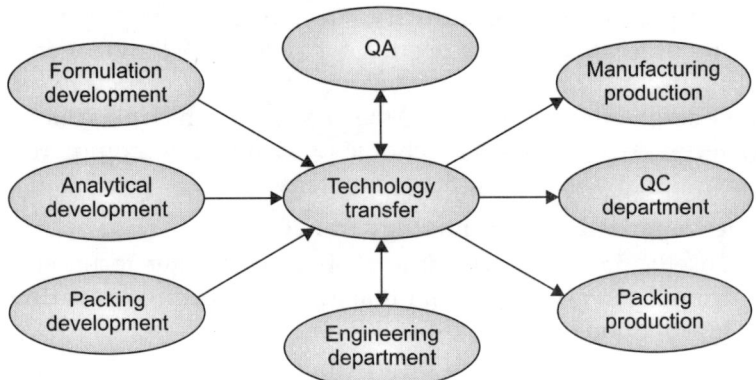

Fig. 27.1: Typical technology transfer flow chart

For a typical research-based pharmaceutical company, drug discovery and development can be broken down into distinct stages which are clearly described in Fig. 27.2.

1. **Research phase**
   a. Quality design.
2. **Development phase**
   a. Research for factory production
   b. Consistency between quality and specification
   c. Assurance of consistency through development and manufacturing
   d. Technology transfer from R and D to production
3. **Production phase**
   a. Validation and production
   b. Feedback from production and technology transfer of marketed products

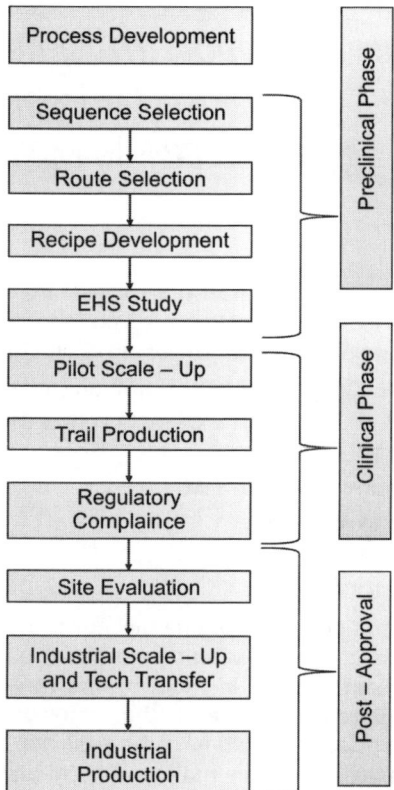

Fig. 27.2: Typical process development work flow in pharmaceutical industry

28 Career Opportunity as Drugs Inspector (6 Posts)
Require B.Pharm, M.Pharm

Online recruitment applications (ORA) are invited from the desirous and eligible candidates for recruitment to various posts in various departments of HP Government up to 11th November, 2013 till 11:59 p.m.

Name of the post: Drugs inspector class-II (Gazetted)

Number of posts: 06 posts (UR = 03, SC of HP = 01, OBC of HP = 01 and UR Ex-SM of HP = 01)

Contractual amount: ₹14,500/- P.M.

Age: Between 18 to 45 years

Essential Qualifications

Bachelor's degree in pharmacy or pharmaceutical chemistry or a post-graduate degree in chemistry with pharmaceutics as essential subject of an University established in India by the law or its equivalent qualification recognized and notified by the central government for such purpose or the associateship diploma of the institution of chemists (India) obtained by passing the examination with "Analysis of drugs and pharmaceuticals" as one of the subject.

OR

Bachelor's degree in science or graduate in medicine of an University recognized for this purpose by the appointing authority and has had at least one year's post-graduate training in a laboratory under (i) a Government analyst appointed under the act, or (ii) a chemical examiner, or (iii) the head of an institution specifically approved for the purpose by the appointing authority, provided that only those inspectors:

(i) Who have not less than 18 months experience in the manufacture of at least one of the substances specified in Schedule-C or

(ii) Who have not less than 18 months experience in testing of at least one of the substances specified in Schedule–C in a laboratory approved for this purpose, by the licensing authority or

(iii) Who have gained experience of not less than three years in the inspection of firm manufacturing any of the substances specified in Schedule-C appended to these rules during the tenure of their service as drugs inspectors shall be authorized to inspect the manufacture of the substances mentioned in schedule-C.

Desirable qualification: Knowledge of customs, manners and dialects of H.P. and suitability for appointment in the peculiar conditions prevailing in the Pradesh.

How to Apply

(a) Desirous/eligible candidates must apply online through the **website hp.gov.in/hppsc**. Applications received through any other mode would not be accepted and summarily rejected. Detailed instructions for filling up online recruitment applications are available on the above mentioned website. (b) Candidates who wish to apply for more than one post should apply separately for each post and pay the fee for each post in the prescribed manner. (c) After submitting the online recruitment application (ORA), the candidates are required to take a printout of the finally submitted online recruitment application and submit the same alongwith requisite attested documents/certificates in support of their eligibility to the commission on the day of screening test for the concerned post. (d) In case the candidate has applied against more than one item, i.e. post published in the advertisement, the candidate is required to submit separate copies of requisite attested documents/certificates alongwith the printout of the online recruitment application of each post on the day of screening test for the respective posts.

Examination Fees

The detail of fee for respective categories is as under:

Sr. no.	Category	Fees
1.	General category {including general physically disabled, i.e. orthopaedically disabled, deaf and dumb, hearing impaired/W.F.F. of HP/Ex-servicemen relieved from defence services on their own request before completion of normal tenure and candidates of other states (including reserved category candidates of other states)}	₹400
2.	S.C. of H.P./S.T. of H.P./O.B.C. of H.P. (including S.C./S.T./O.B.C. Ex-Servicemen of H.P. relieved from defence services on their own requests before completion of normal tenure)	₹100
3.	Ex-Servicemen of H.P. (Ex-Servicemen, who are relieved from defence services after completion of normal tenure)/ Blind of H.P./Visually Impaired of H.P.	No Fee

Mode of payment: The candidates can deposit the requisite fee at any branch of Punjab National Bank through an e-Challan generated through the website of the commission, i.e. **www.hp.gov.in/hppsc** and its transaction no., branch code and date of receipt are required to be updated before the last date in the same login ID in the fee details link. Before applying online, all candidates are advised to go through detailed instructions given on the above mentioned website.

Eligibility Conditions

(i) The date of determining the eligibility of all candidates in terms of essential qualification, experience, etc. shall be reckoned as on the closing date, **11th November, 2013** for submitting the online recruitment applications (ORA) on the **website hp.gov.in/hppsc**.

(ii) The decision of the commission regarding eligibility etc. of a candidate for admission to viva-voice/personality test or selection will be final and no correspondence/personal enquiries will be entertained.

(iii) Onus of proving that a candidate has acquired requisite degree/essential qualification by the stipulated date is on the candidate and in the absence of proof to the contrary, the date as mentioned on the face of certificate/degree or the date of issue of certificate/degree shall be taken as date of acquiring essential qualification. No extra opportunity shall be provided to the candidates to produce appropriate certificates at the time of interview.

(iv) In respect of equivalent clause in essential qualifications, if a candidate is claiming a particular qualification as equivalent qualification as per the requirement of advertisement, then the candidate is required to produce order/letter in this regard, indicating the authority (with number and date) under which it has been so treated otherwise the online recruitment application is liable to be rejected.

Closing date for submission of online recruitment applications (ORA) through ORA website is upto **11th November, 2013 till 11:59 p.m**. After which the link will be disabled (by using the **website hp.gov.in/hppsc**).*

*Date for determining the eligibility of all candidates in every respect shall be the prescribed closing date for submisison of online recruitment application (ORA), i.e. **11th November, 2013**.*

Medical Devices Rules, 2017

No. DCG (I/Misc./2017 (68)
Central Drugs Standard Control Organisation
Directorate General of Health Services
Office of Drugs Controller General India
FDA Bhawan, Kotla Road, New Delhi

Dated: 29th June, 2017

NOTICE

The Drugs & Cosmetics Act, 1940 is an Act to regulate import, manufacture, distribution and sale of drugs and cosmetics. It extends to the whole of India. Further, the Drugs & Cosmetics Rules, 1945 have been put in place which are updated from time to time for uniform implementation of the statutory requirements. The devices intended for internal or external use in the diagnosis, treatment, mitigation or prevention of disease or disorder in human beings or animals, as may be specified from time to time by the Central Govt. by notification in official Gazette, after consultation with the Board, fall under the definition of drug. The list of devices notified so far are appended below:

S. no.   Name of the device
1.   Disposable hypodermic syringes
2.   Disposable hypodermic needles
3.   Disposable perfusion sets
4.   *In vitro* diagnostic devices for HIV, HbsAg and HCV
5.   Cardiac stents
6.   Drug eluting stents
7.   Catheters
8.   Intraocular lenses

9. IV cannulae
10. Bone cements
11. Heart valves
12. Scalp vein set
13. Orthopedic implants
14. Internal prosthetic replacements
15. Ablation device.

The Medical Devices Rules, 2017* have been notified and would come into force with effect from 1st day of January, 2018. Criteria for Classification of medical devices including *in vitro* diagnostics have been specified in Rule 4, Chapter II of the rules which deals with regulation of Medical Devices in India context and in line with International Classification. A draft list of Medical Devices and *in vitro* diagnostics along with their risk based classification is annexed.

It is expected that the importers, manufacturers, distributors and supply chain personnel shall voluntarily adhere with the safety, performance and quality aspects as stated in the said medical devices Rule, 2017 for creating proper eco-system for its effective regulation.

In order to facilitate the process a special cell has also been created consisting of concerned JDC (I), DDC (I) and ADC (I) to address the issues, if any.

Signed
Drug Controller General (India)

To
1. All State/UT Drugs Controllers
2. All Medical Devices and Diagnostic Associations

Copy to:
i. PPS to Secretary (H&FW)/DGHS/AS & DG (CGHS)/JS (R)
ii. CDSCO website

ANNEXURE

DRAFT LIST OF MEDICAL DEVICES AND *IN VITRO* DIAGNOSTICS ALONG WITH THEIR RISK CLASS

A. List of Medical Devices Along with their Risk Class

S. no.	Device Name	Risk Class	Intended Use
1.	Vein ablation device	Class C	It is a non-thermal, minimally-invasive choice for treating the source of varicose veins, providing patients with immediate recovery and a return to normal daily routines
2.	Thermal ablation device	Class C	Destruction of tissue by application of heat. Ablation of the endometrium as a treatment for menorrhagia is performed by placing a balloon filled with hot water in the uterine cavity
3.	Radiofrequency ablation device	Class D	A medical procedure in which part of the electrical conduction system of the heart, tumour or other dysfunctional tissue is ablated using the heat generated from high frequency alternating current
4.	Percutaneous conduction tissue ablation	Class D	Clinical applications using hollow needles (cryoprobes) through which cooled, thermally conductive, fluids are circulated
5.	Suction ablation catheter system	Class D	Intended for use in inactivating portions of the heart's conduction system to prevent abnormal heartbeat rates, comprises a tubular body having an open, distal end and a proximal aperture for applying suction through the catheter and through the distal end
6.	Fiberoptic oximeter catheter	Class D	Intended for monitoring the balance between oxygen delivery and consumption at the bedside

7.	Injector type actuator syringe	Class C	A syringe actuator for an injector is an electrical device that controls the timing of an injection by an angiographic or indicator injector and synchronizes the injection with the electrocardiograph signal
8.	A-V shunt or fistula adapter	Class B	A blood access device and accessories is a device intended to provide access to a patient's blood for haemodialysis or other chronic uses
9.	Enteral infusion pump	Class B	The device designed to provide nutrition to patients who are unable to ingest food, either because of recent surgery or because of the inability of various digestive organs to function properly
10.	Transcervical (aminoscope) endoscope and accessories	Class B	It is a device designed to permit direct viewing of the foetus and amniotic sac by means of an open tube introduced into the uterus through the cervix
11.	Forceps, endoscopic	Class B	Grasping forceps device is intended to be used to grasp tissue, retrieve foreign bodies, and remove tissue from within the gastrointestinal tract
12.	Transabdominal (fetoscope) aminoscope and accessories	Class C	It is a device designed to permit direct visual examination of the foetus by a telescopic system via abdominal entry. The device is used to ascertain foetal abnormalities
13.	Anastomosis device for microvascular surgery	Class C	Suitable in microvascular surgery for repairing severed blood vessels and inserting vein grafts
14.	Anastomosis device for gastroenterology urology use	Class C	It is a surgical procedure to establish communication between two formerly distant portions of the intestine
15.	Anastomotic microvascular device	Class B	It uses in the anastomosis of veins and arteries normally encountered in microsurgical procedures
16.	Anaesthetic conduction kit	Class C	An anaesthesia conduction kit is a device used to administer to a patient conduction, regional, or local anaesthesia. The device may contain syringes, needles, and drugs

17.	Angiographic guide wire and accessories	Class B	It delivers radio-opaque media and therapeutic agents to selected sites in the vascular system. It is also used to lead a guide wire or a catheter into the target site
18.	Cardiac catherization kit	Class D	Cardiac catheterization is a general term for a group of procedures that are performed using this method, such as coronary angiography and left ventricle angiography
19.	Vessel dilator for percutaneous catheterization	Class B	A vessel dilator for percutaneous catheterization is a device which is placed over the guide wire to enlarge the opening in the vessel, and which is then removed before sliding the catheter over the guide wire
20.	Angioscope	Class B	Used to visually examine the interior of a blood vessel
21.	Aspiration needle and syringe	Class B	Used for either laparoscopic aspiration or injection
22.	Ophthalmic laser and accessories	Class C	An ophthalmic laser is an AC-powered device intended to coagulate or cut tissue of the eye, orbit, or surrounding skin by a laser beam
23.	Tracheobronchial suction catheter	Class B	Clearing the airways of mucus, pus, or aspirated materials to improve oxygenation and ventilation
24.	Cervical drain	Class B	The device is used to avoid postoperative wound and respiratory complications such as excessive edema, hematoma, infection, re-intubation, delayed extubation, or respiratory distress
25.	Rectal balloon	Class B	Reducing the intrafraction motion and improving the sparing of rectal wall by reducing the rectal volume in the high-dose region, resulting in significant reduction in rectal toxicity
26.	Balloon for cerebrovascular occlusion	Class D	Balloon used to treat blockage or closing of cerebrovascular vessels/ carotid arteries

27.	Intra-aortic system balloon and control	Class D	It is a mechanical device that increases myocardial oxygen perfusion while at the same time increasing cardiac output
28.	Biliary stone retrieval basket	Class B	Intend to extract stones in an antegrade fashion through an ampullary orifice previously treated by endoscopic sphincterotomy or less commonly with balloon dilation
29.	Contact lens bifola and daily	Class B	Worn to correct vision, or for cosmetic or therapeutic reasons
30.	Blood administration kits	Class B	It is used to administer blood from a container to a patient's vascular system through a needle or catheter inserted into a vein
31.	Biopsy kit	Class B	Involving sampling of cells or tissues for examination
32.	Bolster suture	Class A	Non-latex plastic bolsters are used to hinder pressure of any temporary suture against the body during surgery
33.	Embolic particles system	Class C	Embolization particles are small and irregular flakes of polyvinyl alcohol, which are used for permanent occlusion within a blood vessel
34.	Tracheostomy tube/tracheal tube	Class B	A breathing tube inserted into a tracheotomy used to obtain a closed circuit for ventilation
35.	Irrigating syringes	Class B	Cleaning debris away from the area the dentist is working on
36.	Intravenous cannula	Class B	The IV cannula is a passive device to provide for the infusion of fluids, drugs, and/or blood components, or to facilitate the placement of vascular access devices
37.	Cyclodialysis eye cannula	Class A	It is useful in the treatment of glaucoma where it creates a channel between the anterior chamber of the eye and the subarachnoidal space
38.	Vial adapter	Class B	It is indicated to allow multiple needleless access to injection medication vials for transfer or withdrawal of fluids from the vial

39.	Suprapubic, non-disposable cannula and trocar	Class B	An emergency measure for the relief of acute urinary retention or condition which require temporary and permanent drainage of bladder
40.	Aortic cannula	Class B	The aortic cannula is a passive device to provide for the infusion of fluids, drugs, and/or blood components or to provide access to the aorta
41.	Arterial cannula	Class B	Inserted into an artery, commonly the radial artery, and is used during major operations and in critical care areas to measure beat-to-beat blood pressure and to draw repeated blood samples
42.	Coronary artery cannula	Class B	Cannulation technique for left-sided coronary artery surgery
43.	Arthroscopy drainage cannula	Class B	It is designed to provide maximized outflow, without interruption, during arthroscopic procedures (surgical procedure on a joint)
44.	Lacrimal cannula	Class B	Used for probing and irrigating the lachrymal passages
45.	Hemodialysis cannula	Class B	Allowing the arterial blood to flow to the dialyzer and the dialyzed blood to return from the dialyzer to the circulation through the cannula in the vein
46.	Cannula injection	Class B	It is a small tube with an edge that is not sharp and an extrusion port or pore near the tip which is designed for a traumatic subdermal injections of fluids or gels
47.	Uterine insufflation cannula	Class B	An Injection of radiopaque medium is given to visualize the interior of the uterus and fallopian tubes and air is used for insufflations of fallopian tubes with carbon dioxide to test their patency
48.	Continuous positive airway pressure nasal oxygen cannula	Class B	It is a form of positive airway pressure ventilator, which applies mild air pressure on a continuous basis to keep the airways continuously open in a person who is able to breathe spontaneously on their own

49.	Nasal oxygen cannula	Class B	It is a device used to deliver supplemental oxygen or increased airflow to a patient or person in need of respiratory help
50.	General and plastic surgery cannula	Class B	Used for general surgery and cosmetic surgery
51.	Vena cava cannula	Class B	Inserted into vena cava, taking deoxygenated blood to heart
52.	Venous cannula	Class B	It is intended for use as a single cannula for both venous drainage and reinfusion of blood via an internal jugular vein during extracorporeal life support procedures
53.	Ventricular cannula	Class B	For use in neurosurgical procedures. It is specially designed to penetrate delicate brain tissue and give continued access to brain's ventricular system
54.	Bronchial cannulae	Class B	A cannula used for holding the suction tube during the aspiration of bronchial secretions through a specific diameter bronchoscope
55.	Endoscopic/ laparoscopic surgical instrument	Class B	An electrosurgical cutting and coagulation device and accessories is a device intended to remove tissue and control bleeding by use of high-frequency electrical current
56.	Intrafallopian system cannula	Class B	Cannula inserted inside fallopian tube
57.	A-V shunt cannula	Class C	It is inserted into one of the client's blood vessels to facilitator repeated hemodialysis
58.	Cannulact or lymph duct	Class B	A lymph duct is a great lymphatic vessel that empties lymph into one of the subclavian veins
59.	Nasopharyngeal catheter/ nasopharyngeal	Class A	A catheter (for adults) passed through the nares and advanced to the depth of the nasopharynx to remove air choke or obstruction.
60.	Esophageal obturator	Class B	A resuscitator inserted through a patient's mouth to aid ventilation of the patient during emergency resuscitation by occluding (blocking) the esophagus, thereby permitting positive pressure ventilation through the trachea

61.	Oropharyngeal	Class B	The device inserted into a patient's pharynx through the mouth to provide a patent airway
62.	Cricothyrotomy kit	Class B	Indicated to provide emergency airway access when conventional ventilation by intubation or face mask cannot be performed
63.	Incontinence urosheath device	Class A	A urine collector and accessories is a device intended to collect urine. The device and accessories consist of tubing, a suitable receptacle, connectors, mechanical supports, and may include a means to prevent the backflow of urine or ascent of infection
64.	Balloon catheter for retinal reattachment	Class B	An instrument for reattachment of a detached retina to the inner wall of the eyeball. It can be inserted into the interior of the eyeball
65.	Gastric, colonic, etc.) irrigation and aspiration catheter	Class B	Used for instilling fluids into, withdrawing fluids from, splinting, or suppressing bleeding of the alimentary tract
66.	Suction tip and catheter	Class B	Suction catheters feature a whistle tip and a thumb control port for precise and accurate suctioning
67.	Angiographic catheter	Class B	Designed to provide a pathway for delivering contrast media to selected sites in the device vascular system including the carotid arteries
68.	Arterial catheter	Class B	Intended to be used in conjunction with steerable guidewires in order to access discrete regions of the coronary and peripheral arterial vasculature, to facilitate placement and exchange of guidewires and other interventional devices
69.	Balloon type catheter	Class B	"Soft" catheter with an inflatable "balloon" at its tip which is used during a catheterization procedure to enlarge a narrow opening or passage within the body

70.	Balloon dilation vessel catheter	Class B	Intended for use in percutaneous transluminal angioplasty of the renal, tibial, popliteal, femoral and peroneal arteries. These catheters are not for use in coronary arteries
71.	Bartholin gland catheter	Class B	Catheter is used for the treatment of abscesses and cysts of the Bartholin gland
72.	Bronchography catheter	Class B	Intended to deliver therapeutic and diagnostic agents that are indicated or labeled for airway, tracheal or bronchial delivery into selected and sub-selected regions of the airway tree
73.	Cholangiography catheter	Class B	Diagnostic evaluation of the bile ducts during laparoscopic cholecystectomy procedures
74.	Anesthetic conduction catheter	Class B	An anesthesia conduction catheter is a flexible tubular device used to inject local anesthetics into a patient and to provide continuous regional anesthesia
75.	Anesthesia conduction filter	Class C	A microporous filter used while administering to a patient injections of local anesthetics to minimize particulate (foreign material) contamination of the injected fluid
76.	Anesthesia conduction kit	Class C	Intended for use in the administration of anesthetic agents into the epidural space
77.	Continuous flush catheter	Class B	Intended for the controlled and selective infusion of physician-specified fluids, including thrombolytics, into the peripheral vasculature
78.	Continuous irrigation catheter	Class B	Intended to be used to introduce fluids into body cavities other than blood vessels, drain fluids from body cavities, or evaluate certain physiologic conditions.
79.	Coude catheters	Class B	It is a urinary catheter, It may be used to inject liquids used for treatment or diagnosis of bladder conditions

80.	Depezzer catheter	Class B	A tubular, flexible instrument, passed through body channels for withdrawal of fluids from a body cavity
81.	Double lumen female urethrographic catheter	Class B	Intended for vascular access infusion and withdrawal of blood, blood products, and fluids, plasma pheresis, hyperalimentation, central venous blood sampling and continuous and intermittent drag infusion
82.	Epidural catheter	Class B	Epidural catheter is a very thin, flexible tube that is implanted into spine
83.	Esophageal balloon catheter	Class B	Intended for use in adult and adolescent populations to endoscopically dilate strictures of the esophagus
84.	Eustachian catheter	Class B	It is used to test Eustachian tube patency
85.	Guiding catheter	Class B	The guide catheter provides support for device advancement
86.	Haemodialysis catheter	Class B	A catheter used for exchanging blood to and from the haemodialysis machine from the patient
87.	Intramuscular pressure monitoring catheter	Class B	A modified fibre optic transducer-tipped catheter system for measuring intramuscular pressures during exercise was determined
88.	Introducer sheath	Class C	Intended to provide easier access to the femoral, popliteal and infrapopliteal arteries
89.	Intravenous catheter	Class B	A catheter that is inserted into a vein for supplying medications or nutrients directly into the bloodstream or for diagnostic purposes such as studying blood pressure
90.	Jejunostomy catheter	Class B	Used for intraoperative feeding jejunostomy
91.	Multiple lumen catheter	Class B	Intended for monitoring central venous pressure (CVP), sampling blood, and simultaneous administration of multiple IV solutions or drugs

92.	Nasal oxygen catheter	Class B	It is a device used to deliver supplemental oxygen or increased airflow to a patient or person in need of respiratory help
93.	Nephrostomy catheter	Class B	A nephrostomy is a tube that's used to drain urine from a kidney into a bag outside the body
94.	Peritoneal dialysis catheter	Class B	That allows dialysis fluid to enter the abdominal cavity, dwell inside for a while, and then drain back out again
95.	Radiographic (non-vascular) catheter	Class B	Interventional radiologists obtain images using needles and narrow tubes called catheters, rather than by making large incisions into the body as in traditional surgery
96.	Rectal catheter	Class B	It is inserted into the rectum in order to relieve flatulence which has been chronic and which has not been alleviated by other methods
97.	Retention type catheter	Class B	This type of catheter is placed into the bladder and secured there for a period of time
98.	Retention type balloon catheter	Class B	It has a balloon at the distal end, which is inflated with sterile water or saline to prevent the catheter from slipping out of the bladder
99.	Salpingography catheter	Class B	Used for injection of contrast medium into the fallopian tube(s) for selective salpingography
100.	Single needle hemodialysis catheter/blood lines	Class B	The single-needle dialysis, in which case only one cannula or a single-lumen catheter is used to access the blood
101.	Straight catheter	Class B	It is used in patients with neurogenic bladder or spinal cord injury, lessens the risk of urinary tract infection
102.	Subclavian catheter	Class B	Catheters can be placed in veins in the neck (internal jugular vein), chest (subclavian vein or auxiliary vein)
103.	Suprapubic catheter	Class B	A suprapubic catheter is a thin, sterile tube used to drain urine from bladder

104.	Umbilical artery catheter	Class B	Umbilical artery catheterization provides direct access to the arterial blood supply and allows accurate measurement of arterial blood pressure, a source of arterial blood sampling, and intravascular access for fluids and medications
105.	Umbilical occlusion device	Class A	These devices may be a clip, tie, tape, or other article used to close the blood vessels in the umbilical cord of a newborn infant
106.	Upper urinary tract catheter	Class B	The catheter to the bladder and subsequently to the upper urinary tract
107.	Urethral catheter/ Nelaton catheter/ Foley catheter	Class B	A long, small gauge catheter designed for insertion directly into a ureter, either through the urethra and bladder or posteriorly via the kidney
108.	Urethrographic male catheter	Class B	A catheter used to pass into a man's bladder
109.	Chorionic villus sampling catheter	Class B	An ultrasound guides a thin catheter through the cervix to your placenta. The chorionic villi cells are gently suctioned into the catheter
110.	Percutaneous retrieval device	Class B	Embolization of the occlusion device after percutaneous closure of atrial septal defect (ASD) is a potential disastrous complication
111.	Sclerotherapy needle/catheter	Class B	Sclerotherapy needles are designed to provide access for injection therapy applications and may also be used for polypectomy and endoscopic mucosal resection (EMR)
112.	Water jet renal catheter	Class B	A device used to dislodge stones from renal calyces (recesses of the pelvis of the kidney) by means of a pressurized stream of water through a conduit
113.	Hemodialysis catheter (long-term)	Class C	A dialysis catheter is a catheter used for exchanging blood to and from the hemodialysis machine from the patient. The dialysis catheter contains two lumens: Venous. Arterial

114.	Percutaneous intravascular long-term catheter	Class C	The device allows for repeated access to the vascular system for long-term use of 30 days or more, and it is intended for administration of fluids, medications, and nutrients; the sampling of blood
115.	Percutaneous long-term intraspinal catheter	Class C	To conduct a preimplant intraspinal infusion screening trial procedure prior to implanting a pump
116.	Implanted subcutaneous intravascular port and catheter	Class C	The device allows for repeated access to the vascular system for the infusion of fluids and medications and the sampling of blood
117.	Subcutaneous intraspinal port and catheter	Class C	Catheters used for both epidural intrathecal infusion include short-term externalized catheters and long-term catheters that are tunnelled in the subcutaneous tissue
118.	Peripheral, transluminal angioplasty catheter	Class D	A catheter for treating peripheral vascular diseases
119.	Cardiac thermodilution catheter	Class D	A catheter used in thermodilution for introduction of the cold liquid indicator into the cardiovascular system
120.	Cardiovascular catheter	Class D	A thin, hollow tube called a catheter is inserted into a large blood vessel that leads to heart
121.	Cerebrospinal catheter	Class D	For treatment or prevention of cranial/spinal cerebrospinal fluid fistula
122.	Atherectomy coronary catheter	Class D	A catheter containing a rotating cutter and a collecting chamber for debris, used for atherectomy and endarterectomy
123.	Electrode recording probe, electrode recording catheter	Class D	A cardiac catheter containing one or more electrodes; it may be used to pace the heart or to deliver high energy shocks
124.	Embolectomy catheter	Class D	Indicated for the removal of fresh, soft emboli and thrombi from vessels in the arterial system
125.	Flow directed catheter	Class D	Used for venous sampling and pressure monitoring

126.	Ultrasonic imaging catheter	Class D	Intended for ultrasound examination of peripheral pathology only
127.	Intra-aortic balloon catheter	Class D	It is indicated for use in patients undergoing cardiopulmonary bypass
128.	Intracardiac mapping, high density array catheter	Class D	A high density array catheter once used in the right atrium to map and diagnosis complex arrhythmias and assess the effectiveness of ablation treatment
129.	Intravascular occluding catheter	Class D	It is a catheter with an inflatable or detachable balloon tip that is used to block a blood vessel to treat malformations, e.g. aneurysms of intracranial blood vessels
130.	Intravascular diagnostic catheter	Class D	Used to record intracardiac pressures, to sample blood, and to introduce substances into the heart and vessels
131.	Occlusion catheter	Class D	Insertion of a device or develop at any time during the course of intravenous (IV) therapy
132.	Percutaneous catheter	Class D	A needle catheter getting access to a blood vessel, followed by the introduction of a wire through the lumen (pathway) of the needle
133.	Perfusion catheter	Class D	Perfusion catheter allowing localised perfusion of drugs not only into the vessel lumen, but also directly into the vessel wall at low pressure, during coronary intervention
134.	Pericardium drainage catheter	Class D	Catheter drainage of the pericardium
135.	Atherectomy peripheral catheter	Class D	Intended for use in atherectomy of the peripheral vasculature
136.	Septostomy catheter	Class D	Used to enlarge interatrial openings
137.	Thrombectomy catheter	Class D	Thrombectomy catheter is specifically designed to treat deep vein thrombosis (DVT) in large-diameter upper and lower peripheral veins
138.	Transluminal, coronary angioplasty, percutaneous catheter	Class D	The catheter is placed in the opening or ostium of one the coronary arteries

139.	Ventricular catheter	Class C	It is used to monitor pressure in patients with brain injuries, intracranial bleeds or other brain abnormalities that lead to increased fluid build-up
140.	Balloon repair kit catheter	Class C	A device used to repair or replace the balloon of a balloon catheter. The kit contains the materials, such as glue and balloons, necessary to affect the repair or replacement
141.	Pacemaker lead (catheter)	Class D	A catheter that is inserted near your collarbone or through your leg (groin) artery
142.	Microcatheter	Class C	It is intended to access the peripheral and neurovasculature for the controlled selective infusion of physician-specified therapeutic agents such as embolization materials and or diagnostic materials such as contrast media
143.	Imaging catheter	Class C	Intended for use with the various medical imaging consoles
144.	Central nervous system shunt including neurological catheters and other components	Class D	It is a device or combination of devices used to divert fluid from the brain or other part of the central nervous system to an internal delivery site or an external receptacle for the purpose of relieving elevated intracranial pressure or fluid volume
145.	Angiographic injector and syringe	Class B	It is a device used to inject contrast material into the heart, great vessels, and coronary arteries to study the heart and vessels by X-ray photography
146.	Autotransfusion apparatus	Class B	It is a device used to collect and reinfuse the blood lost by a patient due to surgery or trauma
147.	Colonoscope (Gastrourology)	Class B	The endoscopic examination of the large bowel and the distal part of the small bowel with a CCD camera or a fibre optic camera on a flexible tube passed through the anus
148.	Disposable hypodermic syringes	Class B	Intend to inject fluids into or withdraw fluids from the body

149.	Transfusion or perfusion sets for single use	Class B	Transfusion set is used to administer blood/drugs to a patient's vascular system through a needle or catheter inserted into a vein
150.	Custom perfusion system	Class C	Indicated for use in the extracorporeal circuit during cardiopulmonary bypass surgery procedure
151.	Sealant, pit and fissure	Class C	Sealant is a protective plastic coating, which is applied to the biting surfaces of the back teeth
152.	Contraceptive occlusion tubal device	Class C	A contraceptive tubal occlusion device (TOD) and introducer is a device designed to close a fallopian tube with a mechanical structure. The devices are used to prevent pregnancy
153.	Suture non-absorable synthetic	Class C	Non-absorbable suture is comprised of surgical steel as well as synthetic non-absorbable sutures for use in general soft tissue approximation and ligation
154.	Suture absorable	Class C	The device is intended for use in general soft tissue approximation and ligation
155.	Dialysate tubing and connector	Class B	A tubing connector adapted for peritoneal dialysis connections between tubing sets and containers of dialysate
156.	Semi-automatic peritoneal dialysate delivery system	Class C	The source of dialysate may be sterile prepackaged dialysate or dialysate prepared from dialysate concentrate and sterile purified water
157.	Peritoneal automatic delivery system	Class C	Controls and monitors the dialysate circulating through the dialysate compartment of the dialyzer
158.	Peritoneal dialysis unit	Class B	Peritoneal dialysis (PD) is a treatment for patients with severe chronic kidney disease
159.	Hollow fiber capillary dialyzer	Class C	Intended for single use acute and chronic haemodialysis
160.	Penrose drain	Class B	A penrose drain is a surgical device, placed in a wound to drain fluid

161.	Sump drain	Class B	A drain consisting of an outer tube vented to the outside with a smaller tube within it that is attached to a suction pump; both have multiple perforations that allow fluid and air to be carried away through the suction tube
162.	Vent drain	Class B	To release or discharge (e.g. steam) through an opening
163.	Urinary drainage unit	Class A	A closed urinary drainage system consists of a catheter inserted into the urinary bladder and connected via tubing to a drainage bag
164.	Wound drainage and closed drainage system	Class B	Intended for evacuation of biological fluid from wound or body cavity during surgical procedure or in wound care management
165.	Tympanostomy tube	Class C	It is a small tube inserted into the eardrum in order to keep the middle ear aerated for a prolonged period of time, and to prevent the accumulation of fluid in the middle ear
166.	Embolic protection device	Class D	Embolic protection devices are used to capture and remove debris that becomes dislodged during an interventional procedure
167.	Artificial embolization device	Class D	Used for the treatment of unresectable/inoperable hypervascularized tumours.
168.	Pharynscope	Class A	An instrument for inspecting the pharynx
169.	Anoscope	Class B	It is inserted a few inches into the anus in order to evaluate problems of the anal canal
170.	Choledochoscope	Class B	Used to see into the central bile duct which is a narrow channel
171.	Cystourethroscope	Class B	An endoscope used for the visual examination of the posterior urethra and bladder
172.	Endoscope and accessories	Class B	An endoscope and accessories is a device used to provide access, illumination, and allow observation or manipulation of body cavities, hollow organs, and canals

173.	Fibreoptic endoscope	Class B	An endoscope can consist of A rigid or flexible tube. A light delivery system to illuminate the organ or object under inspection. The light source is normally outside the body and the light is typically directed via an optical fibre system
174.	Neurological endoscope	Class B	A neurological endoscope is an instrument with a light source used to view the inside of the ventricles of the brain
175.	Transcervical (amnioscope) and accessories	Class B	A transcervical endoscope is a device designed to permit direct viewing of the foetus and amniotic sac by means of an open tube introduced into the uterus through the cervix
176.	Oesophagus gastro suodenoscope	Class B	To examine the lining of oesophagus, stomach, and duodenum. The oesophagus is the muscular tube that connects your throat to stomach and the duodenum, which is the upper part of small intestine
177.	Esophagoscope	Class B	An endoscope for inspecting the interior of the oesophagus
178.	Gastroscope	Class B	An endoscope for inspecting the interior of the stomach
179.	Hysteroscope	Class B	An endoscope used for the visual examination of the cervix and interior of the uterus
180.	Laparoscope	Class B	A usually rigid endoscope that is inserted through an incision in the abdominal wall and is used to examine visually the interior of the peritoneal cavity—called also peritoneoscope
181.	Mediastinoscope	Class B	An endoscope used in mediastinoscopy
182.	Panendoscope	Class B	A cystoscope that gives a wide-angle view of the bladder.
183.	Peritoneoscope	Class B	A usually rigid endoscope that is inserted through an incision in the abdominal wall and is used to examine visually the interior of the peritoneal cavity—called also peritoneoscope

184.	Proctoscope	Class B	An instrument used for dilating and visually inspecting the rectum and lower portion of the sigmoid colon
185.	Resectoscope	Class B	An instrument consisting of a tubular fenestrated sheath with a sliding knife within it that is used for surgery within cavities
186.	Fiberoptic intubation scope	Class B	Fiberoptic intubation involves threading an endotracheal tube over the shaft of a flexible fiberoptic scope
187.	Nephroscope	Class B	An endoscope used for inspecting and passing instruments into the interior of the kidney
188.	Sigmoidoscope	Class B	An endoscope designed to be passed through the anus in order to permit inspection, diagnosis, treatment, and photography especially of the sigmoid colon—called also proctosigmoidoscope
189.	Sphyncteroscope	Class B	An endoscope and accessories is a device used to provide access, illumination, and allow observation or manipulation of body cavities, hollow organs, and canals
190.	Ophthalmoscope	Class B	The ophthalmoscope allows easy entry into the eye, and a 5X larger field of view of the fundus in an undilated eye, providing better images of the retinal changes caused by hypertension, diabetic retinopathy, glaucoma, and papilledema
191.	Surgical polymeric mesh	Class C	The polymeric mesh comprises an absorbable polymeric fibre and a non-absorbable polymeric fibre knitted together to form an interdependent, co-knit mesh structure
192.	Absorable hemostatic collagen based	Class D	An absorbable haemostatic agent or dressing is a device intended to produce haemostasis by accelerating the clotting process of blood. It is absorbable

193.	Aspiration and injection needle	Class B	A thin needle is inserted into an area of abnormal-appearing tissue or body fluid. As with other types of biopsies, the sample collected during fine needle aspiration can help make a diagnosis or rule out conditions such as cancer
194.	Insulin injector/ insulin syringes/ insulin needles/pen needles for insulin	Class B	Used to inject insulin for the treatment of diabetes
195.	Medication injector	Class B	A subcutaneous injection is a method of administering medication
196.	Contrast medium automatic injector	Class C	Contrast material are inserted, piston plungers that deliver the contrast from the syringes, and pressure tubing that connects the syringe and vascular system of the patient
197.	Thermal dilution injector	Class C	A thermodilution injector is presented in which a pneumatically powered piston operates the plunger of a syringe to deliver a measured amount of injectate in an accurately predetermined time period
198.	*In vitro* fertilization/ embryo transfer catheter	Class B	A cellular transfer catheter is provided for implantation of cellular material into the uterus of a patient
199.	Dry eye insert	Class B	It is indicated in patients with moderate to severe dry eye syndromes, including kerato-conjunctivitis sicca
200.	Myringotomy tube inserter	Class A	An instrument for grasping securely an aural ventilation tube whilst simultaneously presenting the device at the correct angle for the insertion of an aural ventilation tube
201.	Sacculotomy tack inserter	Class A	The device repetitively ruptures the utricular membrane as the membrane expands under increased endolymphatic pressure
202.	Laryngoscope	Class B	The conventional laryngoscope consists of a handle containing batteries with a light source, and a set of interchangeable blades

203.	Biopsy needle kit	Class B	A set of neurosurgical instruments designed to allow multiple biopsies from one or more targets in one trajectory
204.	Angiographic needle	Class B	Angiographic needle has a unique hub design with an ergonomic feel and a black triangle indicator to orient the bevel
205.	Mammary biopsy needle	Class B	The growth sample is suctioned out through a needle or cut out using a surgical procedure
206.	Blood collecting needle	Class B	Needle used to collect blood through syringe
207.	Bone marrow needle	Class B	Needle inserted in bone marrow to collect sample
208.	Gynaecological cerclage needle	Class B	It is a loop like instrument used to suture the cervix
209.	Cholangiography needle	Class B	The aspirating needle is passed through the patient's skin and liver tissue until the tip penetrates one of the hepatic ducts
210.	Anaesthetic conduction needle	Class B	An anaesthesia conduction needle is a device used to inject local anaesthetics into a patient to provide regional anaesthesia
211.	Dental needle	Class B	Dental needles have the ultra-sharp bevel design with triple faceting, which minimises patient trauma
212.	Emergency airway needle	Class B	Emergency airway puncture is the placement of a hollow needle through the throat into the airway. It is done to treat life-threatening choking
213.	Endoscopic needle	Class B	Used to sample targeted submucosal gastrointestinal lesions through the accessory channel of an ultrasound endoscope
214.	Fistula needle	Class B	To connect blood lines with the blood vessels through needles when dialysis is carried out
215.	Epidural needle	Class B	Intended for transient delivery of anesthetics to provide regional anesthesia or to facilitate placement of an epidural catheter

216.	Vacutainer flashback needles	Class B	Intended to be used with evacuated blood collection tube for collection of venous blood
217.	Y-connector	Class C	It can be used to connect to a perfusion sets or catheter for infusion of contrast media, etc.
218.	Retrieval basket	Class C	To entrap and remove stones from biliary system
219.	3 way stop cock as an accessory	Class B	It is indicated for fluid flow directional control and for providing access port for administration of solution, withdrawal of fluid and pressure monitoring
220.	Detachable coils	Class D	Intended for endovascular embolization of the intracranial aneurysms. Also intended for the embolization of other neurovascular abnormalities
221.	Gastrourology needle	Class B	Intended for gastroenterology biopsy
222.	Single lumen hypodermic needle	Class B	A hypodermic single lumen needle is a device intended to inject fluids into, or withdraw fluids from, parts of the body below the surface of the skin
223.	Neurosurgical suture needle	Class B	A needle used in suturing during neurosurgical procedures or in the repair of nervous tissue.
224.	Oocyte aspiration needle	Class B	Mission to collect the maximum amount of undamaged oocytes in a short-time as possible
225.	Ophthalmic needle	Class B	Needle used for ophthalmic surgery
226.	Pneumoperitoneum simple needle	Class B	Inserting a Veress needle through the abdominal wall inside the peritoneal cavity
227.	Radiographic needle	Class B	Identifying lost surgical needles
228.	Sclerotherapy needle/catheter	Class B	It is designed to provide access for injection therapy applications and may also be used for polypectomy and endoscopic
229.	Oxygen administration kit	Class B	Administered for various cardiac and respiratory emergencies, emergency oxygen kits and supplies are available without a prescription for first aid

230.	Passer wire orthopaedic	Class B	To fit through a small incision on the clavicle and curve around the coracoids
231.	Polymeric surgical mesh	Class C	The polymeric mesh comprises an absorbable polymeric fibre and a non-absorbable polymeric fibre knitted together to form an inter-dependent, co-knit mesh structure
232.	Fluid delivery tubing	Class B	Tube used to deliver fluid in body
233.	Gastrourology probe and director	Class B	Guiding probe, in particular for an endoscope for surgical endoscopy with laser light
234.	Common duct probe	Class B	Guiding probe, in particular for an endoscope for surgical endoscopy with laser light
235.	ENT probe	Class B	Guiding probe, in particular for an endoscope for surgical endoscopy with laser light
236.	Periodontic probe	Class B	A periodontal probe is an instrument in dentistry commonly used in the dental armamentarium
237.	Trabeculotomy probe	Class B	Trabeculotomy probes are a commonly used tool in glaucoma surgeries
238.	Laproscope heating tissue probe	Class B	A heater probe can achieve extreme temperatures that conduct heat to the tissue
239.	Laser probe	Class B	It is a laser-based voltage and timing waveform acquisition system which is used to perform failure analysis on flip-chip integrated
240.	Radiofrequency lesion probe	Class B	A radiofrequency lesion probe is a device connected to a radiofrequency (RF) lesion generator to deliver the RF energy to the site within the nervous system where a lesion is desired
241.	Temperature probe	Class B	Used to measure core body temperature via placement in the oesophagus
242.	Nuclear uptake probe	Class B	A nuclear uptake probe is a device intended to measure the amount of radionuclide taken up by a particular organ or body region

243.	Extravascular blood flow probe	Class C	An extravascular blood flow probe is an extravascular ultrasonic or electromagnetic probe used in conjunction with a blood flow meter to measure blood flow in a chamber or vessel
244.	Ultrasonic probe	Class C	Ultrasonic probe is a very important sensor which generate acoustic signals and also detect returned signals
245.	Pulmonary artery band	Class D	Intended to reduce excessive pulmonary blood flow and protect the pulmonary vasculature from hypertrophy and irreversible (fixed) pulmonary hypertension
246.	Bronchoscope rigid tube	Class B	It is intended to examine or treat the larynx and tracheobronchial tree. It is typically used with a fiberoptic light source and carrier to provide illumination
247.	Gastroplasty calibration tube	Class B	It is used in silastic ring gastroplasty and is based on a tube of the desired size in the lumen
248.	Colon tube	Class B	Colon tubes also called "Tips" or even catheters are inserted from the anus, through the rectum to deliver your enema solution into the colon (large intestine)
249.	Connecting tube	Class B	Used to provide connection to a drainage bag
250.	Decompression tube	Class B	Decompression using a rectal tube may assist in the treatment only if the sigmoid colon is involved
251.	Double lumen for intestinal decompression and/ or intubation tube	Class B	Tracheal intubation, usually simply referred to as intubation, is the placement of a flexible plastic tube into the trachea (windpipe) to maintain an open airway or to serve as a conduit through which to administer certain drugs
252.	Drainage tube	Class B	A surgical drain is a tube used to remove pus, blood or other fluids from a wound. They are commonly placed by surgeons or interventional radiologists

253.	Oesophageal blakemore tube	Class B	It is a medical device inserted through the nose or mouth and used occasionally in the management of upper gastrointestinal hemorrhage due to oesophageal varices
254.	Oesophageal sengtaken tube	Class B	It is used only in emergencies where bleeding from presumed varices is impossible to control with medication alone
255.	Feeding tube	Class C	A feeding tube is a device that's inserted into your stomach through your abdomen. It's used to supply nutrition when you have trouble eating
256.	Gastroenterostomy tube	Class B	Tube is placed through the abdominal wall into the stomach and then through the duodenum into the jejunum
257.	Gastrointestinal tube	Class B	A gastrostomy tube (also called a G-tube) is a tube inserted through the abdomen that delivers nutrition directly to the stomach
258.	Heart-lung bypass unit tube	Class B	A tube will be placed in your heart to drain blood to the machine
259.	Laryngectomy tube	Class B	It is a hollow tube made of metal or plastic. It is put into the breathing tube in your neck called the trachea so you can breathe
260.	Levine tube	Class B	Used for the aspiration of gastric and intestinal contents and administration of tube feedings or medications
261.	Nasogastric tube/ Ryles tube	Class B	It is a special tube that carries food and medicine to the stomach through the nose. It can be used for all feedings or for giving a person extra calories
262.	Nephrostomy tube	Class B	The nephrostomy tube drains urine from kidney into a collecting bag outside the body
263.	Orthodontic tube	Class B	An orthodontic small metal part welded on the outside of a molar bank, which contains slots to holdarchwires, lip bumpers, facebows and other devices used to move the teeth

264.	Rectal tube	Class B	A rectal tube, also called a rectal catheter, is a long slender tube which is inserted into the rectum in order to relieve flatulence
265.	Stomach evaculator (gastric lavage) tube	Class B	Passage of a tube via the mouth or nose down into the stomach followed by sequential administration and removal of small volumes of liquid
266.	Tonsil suction tube	Class B	Used to suck out stones in tonsils
267.	Tracheal (endotracheal) tube	Class B	Inserts the tube with the help of a laryngoscope, an instrument that permits to see the upper portion of the trachea, just below the vocal cords
268.	Anastomosis bypass tube	Class C	It is anchored to mucosa and submucosa 3 centimetres proximal to a site of colocolonic anastomosis and later spontaneously evacuated by way of the rectum
269.	Endolymphatic shunt tube	Class B	During a surgical procedure in which it is placed in the membranous labyrinth of the inner ear to drain excess fluid
270.	Orthodontic guide wire	Class B	A wire conforming to the alveolar or dental arch that can be used with dental braces as a source of force in correcting irregularities in the position of the teeth
271.	Bone wire	Class B	Intended to be used for bone stabilization in the hand and wrist
272.	Intraosseous fixation wire	Class B	Stabilization of fractured bony parts by direct fixation to one another with surgical wires
273.	Ligature wire	Class B	Offer a spot-welded auxiliary hook which may be added to any bracket by simply tying in the arch wire
274.	Surgical staples	Class A	Surgical staples are specialized staples used in surgery in place of sutures to close skin wounds, connect or remove parts of body during surgery
275.	Scalp vein set	Class C	To administer parental fluid/ medication into patient's vascular system

276.	Collection bags	Class A	Bags intended for bile collecting, drainage purpose, stoma collection, urinary collection or for other external collection use
277.	Collection bags	Class B	Intended for breathing, enteral feeding, haemostatic (blood collection), IV container and accessories
278.	Surgical dressings	Class A	Dressing aerosol, non-adherent, dressing, periodontal, kit, dressing pad, dressing
279.	Surgical dressings	Class B	Dressing-gel, dressing-permeable, moisture dressing, tracheostomy tube dressing, wound and burn dressings, hydrogel dressing, wound and burn, occlusive
280.	Cotton grudges and bandages	Class B	Adhesive bandages, gauge bandages, pressure bandages, traction bandages, medical absorbent (fiber) bandages
281.	Sterile drapes	Class B	It is intended for use during various surgeries
282.	Wound dressings/ bacteriostatic wound dressings	Class C	Includes beads, hydrophilics for wound exudate absorption for wound care
283.	Tissue expanders	Class C	Intended to be used in breast reconstruction or treatment of soft tissue deformities such as used following mastectomy or for treatment of underdeveloped breasts
284.	Bio patches	Class C	Intended for reconstruction and repair of defects of pericardium
285.	Casting tapes/ splint rolls	Class B	A prosthetic and orthotic accessory, intended for medical purposes to support, protect, or aid in the use of a cast, orthosis (brace), or prosthesis
286.	Disinfectants and insecticides	Class B	An agent that destroys pathogenic and other kinds of microorganisms by chemical or physical means. A disinfectant destroys most recognized pathogenic micro-organisms, but not necessarily all microbial forms, such as bacterial spores. It is intended to disinfect a medical device

287.	Anticoagulant solutions	Class B	For pre-storage leukocyte reduction of whole blood or blood component initiated between 4 and 7 hours after collection if whole blood is stored at ambient temperature
288.	Manifolds	Class B	Indicated for fluid flow directional control and for providing access port/ports for administration of a solution
289.	Haemostatic gelatine sponge/ haemostat	Class C	Intended for the control of surface bleeding from vascular access sites and percutaneous catheters or tubes
290.	Surgical dressings	Class C	Material dressing, surgical, polylactic acid dressings
291.	Male/female condoms	Class C	Condom with nonoxynol-9, micro-condom, prophylactic (condom)– latex sheath, non-latex, condoms with natural membrane, intra-vaginal condoms
292.	Intra Uterine devices	Class C	Intrauterine device, contraceptive (IUD), introducer, uterine balloon therapy devices
293.	Tubal rings/ fallopian rings	Class C	Contraception devices for female sterilization
294.	Surgical wire	Class B	It is a medical device used to hold body tissues together after an injury or surgery
295.	Vascular clip	Class D	A small titanium or polyglycolic acid vessel clamp used to occlude blood vessels or to perform vascular anastomoses
296.	Pacemaker polymeric mesh bag	Class B	A pacemaker polymeric mesh bag is an implanted device used to hold a pacemaker pulse generator
297.	Vena cava clip	Class D	An implanted extravascular device designed to occlude partially the vena cava for the purpose of inhibiting the flow of thromboemboli through that vessel
298.	Vascular graft/ occluders/cardiac patches	Class D	Intended to repair, replace, or bypass sections of native or artificial vessels, excluding coronary or cerebral vasculature, and to provide vascular access

299.	Vascular embolization device	Class D	It is an intravascular implant intended to control hemorrhaging due to aneurysms, certain types of tumors
300.	Endovascular suturing system	Class C	It is a medical device intended to provide fixation and sealing between an endovascular graft and the native artery
301.	Cardiovascular prosthetic devices	Class D	An intra-cardiac patch or pledgete which is a medical device placed in the heart and is used to repair septal defects, for patch grafting, to repair tissue, and to buttress sutures
302.	Intra-aortic balloon and control system	Class D	It is a medical device which is placed in the aorta to improve cardiovascular functioning during certain life-threatening emergencies
303.	Ventricular bypass (assistive)	Class D	A ventricular bypass (assistive) device is a device that assists the left or right ventricle in maintaining circulatory blood flow
304.	Pacemaker repair or replacement material	Class C	A pacemaker repair or replacement material is an adhesive, a sealant, a screw, a crimp, a battery or any other material used to repair a pacemaker lead or to reconnect a pacemaker lead to a pacemaker pulse generator
305.	Annuloplasty ring	Class C	An annuloplasty ring implanted around the mitral or tricuspid heart valve for reconstructive treatment
306.	Heart valve	Class D	A device intended to perform the function of any of the heart's natural valves
307.	Middle ear mold	Class C	It is a preformed device that is intended to be implanted to reconstruct the middle ear cavity during repair of the tympanic membrane
308.	Total ossicular replacement prosthesis	Class D	It is a device intended to be implanted for the functional reconstruction of segments of the ossicular chain and facilitates the conduction of sound wave from the tympanic membrane to the inner ear

309.	Ear, nose, and throat synthetic polymer material	Class C	It is a device material that is intended to be implanted for use as a space-occupying substance in the reconstructive surgery of the head and neck
310.	Mandibular implant facial prosthesis	Class C	Intended to be implanted for use in the functional reconstruction of mandibular deficits
311.	Sacculotomy tack (cody tack)	Class C	Intended to be implanted to relieve the symptoms of vertigo
312.	Endolymphatic shunt	Class C	Intended to be implanted to relieve the symptoms of vertigo
313.	An endolymphatic shunt tube with valve	Class C	It is a device that consists of a pressure-limiting valve associated with a tube intended to be implanted in the inner ear to relieve symptoms of vertigo and hearing loss
314.	Tympanostomy tube	Class C	Intended to be implanted for ventilation or drainage of the middle ear
315.	Hearing aids	Class C	It is a wearable sound-amplifying device intended to compensate for impaired hearing
316.	Vaginal pessary	Class C	Device is placed in the vagina to support the pelvic organs and is used to treat conditions such as uterine prolapse, uterine retroposition) or gynecologic hernia
317.	Fallopian tube prosthesis	Class C	A device designed to maintain the patency (openness) of the fallopian tube and is used after reconstructive surgery
318.	Vaginal stent	Class C	A device used to enlarge the vagina by stretching, or to support the vagina and to hold a skin graft after reconstructive surgery.
319.	Eye sphere implant	Class D	An eye sphere implant is a device intended to be implanted in the eyeball to occupy space following the removal of the contents of the eyeball with the sclera left intact
320.	Keratoprosthesis	Class D	It is a device intended to provide a transparent optical pathway through an opacified cornea, either intra-operatively or permanently, in an eye

321.	Aqueous shunt	Class C	Intended to reduce intraocular pressure in the anterior chamber of the eye
322.	Bone cap	Class B	Intended to be implanted to cover the end of a bone
323.	Bone fixation cerclage	Class C	Intended to use in the fixation of fractures
324.	Bone heterograft	Class D	Intended to be implanted that is made from bovine bones and used to replace human bone following surgery in the cervical region of the spinal column
325.	Intramedullary fixation rod	Class C	Intended to be implanted into the medullary (bone marrow) canal of long bones for the fixation of fractures
326.	Bone cement	Class C	Intended for use in arthroplastic procedures of the hip, knee, and other joints for the fixation of polymer or metallic prosthetic implants to living bone
327.	Bone fixation appliances and accessories	Class C	Used for fixation of fractures of the proximal or distal end of bones, for fusion of a joint; or for surgical procedures
328.	Dental fillers	Class C	Intended for the purpose of repairing a tooth
329.	Orthopedic implant and accessories	Class C	Intended to replace a missing joint or bone or to support a damaged bone
330.	Endosseous dental implant	Class C	Intended to be surgically placed in the bone of jaw arches to provide support for prosthetic devices, such as artificial teeth
331.	Endosseous dental implant abutment	Class C	Intended for use as an aid in prosthetic rehabilitation
332.	Dental implant and accessories	Class C	A dental implant is a surgical component that interfaces with the bone of the jaw or skull to support a dental prosthesis such as crown, bridge, denture, facial prosthesis or to act as an orthodontic anchor.
333.	Bone grafting material	Class C	Intended to fill, augment, or reconstruct periodontal or bony defects of the oral and maxillofacial region

334.	Total temporomandibular joint prosthesis	Class D	Intended to be implanted in the human jaw to replace the mandibular condyle and augment the glenoid fossa to functionally reconstruct the temporomandibular joint
335.	Glenoid fossa prosthesis	Class D	Intended to be implanted in the temporomandibular joint to augment a glenoid fossa or to provide an articulation surface for the head of a mandibular condyle
336.	Mandibular condyle prosthesis	Class D	Intended to be implanted in the human jaw to replace the mandibular condyle and to articulate within a glenoid fossa
337.	An interarticular disc prosthesis	Class D	Intended to be an interface between the natural articulating surface of the mandibular condyle and glenoid fossa
338.	Pacemaker lead adaptor	Class C	A device used to adapt a pacemaker lead so that it can be connected to a pacemaker pulse generator produced by a different manufacturer
339.	Cardiovascular intravascular filter	Class C	It is placed in the inferior vena cava for the purpose of preventing pulmonary thromboemboli from flowing into the right side of the heart and the pulmonary circulation
340.	Implantable cardiac pacemaker including accessories	Class D	An implantable pacemaker pulse generator is a device that generates a periodic electrical pulse to stimulate the heart
341.	Implantable cardioverter defibrillator	Class D	An implantable cardioverter defibrillator (ICD) is used to treat irregular heartbeats called arrhythmias
342.	Implantable cerebral stimulators	Class D	An implanted cerebellar stimulator is a device used to stimulate electrically a patient's cerebellar cortex related disorders
343.	Implanted intracerebral/ subcortical stimulator for pain relief	Class D	An implanted intracerebral/ subcortical stimulator used to subsurface areas of a patient's brain to treat severe intractable pain

344.	Implanted spinal cord stimulator for bladder evacuation	Class D	It is used to empty the bladder of a paraplegic patient who has a complete transection of the spinal cord and who is unable to empty his or her bladder by reflex means or by the intermittent use of catheters
345.	Implanted neuromuscular stimulator	Class D	It provides electrical stimulation to a patient's nerve to cause muscles in the affecting area of the body to contract, thus improving condition of a patient with a paralyzed organ
346.	Implantable diphragmatic stimulator	Class D	A device that provides electrical stimulation of a patient's phrenic nerve to contract the diaphragm rhythmically and produce breathing in patients who have hypoventilation caused by brainstem disease, high cervical spinal cord injury, or chronic lung disease
347.	Implanted peripheral nerve stimulator for pain relief	Class D	It is used to stimulate electrically a peripheral nerve in a patient to relieve severe intractable pain
348.	Implanted spinal cord stimulator	Class D	A device that is used to stimulate electrically a patient's spinal cord to relieve severe intractable pain
349.	Permanent pacemaker electrode	Class C	A device consisting of flexible insulated electrical conductors with one end connected to an implantable pacemaker pulse generator and the other end applied to the heart
350.	A carotid sinus nerve stimulator	Class D	An implantable device used to decrease arterial pressure by stimulating Hering's nerve at the carotid sinus
351.	Penile inflatable implant	Class C	A penile inflatable implant is a device which is implanted in the penis, connected to a reservoir filled with radiopaque fluid implanted in the abdomen, and a subcutaneous manual pump implanted in the scrotum. This device is used in the treatment of erectile impotence

352.	Penile rigidity implant	Class C	A device that is implanted in the corpora cavernosa of the penis to provide rigidity. It is intended to be used in men diagnosed as having erectile dysfunction
353.	A testicular prosthesis	Class D	A testicular prosthesis is an implanted device that consists of a solid or gel-filled silicone rubber prosthesis that is implanted surgically to resemble a testicle
354.	Implantable infusion pump	Class D	An implantable infusion pump (IIP) is intended to provide long-term continuous or intermittent drug infusion
355.	Artificial urinary sphincters implants	Class C	It is used to prevent incontinence by occluding the urethra
356.	Ureteral stent	Class C	An ureteral stent is a tube-like implanted device that is inserted into the ureter to provide ureteral rigidity and allow the passage of urine
357.	Coronary stent	Class D	A coronary stent is a tube-shaped device placed in the coronary arteries that supply blood to the heart, to keep the arteries open in the treatment of coronary heart disease
358.	Drug eluting stent	Class D	Stent, coronary, drug-eluting—a metal scaffold with a drug coating placed via a delivery catheter into the coronary artery or saphenous vein graft to maintain the lumen. The drug coating is intended to inhibit restenosis
359.	Bioresorbable vascular scaffold (BVS) system	Class D	An absorbable stent which is placed into a blood vessel (coronary artery) during angioplasty to help keep the coronary artery open
360.	Implanted mechanical/hydraulic urinary continence device	Class C	An implanted mechanical/hydraulic urinary continence device is a device used to treat urinary incontinence by the application of continuous or intermittent pressure to occlude the urethra

361.	Implanted electrical urinary continence device	Class D	A device intended for treatment of urinary incontinence that consists of a receiver implanted in the abdomen with electrodes for pulsed-stimulation that are implanted either in the bladder wall or in the pelvic floor, and a battery-powered transmitter outside the body
362.	Implantable transprostatic tissue retractor system	Class C	It is a prescription use device that consists of a delivery device and implant. The delivery device is inserted transurethrally and deploys the implant through the prostate
363.	External infusion pump	Class C	Intended for drug delivery to the patients body
364.	Haemo-dialyzer system	Class D	The dialyzer is intended for the treatment of chronic and acute renal failure by hemodialysis
365.	Intraocular lens	Class C	Intraocular lens (IOL) are lens implanted in the eye used to treat cataracts or myopia
366.	Cochlear implant	Class D	A cochlear implant is an implanted electronic hearing device, designed to produce useful hearing sensations to a person with severe to profound nerve deafness by electrically stimulating nerves inside the inner ear
367.	Retinal implant	Class D	The retinal implant is meant to partially restore useful vision to people who have lost their vision due to degenerative eye conditions
368.	Breast implant	Class C	Breast implant is used to increase the breast size
369.	Hernia surgical mesh implant	Class C	Hernia surgical mesh implant is a medical device that is used to provide additional support to weakened or damaged tissue
370.	Esophageal stent	Class C	An esophageal stent is a stent (tube) placed in the oesophagus to keep a blocked area open so the patient can swallow soft food and liquids

371.	Biliary stents	Class C	Biliary stents provide bile drainage from the gallbladder, pancreas and bile ducts to the duodenum in conditions such as ascending cholangitis due to obstructing gallstones
372.	Glaucoma drainage stents	Class C	Glaucoma drainage stents are recent developments and are awaiting approval in some countries. They are used to reduce intraocular pressure by providing a drainage channel
373.	Duodenal stents	Class C	Duodenal stent is indicated for the palliative treatment of gastroduodenal obstructions
374.	Colonic stent	Class C	A colonic stent is a flexible, hollow tube designed to keep a segment of the colon (large bowel) open when it has become blocked (obstructed). This blockage is commonly caused by a tumour inside the bowel or by outside pressure on the bowel wall
375.	Pancreatic stent	Class C	Pancreatic duct stents are often placed in patients who have chronic pancreatitis
376.	Bifurcation stent	Class C	Intended for improving the side branch luminal diameter of arterial bifurcation liaisons
377.	Carotid stent system	Class C	Indicated for the treatment of patients at high-risk for adverse events from carotid endarterectomy who require carotid revascularization
378.	Peripheral stent system	Class C	A peripheral stent is a tube-shaped device placed in the peripheral arteries that supply blood into body organ
379.	Intervertebral body fusion device	Class D	The device is inserted into the intervertebral body space of the cervical or lumbosacral spine, and is intended for intervertebral body fusion
380.	Pedicle screw spinal system	Class C	It is used to intended to provide immobilization and stabilization of spinal segments

381.	Ankle joint metal/ composite semi-constrained cemented prosthesis	Class C	An ankle joint metal/composite semi-constrained cemented prosthesis is a device intended to be implanted to replace an ankle joint
382.	Ankle joint metal/ polymer non-constrained cemented prosthesis	Class C	A device intended to be implanted to replace an ankle joint. The device limits minimally translation in one or more planes. It has no linkage across-the-joint
383.	Elbow joint metal/ polymer constrained cemented prosthesis	Class C	An elbow joint metal/polymer constrained cemented prosthesis is a device intended to be implanted to replace an elbow joint
384.	Elbow joint metal/ polymer semi-constrained cemented prosthesis	Class C	An elbow joint metal/polymer semi-constrained cemented prosthesis is a device intended to be implanted to replace an elbow joint
385.	Elbow joint radial (hemi-elbow) polymer	Class C	An elbow joint radial (hemi-elbow) polymer prosthesis is a device intended to be implanted made of medical grade silicone elastomer used to replace the proximal end of the radius
386.	Elbow joint humeral (hemi-elbow) metallic uncemented prosthesis	Class C	A device intended to be implanted made of alloys, such as cobalt-chromium-molybdenum, that is used to replace the distal end of the humerus formed by the trochlea humeri and the capitulum humeri
387.	Elbow joint humeral (hemi-elbow) metallic uncemented prosthesis	Class C	A device intended to be implanted made of alloys, such as cobalt-chromium-molybdenum, that is used to replace the distal end of the humerus formed by the trochlea humeri and the capitulum humeri
388.	Finger joint metal/ metal constrained uncemented prosthesis	Class C	A device intended to be implanted to replace a metacarpophalangeal or proximal interphalangeal (finger) joint
389.	Finger joint metal/ metal constrained cemented prosthesis	Class C	A finger joint metal/metal constrained cemented prosthesis is a device intended to be implanted to replace a metacarpophalangeal (finger) joint

390.	Finger joint polymer constrained prosthesis	Class C	A device intended to be implanted to replace a metacarpophalangeal or proximal interphalangeal (finger) joint
391.	Hip joint metal constrained cemented or uncemented prosthesis	Class D	A hip joint metal constrained cemented or uncemented prosthesis is a device intended to be implanted to replace a hip joint
392.	Hip joint metal/polymer constrained cemented or uncemented prosthesis	Class D	A hip joint metal/polymer constrained cemented or uncemented prosthesis is a device intended to be implanted to replace a hip joint
393.	Hip joint metal/metal semi-constrained, with a cemented acetabular component, prosthesis	Class D	It is a prosthesis intended to be implanted to replace a hip joint
394.	hip joint metal/metal semi-constrained, with an uncemented acetabular component, prosthesis	Class D	Intended to be implanted to replace a hip joint
395.	Hip joint metal/composite semi-constrained cemented prosthesis	Class C	A hip joint metal/composite semi-constrained cemented prosthesis is a two-part device intended to be implanted to replace a hip joint
396.	Hip joint metal/ceramic/polymer semi-constrained cemented or nonporous uncemented prosthesis	Class C	Intended to be implanted to replace a hip joint
397.	Hip joint metal/polymer/metal semi-constrained porous-coated uncemented prosthesis	Class C	Intended to be implanted to replace a hip joint

398.	A knee joint femorotibial metallic constrained cemented prosthesis is a device intended to be implanted to replace part of a knee joint	Class C	Intended to be implanted to replace part of a knee joint
399.	Shoulder joint metal/metal or metal/polymer constrained cemented prosthesis	Class C	Intended to be implanted to replace a shoulder joint
400.	Wrist joint carpal lunate polymer prosthesis	Class C	Intended to be implanted to replace the carpal lunate bone of the wrist
401.	Wrist joint metal/ polymer semi-constrained cemented prosthesis	Class C	Intended to be implanted to replace a wrist joint
402.	Wrist joint metal constrained cemented prosthesis	Class C	Intended to be implanted to replace a wrist joint
403.	Wrist joint polymer constrained prosthesis	Class C	Intended to be implanted to replace a wrist joint
404.	Wrist joint carpal trapezium polymer prosthesis	Class C	Intended to be implanted to replace the carpal trapezium bone of the wrist
405.	Wrist joint carpal scaphoid polymer prosthesis	Class C	Intended to be implanted to replace the carpal scaphoid bone of the wrist
406.	Toe joint phalangeal (hemi-toe) polymer prosthesis	Class C	Intended to be implanted to replace the base of the proximal phalanx of the toe
407.	Toe joint polymer constrained prosthesis	Class C	Intended to be implanted to replace the first metatarsophalangeal (big toe) joint
408.	Shoulder joint humeral (hemi-shoulder) metallic uncemented prosthesis	Class C	A shoulder joint humeral (hemi-shoulder) metallic uncemented prosthesis

409.	Shoulder joint glenoid (hemi-shoulder) metallic cemented prosthesis	Class C	It is intended to be implanted to replace part of a shoulder joint
410.	Shoulder joint metal/polymer/metal nonconstrained or semi-constrained porous-coated uncemented prosthesis	Class C	It is a device intended to be implanted to replace a shoulder joint
411.	Shoulder joint metal/polymer semi-constrained cemented prosthesis	Class C	Intended to be implanted to replace a shoulder joint
412.	Shoulder joint metal/polymer non-constrained cemented prosthesis	Class C	Intended to be implanted to replace a shoulder joint
413.	Knee joint tibial (hemi-knee) metallic resurfacing uncemented prosthesis	Class C	Intended to be implanted to replace part of a knee joint
414.	Knee joint patellar (hemi-knee) metallic resurfacing uncemented prosthesis	Class C	Intended to be implanted to replace the retropatellar articular surface of the patellofemoral joint
415.	Knee joint femoral (hemi-knee) metallic uncemented prosthesis	Class C	Intended to be implanted to replace part of a knee joint
416.	Knee joint patellofemorotibial metal/polymer	Class C	Intended to be implanted to replace a knee joint
417.	Knee joint patellofemorotibial polymer/metal/polymer semi-constrained cemented prosthesis	Class C	Intended to be implanted to replace a knee joint
418.	Knee joint patellofemorotibial polymer/metal/metal constrained cemented prosthesis	Class C	Intended to be implanted to replace a knee join

419.	Knee joint patellofemoral polymer/ metal semi-constrained cemented prosthesis	Class C	It is intended to be implanted to replace part of a knee joint in the treatment of primary patellofemoral arthritis or chondromalacia
420.	Knee joint femorotibial (uni-compartmental) metal/polymer porous-coated uncemented prosthesis	Class C	Intended to be implanted to replace part of a knee joint
421.	Knee joint femorotibial metal/ polymer semi-constrained cemented prosthesis	Class C	Intended to be implanted to replace part of a knee joint
422.	Knee joint femorotibial metal/ polymer non-constrained cemented prosthesis	Class C	Intended to be implanted to replace part of a knee joint
423.	Knee joint femorotibial metal/ polymer constrained cemented prosthesis	Class C	Knee joint femorotibial metal/polymer constrained cemented prosthesis
424.	Knee joint femorotibial metal/ polymer constrained cemented prosthesis	Class C	Intended to be implanted to replace part of a knee joint
425.	Knee joint femorotibial metal/ composite semi-constrained cemented prosthesis	Class C	Intended to be implanted to replace part of a knee joint
426.	Knee joint femorotibial metal/ composite non-constrained cemented prosthesis	Class C	Intended to be implanted to replace part of a knee joint
427.	Hip joint metal/ polymer or ceramic/ polymer semi-constrained resurfacing cemented prosthesis	Class C	Intended to be implanted to replace the articulating surfaces of the hip while preserving the femoral head and neck

428.	Hip joint metal/ metal semi-constrained, with a cemented acetabular component, prosthesis	Class D	Intended to be implanted to replace a hip joint
429.	Hip joint metal constrained cemented or uncemented prosthesis	Class D	Intended to be implanted to replace a hip joint
430.	Hip joint metal/ polymer constrained cemented or uncemented prosthesis	Class D	Intended to be implanted to replace a hip joint
431.	Hip joint femoral (hemi-hip) metallic resurfacing prosthesis	Class D	Intended to be implanted to replace a portion of the hip joint
432.	A hip joint femoral (hemi-hip) metal/ polymer cemented or uncemented prosthesis	Class D	Intended to be implanted to replace the head and neck of the femur
433.	A hip joint femoral (hemi-hip) trunnion-bearing metal/ polyacetal cemented prosthesis	Class D	Intended to be implanted to replace the head and neck of the femur
434.	Hip joint femoral (hemi-hip) trunnion-bearing metal/ polyacetal cemented prosthesis	Class D	Intended to be implanted to replace the head and neck of the femur
435.	A hip joint (hemi-hip) acetabular metal cemented prosthesis	Class D	Intended to be implanted to replace a portion of the hip joint
436.	Hip joint femoral (hemi-hip) metallic cemented or uncemented prosthesis	Class D	Intended to be implanted to replace a portion of the hip joint

437.	Orthodontic bands/braket	Class A	Band or belt intended to provide support
438.	Orthopaedic plates, clipers screws	Class B	Cervical orthosis, cervical-thoracic, rigid, limb brace, lumbar, lumbosacral, rib fracture, sacroiliac, thoracic orthosis
439.	Spinal intervertebral body fixation orthosis	Class C	The device is used to apply force to a series of vertebrae to correct "sway back," scoliosis (lateral curvature of the spine), or other conditions
440.	Spinal interlaminal fixation orthosis	Class C	A device intended to be implanted made of an alloy, that consists of various hooks and a posteriorly placed compression or distraction rod. The device is used primarily in the treatment of scoliosis
441.	Resorbable calcium salt bone void filler device	Class C	A resorbable calcium salt bone void filler device is a resorbable implant intended to fill bony voids or gaps of the extremities, spine, and pelvis
442.	Smooth or threaded metallic bone fixation fastener	Class C	It may be used for fixation of bone fractures, for bone reconstructions, as a guide pin for insertion of other implants, or it may be implanted through the skin so that a pulling force (traction) may be applied to the skeletal system
443.	Intrastromal corneal ring	Class C	A small device implanted in the eye to correct vision
444.	Injectable fillers	Class C	Injectable filler (injectable cosmetic filler, injectable facial filler) is a soft tissue filler injected into the skin to help fill in facial wrinkles, restoring a smoother appearance
445.	Tracheal prosthesis	Class C	It is intended to be implanted to restore the structure and/or function of the trachea or tracheobronchial tree
446.	Polytetrafluoroe-thylene with carbon fibers composite implant material	Class C	Intended to be implanted during surgery of the chin, jaw, nose, or bones or tissue near the eye or ear
447.	Chin prosthesis	Class C	Intended to be implanted to augment or reconstruct the chin

448.	Ear prosthesis	Class C	Intended to be implanted to reconstruct the external ear
449.	Nose prosthesis	Class C	Intended to be implanted to augment or reconstruct the nasal dorsum
450.	Esophageal prosthesis	Class C	Intended to be implanted to restore the structure and/or function of the esophagus
451.	Fixation, non-absorbable for pelvic use	Class C	Attaching suture or stapling ligaments of the pelvic floor
452.	Sacroiliac joint fixation	Class C	The sacroiliac joints fixation may serve as protective mechanism for the lumbosacral region
453.	Intraocular lenses (IOL)		
454.	IOL multifocal		
455.	IOL tori optic	Class D	Intended to be implanted to replace the natural lens of an eye
456.	IOL accommodative		
457.	IOL iris reconstruction		
458.	Nebulizer	Class B	Intended to spray liquids in aerosol form into gases that are delivered directly to the patient for breathing includes heated, ultrasonic, gas, venturi, and refillable nebulizers
459.	Adhesive	Class A	Adhesive strip for minor skin cut, adhesive gel used on measuring electrodes or any similar use which does not comes with the body fluids
460.	Tissue adhesive for the topical use	Class C	Intended for topical closure of surgical incisions including laparoscopic incisions and simple traumatic lacerations
461.	Tissue adhesive for non-topical use	Class D	Intended for use in adhesion of internal tissues and vessels, e.g. adhesives used in the embolization of brain arteriovenous malformation or for use in ophthalmic surgery
462.	Dental adhesive system	Class C	Used as dental cement, etchant, primer

B-List of *in vitro* Diagnostic Medical Devices along with their Risk Class

S. no. Category	In vitro diagnostic medical device	Class	Intended use
1. **Instruments, analyzers, receptacles, etc. used for an** *in vitro* **diagnostic procedure exemplified as:**	Slides, mixing sticks, droppers, etc.	A	If it is reagent or an article which possesses any specific characteristic that is intended by its product owner to make it suitable for an *in vitro* diagnostic procedure related to a specific examination
2.	Instruments/ analyzers	A	An instrument intended specifically to be used for an *in vitro* diagnostic procedure
3.	Test tubes, blood collection tubes, Petri dishes, etc.	A	A specimen receptacle
		B	
4. **Clinical chemistry reagents/kits for estimation of various parameters exemplified as:**	Acid phosphatase (total or prostatic) test reagents/kits	B	An acid phosphatase (total or prostatic) test reagent/kit is a medical device, intended for the estimation of acid phosphatase in serum/ plasma
5.	Albumin test reagents/kits	B	An albumin test reagent/kit is a medical device intended for the estimation of albumin in serum/ plasma
6.	Alkaline phosphatase or isoenzymes test reagents/kits	B	An alkaline phosphatase or isoenzymes test reagent/kit is a medical device for the estimation of alkaline phosphatase or its isoenzymes in serum/ plasma
7.	Ammonia test reagents/kits	B	An ammonia test reagent/kit is a medical device intended for the estimation of ammonia levels in blood, serum/ plasma

8.	Amylase test reagents/kits	B	An amylase test reagent/kit is a medical device intended for the estimation of the enzyme amylase in serum, saliva/urine
9.	Bicarbonate/ carbon dioxide test reagents/kits	B	A bicarbonate/carbon dioxide test reagent/kit is a medical device for the estimation of bicarbonate/carbon dioxide in plasma, serum/whole blood
10.	Bilirubin (total and direct) test reagents/kits	B	A bilirubin (total and direct) test reagent/kit is a medical device intended for the estimation of bilirubin (total and direct) in serum/plasma
11.	Calcium test reagents/kits	B	A calcium test reagent/kit is a medical device intended for the estimation of total calcium in serum.
12.	Chloride test reagents/kits	B	A chloride test reagent/kit is a medical device intended for the estimation of chloride in plasma, serum, sweat/ urine
13.	Cholesterol (total) test reagents/kits	B	A cholesterol (total) test reagent/kit is a medical device intended for the estimation of cholesterol in serum or plasma
14.	HDL cholesterol test reagents/kits	B	A HDL cholesterol test reagent/kit is a medical device intended for the estimation of HDL cholesterol in serum/ plasma
15.	LDL cholesterol test reagents/kits	B	A LDL cholesterol test reagent/ kit is a medical device intended for the estimation of LDL cholesterol in serum/ plasma
16.	Lipoproteins test reagents/kits	B	A lipoprotein test reagent/ kit is a medical device intended for the estimation of lipoproteins in serum/ plasma

17.	Cholinesterase test reagents/kits	B	A cholinesterase test reagent/kit is a medical device intended for the estimation of cholinesteral in serum/plasma
18.	Creatine kinase and its isoenzymes test reagents/kits	B	A creatine phosphokinase/ creatine kinase or isoenzymes including CKMB, CKBB and CKMM test reagent/kit is a medical device intended for the estimation of the enzyme creatine phosphokinase or its isoenzymes in serum/ plasma
19.	Copper test reagents/kits	B	Copper test reagent/kit is a medical device intended for the estimation of copper in plasma, serum/urine
20.	Creatinine test reagents/kits	B	A creatinine test reagent/ kit is a medical device intended for the estimation of creatinine in serum, plasma/urine
21.	Gamma glutamyl transferase (GGT) and isoenymes test reagents/kits	B	A gamma glutamyl transferase (GGT) and isoenzymes test reagent/ kit is a medical device intended for the estimation of the enzyme gamma glutamyl transferase (GGT) in serum/plasma
22.	Glucose test reagents/kits	B	A Glucose test reagent/kit is a medical device intended for the estimation of glucose in blood/plasma/body fluids
23.	Glucose-6-Phosphate dehydrogenase (G6PD) and its isoenzymes test reagents/kits	B	A glucose-6-phosphate dehydrogenase (G6PD) test reagents/kit is a medical device intended for the estimation of glucose-6-phosphate dehydrogenase or its isoenzymes in serum/ plasma

24.	Glycosylated hemoglobin or its variants test reagents/kits	B	Glycosylated hemoglobin or its variants test reagents/ kits are medical devices intended for the estimation of glycosylated hemoglobin or its variants including A1a, A1b, and A1c in blood
25.	Hemoglobin test reagents/ kits	B	A hemoglobin test reagent/ kit is a medical device intended for the estimation of hemoglobin in blood
26.	Iron test reagents/ kits	B	An iron test reagent/kit is a medical device intended for the estimation of iron in serum/plasma
27.	Ferritin test reagents/kits		A ferritin test reagent/ kit is a medical device intended for the estimation of ferritin in serum/plasma
28.	Iron-binding capacity test reagents/kits	B	Iron-binding capacity test reagents/kits are medical devices intended for the estimation of iron-binding capacity in serum/plasma
29.	Lactate dehydrogenase and its isoenzymes test reagents/kits	B	A lactate dehydrogenase and its isoenzymes test reagent/kit is a medical device intended for the estimation of enzyme lactate dehydrogenase and its isoenzymes in serum/plasma
30.	Lipase test reagents/kits	B	A lipase test reagent/kit is a medical device intended for the estimation of lipase in serum/plasma
31.	Magnesium test reagents/kits	B	A magnesium test reagent/ kit is a medical device intended for the estimation of magnesium levels in serum/plasma
32.	Phosphorus (inorganic) test reagents/kits	B	A phosphorus (inorganic) test reagent/kit is a medical device intended for the estimation of inorganic phosphorus in serum, plasma/urine

33.	Potassium test reagents/kits	B	A potassium test reagent/kit is a medical device intended for the estimation of potassium in serum, plasma/urine
34.	Aspartate amino transferase (AST/SGOT) test reagents/kits	B	An aspartate amino transferase (AST/SGOT) test reagent/kit is a medical device intended for the estimation of the enzyme aspartate amino transferase (AST/SGOT) in serum/plasma
35.	Alanine amino transferase (ALT/SGPT) test reagents/kits	B	An alanine amino transferase (ALT/SGPT) test reagent/kit is a medical device intended for the estimation of enzyme alanine amino transferase (ALT/SGPT) in serum/plasma
36.	Sodium test reagents/kits	B	A sodium test reagent/kit is a medical device intended for the estimation of sodium in serum/plasma/urine
37.	Total protein test reagents/kits	B	A total protein test reagent/kit is a medical device intended for the estimation of total protein(s) in serum/plasma
38.	Protein (fractionation) test reagents/kits	B	A protein (fractionation) test reagent/kit is a medical device intended for the estimation of protein fractions in blood, urine, cerebrospinal fluid/other body fluids
39.	Protein-bound iodine test reagents/kits	B	A protein-bound iodine test reagent/kit is a medical device intended for the estimation of protein-bound iodine in serum/plasma
40.	Triglycerides test reagents/kits	B	A triglyceride test reagent/kit is a medical device intended for the estimation of triglycerides in serum/plasma

41.		Urea (BUN) test reagents/kits	B	A urea (BUN) test reagent/ kit is a medical device intended for the estimation of urea/blood urea nitrogen (BUN) in plasma/serum/urine
42.		Uric acid test reagents/kits	B	A uric acid test reagent/ kit is a medical device intended for the estimation of uric acid in serum/ plasma/urine
43.		Microprotein test reagents/kits	B	A Microprotein test reagent/kit is a medical device intended for the estimation of microproteins including microalbumin in urine
44.		Zinc test reagents/kits	B	A zinc test reagent/kit is a medical device intended for the estimation of zinc in serum/plasma
45.		Other clinical chemistry test reagents/kits	B*	Clinical chemistry test reagent/kit intended for the estimation of analytes/ parameters (other than listed above) in serum/ plasma/urine or other body fluids
	Hematology reagents/kits			
46.	**for estimation of complete blood counts, exemplified as:**	Blood cell diluents	B	A blood cell diluent is a medical device used to dilute blood for further testing, such as complete blood count (CBC)
47.		Lyse reagents/kits for differential counts	B	A lyse reagent/kit is a medical device used for lysing of cells for the estimation of complete blood count (CBC)
48.		Rinse/detergent/ cleaners reagents/ kits	B	A rinse/detergent/cleaner reagent/kit is a medical device used for cleaning various parts of Hematology analyzers like probes, needles, baths, tubing, etc.

	Reagents/Kits for estimation		
49.	of parameters in the urine, exemplified as:	Ascorbic acid/ bilirubin/blood cells/glucose/ ketone/ leukocyte peroxidase/ specific gravity/ urobilinogen nitrite/pH/protein/ albumin and other urinary analytes test reagents/ strips/kits	B	Ascorbic acid/bilirubin/ blood cells/glucose/ ketone/leukocyte peroxidase/specific gravity/ urobilinogen nitrite/pH/ protein/albumin and other urinary analytes test reagents/strips/kits, are medical devices intended for the preliminary estimation of diagnostic markers in urine
50.	*In-vitro* diagnostic medical devices for self-testing	Glucose test reagents/kits	B	A glucose test reagent/kit is a medical device intended for the preliminary self testing of glucose levels in blood/body fluids
51.		Human chorionic gonadotropin (hCG) test reagents/kits	B	A human chorionic gonadotropin (hCG) test reagent/kit is a medical device intended for the preliminary self-testing of hCG in urine/body fluids
52.		Luteinizing hormone (LH) test reagents/kits	B	A luteinizing hormone (LH) test reagent/kit is a medical device intended for the preliminary self-testing of luteinizing hormone (LH) in urine/body fluids
53.		Glycosylated hemoglobin or its variants test reagents/kits	B	Glycosylated hemoglobin or its variants test reagents/ kits are medical devices intended for the preliminary self-testing of glycosylated hemoglobin or its variants including A1a, A1b, and A1c in blood
54.		Cholesterol test reagents/kits	B	A cholesterol test reagent/ kit is a medical device intended for preliminary self testing of cholesterol in blood /body fluids

55.		Follicle stimulating hormone (FSH) test reagents/kits	B	A follicle stimulating hormone (FSH) test reagent/kit is a medical device intended for the preliminary self-testing of follicle stimulating hormone (FSH) in urine/body fluids
56.		Other *in vitro* diagnostic medical devices for self-testing	B	
57.	*In-vitro* **diagnostic**		C	
58.	**medical device for near patient testing**	Blood gas analysis test reagents/kits	C	A blood gas analysis test reagent/kit for near patient testing, is a medical device intended for the estimation of certain gases (such as oxygen and carbon dioxide, etc.) dissolved in arterial blood
59.		Anticoagulant monitoring test reagents/kits	C	An anticoagulant monitoring test reagent/kit for near patient testing, is a medical device intended for the estimation of coagulation parameters (such as PT, TT, APTT, etc.) in plasma/blood
60.		Diabetes management test reagents/kits	C	A diabetes management test reagent/kit for near patient testing, is a medical device intended for the monitoring of diabetes in body fluids
61.		C-reactive protein (CRP) test reagents/kits	C	A C-reactive protein (CRP) test reagent/kit for near patient testing, is a medical device intended for the estimation of C-reactive protein (CRP) in serum and other body fluids
62.		*H. pylori* test reagents/kits	C	An *H. pylori* test reagent/kit for near patient testing, is a medical device intended for the estimation of *H. pylori* in blood/body fluids

63.	Troponin test reagents/kits	C	A troponin test reagent/kit for near patient testing, is a medical device intended for the estimation of Troponin T, I and its variants in blood/body fluids
64.	Other *in vitro* diagnostic medical devices for near patient test reagents/kits	C	*In vitro* diagnostic medical device for near patient test reagent/kit intended for the estimation of analytes/ parameters (other than listed above) in serum, plasma, urine or other body fluids
65.	**Reagents/kits for estimation of parameters of ToRCH and other infectious agents exemplified as under:**	C	
	Toxoplasma gondii test reagents/kits	C	A *Toxoplasma gondii* test reagent/kit is a medical device intended for the detection of *Toxoplasma gondii* in serum/body fluids
66.	Rubella virus I test reagents/kits	C	A rubella virus test reagent/ kit is a medical device intended for the detection of rubella virus in serum/body fluids
67.	Cytomegalovirus test reagents/kits	C	A cytomegalovirus test reagent/kit is a medical device intended for the detection of cytomegalovirus in serum/body fluids
68.	Herpes simplex virus reagents/kits	C	A Herpes simplex virus test reagent/kit is a medical device intended for the detection of Herpes simplex virus in serum/ body fluids
69.	*Chlamydia pneumoniae* test reagents/kits	C	A *Chlamydia pneumoniae* test reagent/kit is a medical device intended for the detection of *Chlamydia pneumonia* in serum/body fluids

70.		Methicillin-resistant *Staphylococcus aureus* test reagents/kits	C	A Methicillin-resistant *Staphylococcus aureus* test reagent/kit is a medical device intended for the detection of Methicillin-resistant *Staphylococcus aureus* in serum/body fluids
71.		Enterovirus test reagents/kits	C	An enterovirus test reagent/kit is a medical device intended for the detection of enterovirus) in serum/body fluids
72.	**Reagents/kits for detection of cancer markers exemplified as:**		C	
		Alpha-fetoprotein test reagents/kits	C	An alpha-fetoprotein test reagent/kit is a medical device intended for the detection of alpha-fetoprotein in serum/body fluids
73.		Beta-2 microglobulin test reagents/kits	C	A beta-2 microglobulin test reagent/kit is a medical device intended for the detection of beta-2 microglobulin in serum/body fluids
74.		Bladder tumour antigen (BTA) test reagents/kits	C	A bladder tumour antigen (BTA) test reagent/kit is a medical device intended for the detection of bladder tumour antigen (BTA) in serum/body fluids
75.		CA15-3 test reagents/kits	C	A CA15-3 antigen (BTA) test reagent/kit is a medical device intended for the detection of CA15-3 in serum/body fluids
76.		CA27.29 test reagents/kits	C	A CA27.29 test reagent/kit is a medical device intended for the detection of CA27.29 in serum/body fluids
77.		CA125 test reagents/kits	C	A CA125 test reagent/kit is a medical device intended for the detection of CA125 in serum/body fluids

78.	CA72-4 test reagents/kits	C	A CA72-4 test reagent/kit is a medical device intended for the detection of CA72-4 in serum/body fluids
79.	CA19-9 test reagents/kits	C	A CA19-9 test reagent/kit is a medical device intended for the detection of CA19-9 in serum/body fluids
80.	Calcitonin test reagents/kits	C	A calcitonin test reagent/kit is a medical device intended for the detection of calcitonin in serum/body fluids
81.	Carcinoembryonic antigen (CEA) test reagents/kits	C	A carcinoembryonic antigen (CEA) test reagent/kit is a medical device intended for the detection of carcinoembryonic antigen (CEA) in serum/body fluids
82.	Chromogranin A test reagents/kits	C	A chromogranin A test reagent/kit is a medical device intended for the detection of chromogranin A in serum/body fluids
83.	Estrogen/ progesterone receptors test reagents/kits	C	A estrogen/progesterone test reagent/kit is a medical device intended for the detection of estrogen/ progesterone in serum/ body fluids
84.	HER2 (human epidermal growth factor) receptor, test reagents/kits	C	A HER2 (human epidermal growth factor-receptor test reagent/kit is a medical device intended for the detection of HER2 (human epidermal growth factor receptor in serum/body fluids
85.	Human chorionic gonadotropin (hCG) test system test reagents/kits		A human chorionic gonadotropin (hCG) test reagent/kit is a medical device intended for the detection of human chorionic gonadotropin (hCG) in serum/body fluids

86.	Lipid associated sialic acid test reagents/kits	C	A lipid associated sialic acid test reagent/kit is a medical device intended for the detection of lipid associated sialic acid in serum/body fluids
87.	Neuron-specific enolase (NSE) test reagents/kits	C	A neuron-specific enolase (NSE) test reagent/kit is a medical device intended for the detection of neuron-specific enolase (NSE) in serum/body fluids
88.	NMP22 test reagents/kits	C	A NMP22 test reagent/kit is a medical device intended for the detection of NMP22 in serum/body fluids
89.	Prostate-specific antigen (PSA) test reagents/kits	C	A prostate-specific antigen (PSA) test reagent/kit is a medical device intended for the detection of prostate-specific antigen (PSA) in serum/body fluids
90.	Prostatic acid phosphatase (PAP) test reagents/kits	C	A prostatic acid phosphatase (PAP) test reagents/kits test reagent/kit is a medical device intended for the detection of prostatic acid phosphatase (PAP) test reagents/kits in serum/body fluids
91.	Prostate cancer antigen 3 gene (PCA 3) test reagents/kits	C	A prostate cancer antigen 3 gene (PCA 3) test reagent/kit is a medical device intended for the detection of prostate cancer antigen 3 gene (PCA 3) in serum/body fluids
92.	Prostate-specific membrane antigen (PSMA) test reagents/kits	C	A prostate-specific membrane antigen (PSMA) test reagent/kit is a medical device intended for the detection of prostate-specific membrane antigen (PSMA) in serum/body fluids

93.		S-100 test reagents/kits	C	A S-100 test reagent/kit is a medical device intended for the detection of S-100 in serum/body fluids
94.		TA-90 test reagents/kits	C	A TA-90 test reagent/kit is a medical device intended for the detection of TA-90 in serum/body fluids
95.		Thyroglobulin test reagents/kits	C	A thyroglobulin test reagent/kit is a medical device intended for the detection of thyroglobulin in serum/body fluids
96.		Tissue polypeptide Antigen (TPA) test reagents/kits	C	A tissue polypeptide antigen (TPA) test reagent/kit is a medical device intended for the detection of tissue polypeptide antigen (TPA) in serum/body fluids
97.		Other reagents/ kits for detection of cancer markers	C	
98.	**Reagents/ kits for estimation of coagulation parameters exemplified as:**	PT (prothrombin time) test reagents/kits	C	A prothrombin time (PT) test reagent/kit is a medical device intended for the estimation of prothrombin time in plasma/body fluids
99.		TT (thrombin time) test reagents/kits	C	A thrombin time (TT) test reagent/kit is a medical device intended for the estimation of thrombin time in plasma/body fluids
100.		Activated partial thromboplastin time (APTT) tests reagents/ kits	C	A activated partial thromboplastin time (APTT) test reagent/kit is a medical device intended for the estimation of activated partial thromboplastin time in plasma/body fluids

101.			Activated whole blood clotting time tests reagents/kits		A activated whole blood clotting time test reagent/kit is a medical device intended for the estimation of activated whole blood clotting time in plasma/body fluids
102.			Fibrinogen/fibrin degradation products tests reagents/kits	C	A fibrinogen/fibrin degradation products test reagent/kit is a medical device intended for the estimation of fibrinogen/fibrin degradation products in plasma/body fluids
103.			D-dimer tests reagents/kits	C	A D-dimer test reagent/kit is a medical device intended for the estimation of D-dimer test in plasma/body fluids
104.			Other reagents/kits for estimation of coagulation parameters	C	
	Reagents/ kits for monitoring			C	
105.	**of drug levels used for therapy or abuse exemplified as under**		Aminoglycoside antibiotics test reagents/kits	C	Aminoglycoside antibiotics test reagents/kits are medical devices intended for the estimation of aminoglycoside antibiotics in serum/body fluids
106.			Antiepileptics test reagents/kits	C	Antiepileptics test reagents/kits are medical devices intended for the estimation of antiepileptics in serum/body fluids
107.			Antipsychotics test reagents/kits	C	Antipsychotics test reagents/kits are medical devices intended for the estimation of antipsychotics in serum/body fluids
108.			Mood stabilisers, test reagents/kits	C	Mood stabilisers test reagents/kits are medical devices intended for the estimation of mood stabilisers in serum/body fluids

109.	Biologic monoclonal antibody drugs test reagents/kits	C	Biologic monoclonal antibody drugs test reagents/kits are medical devices intended for the estimation of biologic monoclonal antibody drugs in serum/body fluids
110.	Buprenorphine (BUP) test reagents/kits	C	Buprenorphine (BUP) test reagents/kits are medical devices intended for the estimation of buprenorphine (BUP) in serum/body fluids
111.	Amphetamine (AMP) test reagents/kits	C	Amphetamine (AMP) test reagents/kits are medical devices intended for the estimation of amphetamine (AMP) in serum/body fluids
112.	Barbiturates (BAR) test reagents/kits	C	Barbiturates (BAR) test reagents/kits are medical devices intended for the estimation of barbiturates (BAR) in serum/body fluids
113.	Opiate test system test reagents/kits	C	Opiate test reagents/kits are medical devices intended for the estimation of opiates in serum/body fluids
114.	Benzodiazepines (BZO) test reagents /kits	C	Benzodiazepines (BZO) test reagents/kits are medical devices intended for the estimation of benzodiazepines (BZO) in serum/body fluids
115.	Cocaine (COC) test reagents/kits	C	Cocaine (COC) test reagents/kits are medical devices intended for the estimation of cocaine (COC) in serum/body fluids
116.	Cotinine (COT) test reagents/ kits	C	Cotinine (COT) test reagents/ kits are medical devices intended for the estimation of cotinine (COT) in serum/ body fluids

117.	Ketamine (KET) test reagents/kits	C	Ketamine (KET) test reagents/ kits are medical devices intended for the estimation of ketamine (KET) in serum/body fluids
118.	Ecstasy (MDMA) test reagents/kits	C	Ecstasy (MDMA) test reagents/kits are medical devices intended for the estimation of ecstasy (MDMA) in serum/body fluids
119.	Methamphetamine (MET) test reagents/kits	C	Methamphetamine (MET) test reagents/kits are medical devices intended for the estimation of methamphetamine (MET) in serum/body fluids
120.	Morphine (MOP) test reagents/kits	C	Morphine (MOP) test reagents/kits are medical devices intended for the estimation of morphine (MOP) in serum/body fluids
121.	Methaqualone (MQL) test reagents/kits	C	Methaqualone (MQL) test reagents/kits are medical devices intended for the estimation of methaqualone (MQL) in serum/body fluids
122.	Methadone (MTD) test reagents/kits	C	Methadone (MTD) test reagents/kits are medical devices intended for the estimation of methadone (MTD) in serum/body fluids
123.	Oxycodone (OXY) test reagents /kits	C	Oxycodone (OXY) test reagents/kits are medical devices intended for the estimation of oxycodone (OXY) in serum/body fluids
124.	Phencyclidine (PCP) test reagents/kits	C	Phencyclidine (PCP) test reagents/kits are medical devices intended for the estimation of phencyclidine (PCP) in serum/body fluids

125.	Propoxyphene (PPX) test reagents /kits	C	Propoxyphene (PPX) test reagents/kits are medical devices intended for the estimation of propoxyphene (PPX) in serum/body fluids
126.	Tricyclic antidepressants (TCA) test reagents/kits	C	Tricyclic antidepressants (TCA) test reagents/kits are medical devices intended for the estimation of tricyclic antidepressants (TCA) in serum/body fluids
127.	Marijuana (THC) test reagents /kits	C	Marijuana (THC) test reagents/kits are medical devices intended for the estimation of Marijuana (THC) in serum/body fluids
128.	Tramadol (TRA) test reagents/kits	C	Tramadol (TRA) test reagents/kits are medical devices intended for the estimation of tramadol (TRA) in serum/body fluids
129.	Fentanyl (FEN) test reagents/kits	C	Fentanyl (FEN) test reagents/kits are medical devices intended for the estimation of fentanyl (FEN) in serum/body fluids
130.	Methadone metabolite (EDDP) test reagents/kits	C	Methadone metabolite (EDDP) test reagents/kits are medical devices intended for the estimation of methadone Metabolite (EDDP) in serum/body fluids
131.	Other reagents/ kits for monitoring of drug levels used for therapy or abuse	C	
	Reagents/	B	
132.	**kits for detection of autoimmune disorders exemplified as:** Antinuclear antibodies test reagents/kits	B	Antinuclear antibodies test reagent/kit is a medical device for the screening of auto-antibodies to nuclear antigens in human specimens

133.	Antitransglutaminase antibodies test reagents/kits	B	Antitransglutaminase antibodies test reagent/kit is a medical device for the screening of auto-antibodies to transglutaminase in human specimens
134.	Antiganglioside antibodies test reagents/kits	B	Antiganglioside antibodies test reagent/kit is a medical device for the screening of auto-antibodies to ganglioside in human specimens
135.	Anticyclic citrullinated peptide (CCP) antibodies test reagents/kits	B	Anticyclic citrullinated peptide (CCP) antibodies test reagent/kit is a medical device for the screening of CCP auto-antibodies in human specimens
136.	Rheumatoid factor (RF) immunological test reagents/kits	B	Rheumatoid factor (RF) immunological test reagent/kit is a medical device for the screening of rheumatoid factor in human specimens
137.	Anti smooth muscle antibody test reagents/kits	B	Anti smooth muscle antibody test reagent/kit is a medical device for the screening of auto-antibodies to smooth muscles in human specimens
138.	Glutamic acid decarboxylase (GAD) antibody test reagents/kits	B	Glutamic acid decarboxylase (GAD) antibody test reagent/kit is a medical device for the screening of autoantibodies to glutamic acid decarboxylase (in human specimens)
139.	Anti-ovary antibodies test reagents/kits	B	Anti-ovary antibodies test reagent/kit is a medical device for the screening of auto-antibodies to ovarian antigens in human specimens

140.	Anti-sperm antibodies test reagents/kits	B	Anti-sperm antibodies test reagent/kit is a medical device for the screening of auto-antibodies to spermatozoa in human specimens
141.	Anti-IA2 test reagents/kits	B	Anti-IA-2 antibodies test reagent/kit is a medical device for the screening of auto-antibodies to IA-2 (tyrosine phosphatase) in human specimens
142.	Anti-acetylcholine receptor test reagents/kits	B	Anti-acetylcholine receptor test reagent/kit is a medical device for the screening of auto-antibodies to acetylcholine receptor in human specimens
143.	Anti-thyroid gland antibody test reagents/kits	B	Anti-thyroid gland antibodies test reagent/kit is a medical device for the screening of auto-antibodies to thyroid gland antigens in human specimens
144.	ANCA test reagents/kits	B	The ANCA test reagent/kit is a medical device for the screening of anti-neutrophil cytoplasmic antibodies (ANCA) in human specimens
145.	Anti-double stranded DNA (anti-dsDNA) test reagents/kits	B	The anti-double stranded DNA (anti-dsDNA) test reagent/kit is a medical device for the screening of auto-antibodies to double stranded DNA in human specimens
146.	Anti-extractable nuclear antigen (Anti-ENA) test reagents/kits	B	The anti-extractable nuclear antigen (anti-ENA) test reagent/kit is a medical device for the screening of auto-antibodies to Extractable Nuclear antigens like Smith (Sm) antigens, ribonuclears protein (RNP), anti SSA (Ro), etc. in human specimens

147.	Anti-intrinsic factor test reagents/kits	B	The anti-intrinsic factor test reagent/kit is a medical device for the screening of antibodies against intrinsic factor in human specimens
148.	Anti-*Saccharomyces cerevisiae* antibodies (ASCA) test reagents/kits	B	The anti-*Saccharomyces cerevisiae* antibodies (ASCA) test reagent/kit is a medical device for the screening of antibodies against *Saccharomyces cerevisiae* in human specimens
149.	Other reagents/ kits for detection of autoimmune disorders	B	
150. **Reagents/ kits for detection of markers for**		C	
151. **congenital disorders exemplified as under:**	Triple Screen Test reagents/kits for Down's Syndrome	C	Triple screen test reagent/ kit for Down's syndrome is a medical device intended for the screening of Down's syndrome in serum/plasma
152.	Quadruple screen test reagents/kits for Down's syndrome	C	Quadruple screen test reagent/kit for Down's syndrome is a medical device intended for the screening of Down's
153.	Chorionic villus sample test reagents/kits for Down's syndrome	C	Chorionic villus sample test reagent/kit for Down's syndrome is a medical device intended for the detection of Down's Syndrome in body fluids
154.	Maternal serum alpha-fetoprotein (MSAFP) test reagents/kits for spina bifida	C	Maternal serum alpha-fetoprotein (MSAFP) test reagents/kits for is a medical device intended for the screening of spina bifida in serum
155.	Others reagents/ kits for detection of congenital disorders	C	

	Reagents/ kits for detection of cardiac	B or C	
156.	**markers exemplified as under:**	B	Creatine kinase (CK) and CKMB test reagents/kits	Creatine kinase (CK) and CKMB test reagent/kit are medical devices intended for the estimation of creatine kinase (CK) and CKMB in blood/body fluids
157.		B	Myoglobin test reagents/kits	Myglobin test reagent/kit for is a medical device intended for the estimation of myglobin in blood/body fluids
158.		C	Troponin test reagents/kits	A troponin test reagent/kit for near patient testing, is a medical device intended for the estimation of troponin T, I and its variants in blood/body fluids
159.		C	BNP and NT pro BNP test reagents/kits	BNP and NT pro BNP test reagent/kit for is a medical device intended for the estimation of BNP and NT pro BNP in blood/body fluids
	Reagents/ kits for human	C		
160.	**genetic testing exemplified as:**	C	Genetic test reagents/kits for cystic fibrosis	Genetic test reagent/kit for cystic fibrosis is a medical device intended for the detection of cystic fibrosis in human specimens
161.		C	Genetic test for Huntington's chorea	Genetic test reagent/kit for Huntington's chorea is a medical device intended for the detection of Huntington's chorea in human specimens
162.		C	Other reagents/ kits for human genetic testing	

	Reagents/ kits for the management	C	
163.	of life-threatening infections exemplified as under:	HIV viral load test reagents/ kits	C	HIV viral load test reagent/ kit is a medical device intended for the estimation of HIV viral load in blood/ body fluids
164.		HBV viral load test reagents/kits	C	HBV viral load test reagent/kit is a medical device intended for the estimation of HBV viral load in blood/body fluids
165.		HCV viral load test reagents/kits	C	HCV viral load test reagent/kit is a medical device intended for the estimation of HCV viral load in blood/body fluids
166.		CD4 Count and % test reagents/ kits	C	CD4 count and % test reagent/kit is a medical device intended for the estimation of CD4 count and % in blood/body fluids
167.		CD8 count and % test reagents/kits	C	CD8 count and % test reagent/kit is a medical device intended for the estimation of CD8 count and % in blood/body fluids
168.		CD4/CD8 ratio test reagents/kits	C	CD4/CD8 ratio test reagent/ kit are a medical device intended for the estimation of CD4/CD8 ratio in blood/ body fluids
169.		Other reagents/ kits for the management of life-threatening infections	C	
	Reagents/ kits for the		C	
170.	detection of sexually transmitted agent exemplified as under:	*Treponema pallidum* test reagents and kits	C	*Treponema pallidum* test reagent/kit is a medical device intended for the detection of *Treponema pallidum* in blood/body fluids

171.		*Neisseria gonorrhoeae* test reagents and kits	C	*Neisseria gonorrhoeae* test reagent/kit is a medical device intended for the detection of *Neisseria gonorrhoeae* in blood/body fluids
172.		Human Papilloma Virus (HPV) test reagents and kits	C	Human Papilloma Virus (HPV) test reagent/kit is a medical device intended for the detection of Human Papilloma Virus in blood/body fluids
173.		Chlamydia test reagents and kits	C	Chlamydia test reagent/kit is a medical device intended for the detection of Chlamydia in blood/body fluids
174.		Herpes virus test reagents and kits	C	Herpes virus test reagent/kit is a medical device intended for the detection of herpes virus in blood/body fluids
175.		Other reagents/kits for the detection of sexually transmitted agent	C	
176.	**Reagents/kits for the antigen**		C	
177.	**detection of infectious agents with a risk of limited propagation exemplified as:**	Malaria antigen test reagents and kits	C	Malaria antigen test reagent/kit is a medical device intended for the detection of malaria antigen in blood/body fluids
178.		Dengue virus antigen test reagents and kits	C	Dengue virus antigen test reagent/kit is a medical device intended for the detection of dengue virus antigen in blood/body fluids
179.		Chikungunya antigen test reagents and kits	C	Chikungunya antigen test reagent/kit is a medical device intended for the detection chikungunya antigen of in blood/body fluids

180.	Leptospira antigen test reagents and kits	C	Leptospira antigen test reagent/kit is a medical device intended for the detection of Leptospira antigen in blood/body fluids
181.	Japanese encephalitis antigen test reagents and kits	C	Japanese encephalitis antigen test reagent/kit is a medical device intended for the detection of Japanese encephalitis antigen in blood/body fluids
182.	Typhoid antigens test reagents and kits	C	Typhoid antigens test reagent/kit is a medical device intended for the detection of typhoid antigens in blood/body fluids
183.	Influenza A antigen test reagents and kits	C	Influenza A antigen test reagent/kit is a medical device intended for the detection of influenza A antigen in blood/body fluids
184.	Influenza B antigen test reagents and kits	C	Influenza B antigen test reagent/kit is a medical device intended for the detection of Influenza B antigen in blood/body fluids
185.	Strep A antigen test reagents and kits	C	Strep A antigen test reagent/kit is a medical device intended for the detection of strep A antigen in blood/body fluids
186.	Strep B antigen test reagents and kits	C	Strep B test antigen reagent/kit is a medical device intended for the detection of Strep B antigen in blood/body fluids
187.	Chagas' antigen test reagents and kits	C	Chagas' disease antigen test reagent/kit is a medical device intended for the detection of Chagas' disease antigen in blood/body fluids

188.	Filariasis antigen test reagents and kits	C	Filariasis test antigen reagent/kit is a medical device intended for the detection of filariasis antigen in blood/body fluids
189.	Kala-azar antigen test reagents and kits gen	C	Kala-azar antigen test reagent/kit is a medical device intended for the detection of kala-azar antigen in blood/body fluids
190.	Rotavirus antigen test reagents and kits	C	Rotavirus antigen test reagent/kit is a medical device intended for the detection of rotavirus antigen in blood/body fluids
191.	*S. pneumonia* antigen test reagents and kits	C	*S. pneumonia* antigen test reagent/kit is a medical device intended for the detection of *S. pneumonia* antigen in blood/body fluids
192.	*H. pylori* antigen test reagents and kits antigen	C	*H. pylori* antigen test reagent/kit is a medical device intended for the detection of *H. pylori* antigen in blood/body fluids
193.	Other reagents/ kits for the detection of infectious agents with a risk of limited propagation	C	Reagents/kits, other than above, for the antigen detection of infectious agents with a risk of limited propagation
194.	**Reagents/kits for the detection of antibodies to infectious agents with a risk of limited propagation exemplified as under:**	B	
195.	Malaria antibody test reagents and kits	B	Malaria antibody test reagent/kit is a medical device intended for the detection of malaria antibody in blood/body fluids

196.	Dengue antibody test reagents and kits	B	Dengue antibody test reagent/kit is a medical device intended for the detection of dengue antibody in blood/body fluids
197.	Chikungunya antibody test reagents and kits	B	Chikungunya antibody test reagent/kit is a medical device intended for the detection of chikungunya antibody in blood/body fluids
198.	Leptospira antibody test reagents and kits	B	Leptospira antibody test reagent/kit is a medical device intended for the detection of Leptospira antibody in blood/body fluids
199.	Japanese encephalitis antibody test reagents and kits	B	Japanese encephalitis antibody test reagent/kit is a medical device intended for the detection of Japanese encephalitis antibody in blood/body fluids
200.	Typhoid antibody test reagents and kits	B	Typhoid antibody test reagent/kit is a medical device intended for the detection of typhoid antibody in blood/body fluids
201.	*Cryptococcus neoformans* antibody test reagents and kits	B	*Cryptococcus neoformans* antibody test reagent/kit is a medical device intended for the detection of *Cryptococcus neoformans* antibody in blood/body fluids
202.	*Neisseria meningitides* antibody test reagents and kits	B	*Neisseria meningitides* antibody test reagent/kit is a medical device intended for the detection of *Neisseria meningitides* antibody in blood/body fluids

203.	Vibrio cholera antibody test reagents and kits	B	Vibrio cholera antibody test reagent/kit is a medical device intended for the detection of vibrio cholera antibody in blood/body fluids
204.	Influenza A antibody test reagents and kits	B	Influenza A antibody test reagent/kit is a medical device intended for the detection of influenza A antibody in blood/body fluids
205.	Influenza B antibody test reagents and kits	B	Influenza B antibody test reagent/kit is a medical device intended for the detection of influenza B antibody in blood/body fluids
206.	Strep A antibody test reagents and kits	B	Strep A antibody test reagent/kit is a medical device intended for the detection of Strep A antibody in blood/body fluids
207.	Strep B antibody test reagents and kits	B	Strep B antibody test reagents/kit is a medical device intended for the detection of Strep B antibody in blood/body fluids
208.	Chagas' antibody test reagents and kits	B	Chagas' antibody test reagent/kit is a medical device intended for the detection of Chagas' antibody in blood/body fluids
209.	Filariasis antibody test reagents and kits	B	Filariasis antibody test reagent/kit is a medical device intended for the detection of filariasis antibody in blood/body fluids
210.	Kala-azar antibody test reagents and kits	B	Kala-azar antibody test reagents/kits is a medical device intended for the detection of Kala-azar antibody in blood/body fluids

211.	Rotavirus antibody test reagents and kits	B	Rotavirus antibody test reagents/kits is a medical device intended for the detection of rotavirus antibody in blood/body fluids
212.	*S. pneumonia* antibody test reagents and kits	B	*S. pneumonia* antibody test reagent/kit is a medical device intended for the detection of *S. pneumonia* antibody in blood/body fluids
213.	*H. pylori* antibody test reagents and kits	B	*H. pylori* antibody test reagent/kit is a medical device intended for the detection of *H. pylori* antibody in blood/body fluids
214.	Other reagents/ kits for the detection of antibodies to infectious agents with a risk of limited propagation	B	
	In vitro **diagnostic medical devices for blood grouping or tissue typing**	C	
215.	All other than, the ABO system; the Duffy system; the Kell system; the Kidd system; the Rhesus system, test reagents/kits.	C	
216.	*In vitro* **diagnostic medical** ABO system test reagents/kits	D D	Intended for blood grouping or tissue typing

217.	devices for blood	Rhesus (D) system test reagents/kits	D	
218.	grouping or tissue	The Duffy system test reagents/kits	D	
219.	typing	The Kell system test reagents/kits	D	
220.		The Kidd system test reagents/kits	D	
221.		HLA test reagents/kits	D	
	Reagents/		**D**	
222.	**kits for the detection of transmissible agents-**	HIV test reagents/kits	D	HIV test reagents/kits is a medical device intended for the detection of HIV in blood/body fluids
223.	**screening and confirmatory**	HBV test reagents/kits	D	HBV test reagents/kits is a medical device intended for the detection of HBV in blood/body fluids
224.		HCV test reagents/kits	D	HCV test reagents/kits is a medical device intended for the detection of HCV in blood/body fluids
225.		Syphilis screening reagents/kits	D	Syphilis test reagents/kits is a medical device intended for the screening of syphilis in blood/body fluids
226.		Malaria screening reagents/kits	D	Malaria test reagents/kits is a medical device intended for the screening of malaria in blood/body fluids
	Other *in vitro* medical		**B**	
227.	**devices**	TSH test reagents/kits	B	TSH test reagent/kit is a medical device intended for the estimation TSH in blood/body fluids
228.		Total/free triiodothyronine (T_3) test reagents/kits	B	Total/free triiodothyronine (T_3) test reagent/kit is a medical device intended for the estimation total/free triiodothyronine (T_3) in blood/body fluids

229.	Total/free thyroxine (T_4) test reagents/ kits	B	Total/free thyroxine (T_4) test reagent/kit is a medical device intended for the estimation of total/free thyroxine (T_4) in blood/body fluids
230.	Dehydroepiandros-terone (DHEA-S) (free and sulfate) test reagents/kits	B	Dehydroepiandrosterone (DHEA-S) (free and sulfate) test reagent/kit is a medical device intended for the estimation of DHEA-S (free and sulfate) in blood/body fluids
231.	Estrogen test reagents/kits	B	Estrogen test reagent/kit is a medical device intended for the estimation of estrogen in blood/body fluids
232.	Progesterone test reagents/kits	B	Progesterone test reagent/ kit is a medical device intended for the estimation of progesterone in blood/ body fluids
233.	Testosterone (free and total) test reagents/kits	B	Testosterone (free and total) test reagent/kit is a medical device intended for the estimation of testosterone (free and total) in blood/body fluids
234.	Sex hormone binding globulin (SHBG) test reagents/kits	B	Sex hormone binding globulin (SHBG) test reagent/kit is a medical device intended for the estimation of sex hormone binding globulin (SHBG) in blood/body fluids
235.	Cortisol test reagents/kits	B	Cortisol test reagent/kit is a medical device intended for the estimation of cortisol in blood/body fluids
236.	Insulin test reagents/kits	B	Insulin test reagent/kit is a medical device intended for the estimation of insulin in blood/body fluids

237.	Luteinizing hormone (LH) test reagents/ kits	B	Luteinizing hormones (LH) test reagent/kit is a medical device intended for the estimation of luteinizing hormone (LH) in blood/ body fluids
238.	Follicle stimulating hormone (FSH) test reagents/kits	B	Follicle stimulating hormone (FSH) test reagent/kit is a medical device intended for the estimation of follicle stimulating hormone (FSH) in blood/body fluids
239.	Prolactin test reagents/kits	B	Prolactin test reagent/kit is a medical device intended for the estimation of prolactin in blood/body fluids
240.	Other test reagents/kits for hormones	B	Test reagents/kits for the estimation of other than above hormones in blood/ body fluids
241.	Vitamin B test reagents/kits	B	Vitamin B test reagent/kit is a medical device intended for the estimation of vitamin B in blood/body fluids
242.	Vitamin D test reagents/kits	B	Vitamin D test reagent/kit is a medical device intended for the estimation of vitamin D in blood/body fluids
243.	Vitamin A test reagents/kits	B	Vitamin A test reagent/kit is a medical device intended for the estimation of vitamin A in blood/body fluids
244.	Vitamin E test reagents/kits	B	Vitamin E test reagent/kit is a medical device intended for the estimation of vitamin E in blood/body fluids
245.	Vitamin K test reagents/kits	B	Vitamin K test reagent/kit is a medical device intended for the estimation of vitamin K in blood/body fluids
246.	Other test reagents/kits for vitamins	B	Test reagents/kits for the estimation of other than above vitamins in blood/ body fluids

247.		Homocystein test reagents/kits	B	Homocystein test reagent/kit is a medical device intended for the estimation of homocystein in blood/body fluids
248.		Allergens test reagents/kits	B	Test reagents/kits intended for the estimation of allergens in blood/body fluids
249.	**Calibrators/controls for above all *in vitro* diagnostic medical devices**	Calibrators		Calibrators intended to be used with a reagent should be treated in the same class as the *in vitro* diagnostic medical device reagent
250.		Controls		Controls intended to be used with a reagent should be treated in the same class as the *in vitro* diagnostic medical device reagent

30 The Drugs and Magic Remedies (Objectionable Advertisements) Act, 1954

(Act No 21 of 1954)[1]

An Act to control the advertisements of drugs in certain cases, to prohibit the advertisement for certain purposes of remedies alleged to possess magic qualities and to provide for matters connected therewith.

(30th April 1954)

Be it enacted by Parliament as follows:

1. *Short title, extent and commencement:*
   a. This Act may be called the Drugs and Magic remedies (Objectionable Advertisements) Act, 1954.
   b. It extends to the whole of India[2] except the State of Jammu and Kashmir, and applies to persons domiciled in the territories to which this Act extends who are out side the said territories.
   c. It shall come into force on such date[3] as the Central Government may, by notification in the Official Gazette, appoint.

2. *Definitions*: In this Act, unless the context otherwise requires.
   a. "Advertisement" includes any notice, circular, label, wrapper, or other document, and any announcement made orally or by any means of producing or transmitting light, sound or smoke.

---

1. Extended to Pondicherry by Reg.7 of 1963, Sec3 w.e.f. 01.10.1963
2. Extended to Sikkim by S.O. 852(E) dated 26.10.1989 w.e.f. 01.11.1989.
3. 1st April 1955 vide G.O.I. Notification S.R.O.511 dated 26.2.1955

b. "Drug" includes:

i. A medicine for internal or external use of human beings or animals.

ii. Any substance intended to be used for or in the diagnosis, cure, mitigation, treatment or prevention of disease in human beings or animals.

iii. Any article, other than food, intended to affect or influence in any way the structure or any organic function of the body of human beings or animals.

iv. Any article intended for use as component of any medicine substance or article, referred to in sub-clauses (i), (ii), and (iii).

c "Magic remedy" includes a talisman, *mantra, kavacha,* and any other charm of any kind which is alleged to possess miraculous powers for or in the diagnosis, cure, mitigation, treatment or prevention of any disease in human beings or animals or for affecting or influencing in anyway the structure or any organic function of the body of human beings or animals.

[1](cc) "registered medical practitioner" means any person.

i. Who holds a qualification granted by an authority specified in, or notified under Sec. 3 of the Indian Medical Degrees Act, 1916 (7 of 1916) or specified in the schedules to the Indian Medical Councils Act, 1956 (102 of 1956); or

ii. Who is entitled to be registered as a registered medical practitioner under any law for the time being in force in any State to which this Act extends relating to the registration of medical practitioner.

d. "Taking part in the publication of any advertisement" includes:

i. The printing of the advertisement.

ii. The publication of the advertisement outside the territories to which this Act extends by or at the

---

1. Ins.by Act 42 of 1963

instance of a person residing within the said territories. [2][* * *]

3. Prohibition of advertisement of certain drugs for treatment of certain diseases and disorders: Subject to the provisions of this Act, no person shall take part in the publication of any advertisement referring to any drug in terms which suggests or are calculated to lead the use of that drug for:

   a. The procurement of miscarriage in women or prevention of conception in women; or

   b. The maintenance or improvement of the capacity of human beings for sexual pleasure;

   c. The correction of menstrual disorders in women; or

3[(d) The diagnosis, cure, mitigation, treatment or prevention of any disease, disorder or condition specified in the schedule, or any disease, disorder or condition (by what so ever name called) which may be specified in the rules made under this Act:

Provided that no such rule shall be made except:

   i. In respect of any disease, disorder or condition which requires timely treatment in consultation with a registered medical practitioner or for which there are no accepted remedies.

   ii. After consultation with the Drugs Technical Advisory Board constituted under the Drugs and Cosmetics Act, 1940 (23 of 1940), and, if the Central Government considers necessary, with such other persons having special knowledge or practical experience in respect of Ayurvedic or Unani systems of medicines as that Government deems fit.]

4. *Prohibition of misleading advertisements relating to drugs:* Subject to the provisions of this Act, no person shall take part in the publication of any advertisement relating to

---

2. Clause (c) omitted by Act 42 of 1963, Sec. 2
3. Subs. by Act 42 of 1963

a drug if the advertisement contains any matter which:
a. Directly or indirectly gives a false impression about the true character of the drug; or
b. Makes a false claim for the drug; or
c. Is false or misleading in any material particular.

5. *Prohibition of advertisement of magic remedies for certain diseases and disorders:* No person carrying on or purporting to carry on the profession of administering magic remedies shall take part in the publication of any advertisement referring to any magic remedy which directly or indirectly claims to be efficacious for any of the purposes specified in Sec.3.

6. *Prohibition of import into, and export from, India of certain advertisements*: No person shall import into, or export from, the territories to which this Act extends, any document containing any advertisement of the nature referred to in Sec. 3, or in Sec A or Sec. 5, and any document containing any such advertisement shall be deemed to be goods of which the import or export has been prohibited under Sec. 19 of the Sea Customs Act, 1878 (8 of 1878) and all the provisions of that Act shall have effect accordingly, except that Sec. 183 thereof shall have effect as if for the word "shall" therein the word "may" were substituted.

7. *Penalty*: Whoever contravenes the provisions of this Act[1] [or the rules made there under] shall, on conviction, be punishable:
a. In the case of first conviction, with imprisonment which may extend to six months, or with fine, or with both.
b. In the case of subsequent conviction, with imprisonment which may extend to one year, or with fine, or with both.

8. [2][*Powers of entry, search etc.*: (1). Subject to the provisions of any rules made in this behalf, any Gazetted officer authorized by the State Government may, within the local limits of the area for which he is so authorized:
a. Enter and search at all reasonable times, with such assistance, if any, as he considers necessary, any place

---

1. Ins. by Act 42 of 1963
2. Subs. by Act 42 of 1963

in which he has reason to believe that an offence under this Act has been or is being committed.

b. Seize any advertisement which he has reason to believe contravenes any of the provisions of this Act.

Provided that the power of seizure under this clause may be exercised in respect of any document, article or thing which contains any such advertisement, including the contents, if any, of such document, article or thing, if the advertisement cannot be separated by reason of it being embossed or otherwise from such document, article or thing without affecting the integrity, utility or saleable value thereof.

c. Examine any record, register, document or any other material object found in any place mentioned in clause (a) and seize the same if he has reason to believe that it may furnish evidence of the commission of an offence punishable under this Act.

(2) The provisions of the Code of Criminal Procedure, 1973 (2 of 1974), shall, so for as may be, apply to any search or seizure under this Act as they apply to any search or seizure made under the authority of a warrant issued under Section 98 of the said Code.

(3) Where any person seizes any thing under clause (b) or clause (c) of subsection (1), he shall, as soon as may be, inform a Magistrate and take his orders as to the custody thereof.]

9. *Offences by companies:* (1) If the person contravening any of the provisions of this Act is a company, every person who at the time the offence was committed, was incharge of and was responsible to the conduct of the business of the company as well as the company shall be deemed to be guilty of the contravention and shall be liable to be proceeded against and punished accordingly:

Provided that nothing contained in this sub-section shall render any such person liable to any punishment provided in this Act if he proves that the offence was committed without his knowledge or that he exercised all due diligence to prevent the commission of the offence. (2) Notwithstanding anything contained in sub-section (1) where an offence under this Act has been committed by a company with the consent or connivance of, or attributable to any neglect on the part, of any director or manager, secretary or other officer of the company, such director, manager, secretary or other officer of the company shall also be deemed guilty of the offence and shall be liable to be proceeded against and punished accordingly.

Explanation: For the purposes of this section:
a. "Company" means any body corporate and includes a firm or other association of individuals.
b. "Director" in relation to a firm means a partner in the firm.

[1][9-A. *Offences to be cognizable:* Notwithstanding anything contained in the Code of Criminal procedure, 1973 (2 of 1974), an offence punishable under this Act shall be cognizable.]

10. *Jurisdiction to try offences:* No Court inferior to that of a Presidency Magistrate or a Magistrate of the first class shall try any offence punishable under this Act.

[2][10-A. *Forfeiture:* Where a person has been convicted by any Court for contravening any provisions of this Act or any rule made there under, the Court may direct hat any document (including all copies thereof), article or thing, in respect of which the contravention is made, including the contents there of where such contents are seized under clause (b) of sub-section (1) of Section 8, shall be forfeited to the Government.]

11. *Officers deemed to be public servants:* Every person authorized under Section 8 shall be deemed to be a public servant within the meaning of section 21 of the Indian Penal Code (45 of 1860).

12. *Indemnity:* No suit, prosecution or other legal proceeding shall lie against any person for anything which is in good faith done or intended to be done under this Act.

13. *Other laws not affected:* The provisions of this Act are in addition to, and not in derogation of the provisions of any other law for the time being in force.

14. *Savings:* Nothing in this Act shall apply to:

   a. Any sign board or notice displayed by a registered medical practitioner on his premises indicating that treatment for any disease, disorder or condition specified in Sec.3, the schedule or the rules made under this Act, is undertaken in those premises; or

   b. Any treatise or book dealing with any of the matters specified in Sec.3 from a *bonafide* scientific or social stand point; or

   c. Any advertisement relating to any drug sent confidentially in the manner prescribed under Sec.16 only to a registered medical practitioner; or

   d. Any advertisement relating to a drug printed or published by the Government; or

   e. Any advertisement relating to a drug printed or published by any person with the previous sanction of the Government granted prior to the commencement of the Drugs and Magic Remedies (Objectionable Advertisements) Amendment Act, 1963(42 of 1963):

   Provided that the Government may, for reasons to be recorded in writing, withdraw the sanction after giving the person an opportunity of showing cause against such withdrawal.

15. *Power to exempt from application of Act.:* (1) If in the opinion of the Central Government public interest requires that the advertisement of any specified drug or class of drugs[1] [or any specified class of advertisement relating to drugs] should be permitted, it may, by notification in the Official Gazette, direct that the provisions of Sections 3, 4, 5 and 6 or anyone of such provisions shall not apply or shall apply subject to such conditions as may be specified in the notification to or in relation to the advertisement of any such drug or classes of drugs, [1][or any such advertisement relating to drugs.]

---

1. Ins. by Act 42 of 1963

16. *Power to make rules*:

1. The Central Government may, by notification in the Official Gazette, make rules for carrying out the purposes of this Act.

2. In particular and without prejudice to the generality of the fore going power, such rules may:

   a. Specify any disease, disorder or condition to which the provisions of Sec. 3. shall apply.

   b. Prescribe the manner in which advertisements of articles or things referred to in Cl. (c) of Sec.14 may be sent confidentially.

3. Every rule made under this Act shall be laid as soon as may be after it is made before each House of Parliament while it is in session for a total period of thirty days which may be comprised in one session or in two or more successive sessions, and before the expiry of the session in which it is so laid or the successive sessions aforesaid, both Houses agree in making any modification in the rule or both the Houses agree that the rule shall not be made, the rule shall thereafter have effect only in such modified form or be of no effect, as the case may be; so however, that any such annulment shall be without prejudice to the validity of anything previously done under that rule.

THE SCHEDULE

[See Secs. 3 (d) and 14]

S.No	Name of the disease, disorder or condition
1	Appendicitis
2	Arteriosclerosis
3	Blindness
4	Blood poisoning
5	Bright's disease
6	Cancer
7	Cataract
8	Deafness
9	Diabetes
10	Diseases and disorders of the brain

11	Diseases and disorders of the optical system
12	Diseases and disorders of the uterus
13	Disorders of menstrual flow
14	Disorders of the nervous system
15	Disorders of the prostatic gland
16	Dropsy
17	Epilepsy
18	Female diseases in general
19	Fevers (in general)
20	Fits
21	Form and structure of the female bust
22	Gallstones, kidney stones and bladder stones
23	Gangrene
24	Glaucoma
25	Goitre
26	Heart diseases
27	High or low blood pressure
28	Hydrocele
29	Hysteria
30	Infantile paralysis
31	Insanity
32	Leprosy
33	Leucoderma
34	Lockjaw
35	Locomotor atoxia
36	Lupus
37	Nervous debility
38	Obesity
39	Paralysis
40	Plague
41	Pleurisy
42	Pneumonia
43	Rheumatism
44	Ruptures
45	Sexual impotence
46	Smallpox
47	Stature of persons
48	Sterility in women
49	Trachoma
50	Tuberculosis

51	Tumors
52	Typhoid fever
53	Ulcers of the gastrointestinal tract
54	Venereal diseases, including syphilis, gonorrhoea, soft chancre, venereal granuloma and lympho granuloma

DRUGS AND MAGIC REMEDIES (OBJECTIONABLE ADVERTISEMENTS) RULES, 1955

1. *Short title and commencement*
   i. These rules may be called the Drugs and Magic Remedies (Objectionable Advertisements) Rules, 1955.
   ii. They shall come into force on such date as the Central Government may, by notification in the Official Gazette, appoint.
2. *Definitions*: In these rules, unless the context otherwise requires:
   i. The "Act" means the Drugs and Magic Remedies (Objectionable Advertisements) Act, 1954 (21 of 1954); and
   ii. "Section" means a section of the Act.
3. *Scrutiny of misleading advertisements relating to drugs*: Any person authorized by the State Government in this behalf may, if satisfied that the advertisement relating to a drug contravenes the provisions of Sec. A, by order, require the manufacturer, packer, distributor or seller of the drug to furnish, within such time as may be specified in the order of such regarding the composition of the drug or the ingredients thereof or such information in regard to that drug as he deems necessary for holding the scrutiny of the advertisement and where such order is made, it shall be the duty of the manufacturer, packer, distributor or seller of the drug to which the advertisement relates to comply with the order. Any failure to comply with such order shall, for the purposes of Sec. 7, be deemed to be a contravention of the provisions of Sec. 4:
   Provided that no publisher or advertising agency of any medium for the dissemination of any advertisement relating to a drug shall be deemed to have made any

contravention merely by the reason of the dissemination by him or if any such advertisement, unless such publisher or advertising agency has failed to comply with any discretion made by the authorized person in this behalf calling upon him or it to furnish the name and address of the manufacturer, packer, distributor, or seller or advertising agency, as the case may be, who or which caused such advertisement to be disseminated.

4. Procedure to be followed in prohibited import into, and export from India of certain advertisements:

   i. If the Customs Collector has reasons to believe that any consignment contains documents of the nature referred to in Sec. 6, he may, and if requested by an officer appointed for the purpose by the Central Government, shall detain the consignment and dispose it of in accordance with the provisions of Sea Customs Act, 1978 (7 of 1878), and the rules made thereunder, and shall also inform the importer or the exporter, of the order so passed:

      Provided that if the importer or exporter feels aggrieved by an order passed by the Customs Collector under this sub-rule and makes a representation to him within one week of the date of the order and has given an undertaking in writing not to dispose of the consignment without the consent of the Customs Collector and to return the consignment when so required by the Customs Collector, the Customs Collector shall pass an order making over the consignment to the importer or the exporter, as the case may be:

      Provide further that before passing any order under this sub-rule or under the first proviso thereto; the Customs Collector shall consult the officer appointed for the purpose by the Central Government.

   ii. If the importer or the exporter who has given an undertaking under the first proviso to sub-rule (1) is required by the Customs Collector to return the consignment or any portion thereof within ten days of the receipt of the notice.

5. *Manner in which advertisements may be sent confidentially:* All documents containing advertisements relating to drugs referred to in clause (c) of sub-section (1) of Section 14, shall be sent by post to a registered medical practitioner by name or to a wholesale or retail chemist, the address of such registered medical practitioner or to wholesale or retail chemist being given. Such document shall bear at the top, printed in indelible ink in a conspicuous manner the words "for the use of a registered medical practitioner or a hospital or a laboratory".

6. *Procedure to be followed in obtaining previous sanction of the Government for publishing an advertisement:* Any person intending to obtain the previous sanction of the Government to publish advertisements under clause (d) of sub-section (10 of Section 14 shall make an application to such officer as may be authorized by the Central Government, or the state Government, as the case may be in this behalf, and any such application shall mention the registered name and the trade mark of the drug, its detailed composition and any special reasons justifying the sanction of the Government and shall be submitted by the officer aforesaid to the Central Government or, as the case may be, the State Government for sanction.

Index